Heritage Landscapes
of the
Irish Midlands

and selected itineraries

P. J. Gibson

Preface

The midland counties of Ireland contain a wealth of natural, archaeological and historical features. Some of these, such as Clonmacnoise, are well-known regionally or nationally, while the location and importance of others, such as St. Manchan's Shrine, although known locally and within academic circles, may be more closely guarded secrets, not having received the publicity of tourism promotion. Accordingly, this book aims not only to describe the well-known but also the many hidden jewels within this central area of Ireland. Discussion of aspects of the physical landscape, such as the rivers and glacial landforms, will interest geologists, geographers and hydrologists, while the information regarding the human heritage landscape will appeal to the archaeologists and historians. However, the book's presentation style makes it accessible to a much wider readership, including local historians, students or tourists.

The book is unique in its treatment of the Irish Midlands, in that, it integrates three landscape themes: physical, archaeological and historical. One theme cannot be considered in isolation from the other two.

The first two sections provide background discussions of the themes; section I relates to physical aspects of the midland landscape, while section II concerns its temporal archaeological and historical development. These set the scene for section III, the major part of the book, where the themes are fully integrated into the itineraries.

The nine selected driving tours through the Irish Midlands collectively amount to a distance of over 1,000 kilometres. Two criteria were involved in choosing the routes. The first was a geographical dimension, so that all the midland counties are represented, and itineraries pass through the major towns: Portlaoise, Longford, Mullingar, Roscommon, Nenagh, Tullamore, Athlone and Carlow. The second was to include a wide range of features, both natural and anthropogenic.

If this book has one aim, it is that the cultural richness revealed within its pages will enthuse readers to go and explore the Irish Midlands for themselves.

Contents

Introduction to the Irish Midlands

The Irish Midlands represent a relatively unknown part of Ireland to many people and are often viewed as flat areas of little interest. However, the midlands contain unique components of Ireland's physical, archaeological and historical heritage. They are characterised by some of the best examples of glacial depositional landforms in Ireland, are drained by the largest river system in Ireland and contain most of Ireland's raised bogs and their unique ecosystems. We also find sites of major archaeological and historical interest such as the Clonmacnoise monastic site in County Offaly, the Celtic landscape around Rathcroghan in County Roscommon, the passage tomb cemetery at Loughcrew in County Meath and Fore ecclesiastical centre in County Westmeath. In addition, there are many less well known sites within the Irish Midlands such as the Timoney Stones in north Tipperary, Clonard in County Meath, the Hill of Uisneach in County Westmeath, the French Church in County Laois and St. Manchan's Shrine and Rahan monastic site in County Offaly – each have their own story to tell.

Three important aspects of the heritage of the Irish Midlands are considered in this book: the physical landscape, the archaeological landscape and the historical landscape. The first section of the book outlines the main physical attributes of the Irish Midlands such as, topography, geology, glacial processes and drainage systems. The second section considers the major events that have helped shape the archaeological and historical landscapes such as the development of Christianity, Anglo-Norman invasion and plantation. The third section of the book comprises nine driving tours through different parts of the Irish Midlands, which encompass a range of physical, archaeological and historical features. Collectively these tours amount to *c.* 1,000 kilometres.

The area covered by this book takes in all of Counties Westmeath, Offaly and Laois and parts of Counties, Roscommon, Kilkenny, Galway, Tipperary, Longford, Carlow, Clare, Meath and Kildare, Figure 1. In all, the area is approximately 100 kilometres wide in an east-west direction and 115 kilometres long in a north-south direction. It stretches from Carlow Town in the south to Longford Town in the north and from Kells in the east to Killaloe in the west, Figure 2. The major towns in the midlands are Athlone (population *c.* 19,000) and Mullingar (*c.* 19,000), County Westmeath; Tullamore (*c.* 13,000), County Offaly; Portlaoise (*c.* 14,000), County Laois; Carlow (*c.* 20,000), County Carlow; Ballinasloe (*c.* 6,000), County Galway; Roscommon Town (*c.* 6000), County Roscommon; Longford (*c.* 9,000), County Longford and Nenagh (*c.* 7,000), County Tipperary. Plate 1 is a false colour satellite image of the central midlands of Ireland. Good healthy vegetation, mainly pasture, used for grazing livestock is shown in shades of red in this image. The average

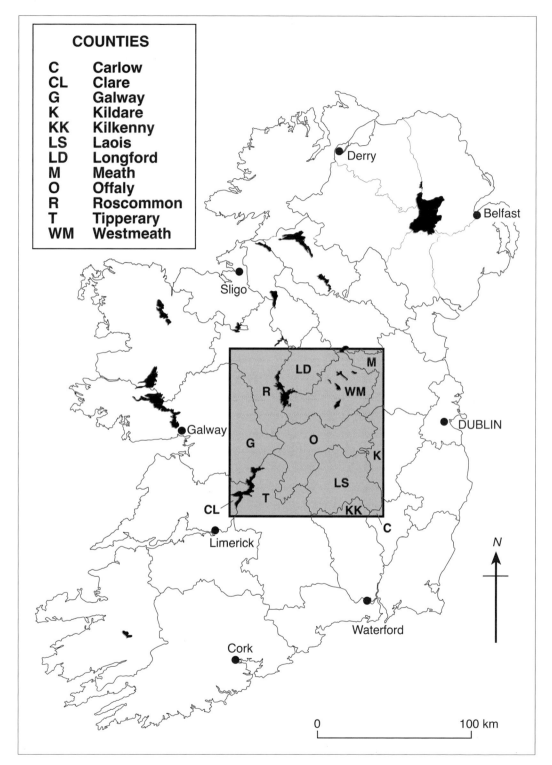

COUNTIES

C	Carlow
CL	Clare
G	Galway
K	Kildare
KK	Kilkenny
LS	Laois
LD	Longford
M	Meath
O	Offaly
R	Roscommon
T	Tipperary
WM	Westmeath

Figure 1:
Geographical location of the Irish Midlands.
Area covered by book shown in green rectangle.

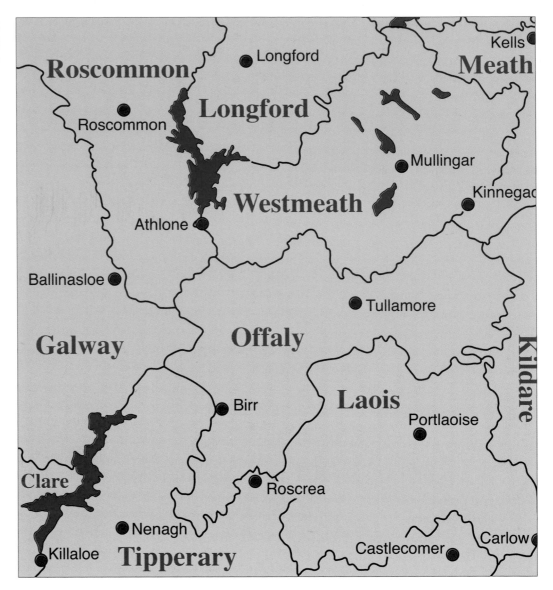

Figure 2:
Map of Irish Midlands showing counties and main towns.

farm size in this region is about 25 hectares. Beef cattle tend to be more important in northern Offaly, Westmeath and Longford whereas in Laois and northern Tipperary and southern Offaly dairying and tillage are more important (Lafferty et al., 1999). About 40% of the farms have sheep. Towns tend to be small and scattered and there are few major urban centres. Water bodies, such as loughs, are shown in black on the satellite image. The region has two large loughs in the west, Lough Ree and Lough Derg, which are connected by the River Shannon, and a number of smaller ones around Mullingar. Other colours are also evident on the image. The Slieve Bloom Mountains are not associated with pasture, the vegetation consists largely of upland scrub and forest plantations and consequently is shown by a different colour (green). The pale blue area to the east of the Slieve Bloom Mountains represents fallow fields. Green areas around Tullamore in County Offaly are where peat extraction has taken place. More detailed satellite images of the Irish Midlands are included later in the book (see Plates 15, 24, 25 and F1).

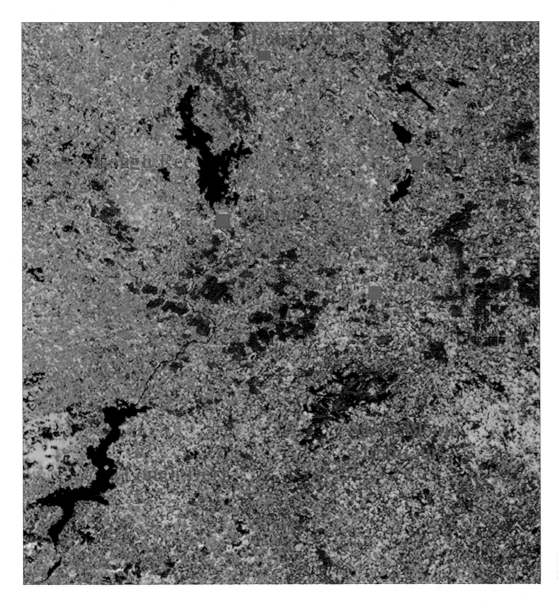

Plate 1:
Satellite image of the Irish Midlands.

SECTION I

Physical Landscape
of the
Irish Midlands

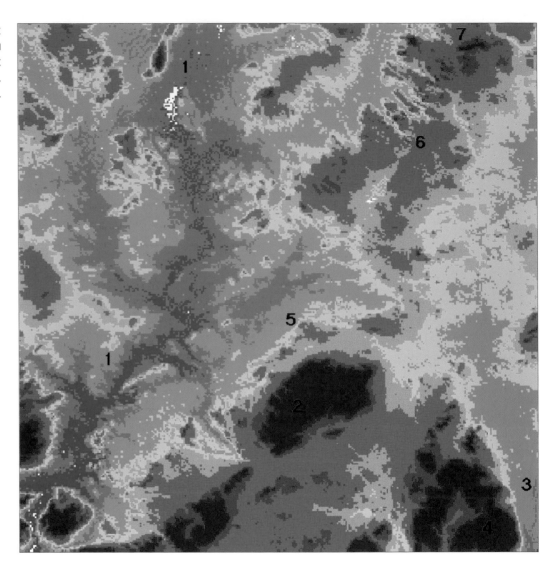

Plate 2:
Colour-coded image showing topographic variations in
the Irish Midlands. Blue: low elevation; green/yellow:
intermediate elevation; red/orange: high elevations.
Data courtesy of NASA.

Topography of the Irish Midlands

There is an inextricable link between the geology and the topography of the Irish
Midlands. Plate 2 shows a colour-coded topographic image of the midlands, which has
been produced from space, using a radar system onboard the Space Shuttle. Low
elevations are shown in shades of blue, intermediate elevations in green and yellow and
the greatest heights in red and orange. The lowest elevations (dark blue) are associated
with the River Shannon drainage system, which occupies the north-south zone in the
western, half of the image (1, Plate 2). The height above sea level for the River Shannon

is about 37m in the north and 30m in the south, a fall of only 7m in 115 kilometres. The highest elevations are located in the southern midlands, with the highest in the Slieve Bloom Mountains (2, Plate 2). This is at Arderin (527m) at Irish Grid reference: S233 989.

The rocks in the Slieve Bloom Mountains (Devonian and Silurian sediments) are much harder than the Carboniferous limestone that underlies much of the midland and consequently are more difficult to erode. The blue zone in the southeast (3, Plate 2) is the course of the River Barrow which is overlooked to the west by the upland basin of the Castlecomer Plateau with elevations of around 250-320m (4, Plate 2). This region is formed

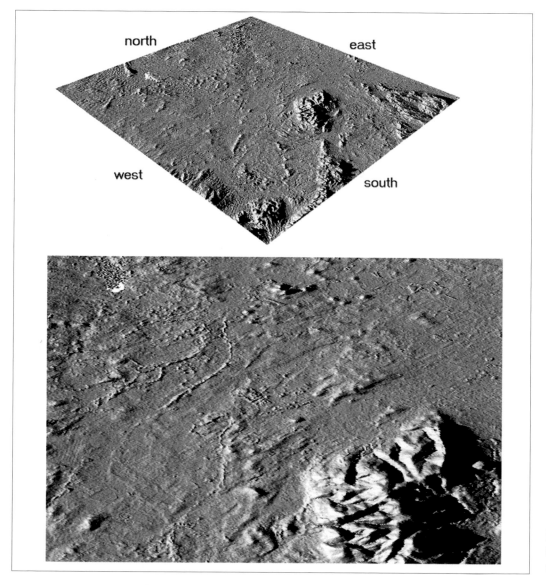

Plate 3:
3D images showing topographic
variations in the Irish Midlands.

of younger Upper Carboniferous rocks. Elevations are relatively low (50-100m) north of the Slieve Bloom Mountains in the boglands of County Offaly (5, Plate 2), though increase northeastward (100-150m) due to the presence of thick glacial sediments (6, Plate 2). The highest elevation (276m) in this region is found on the east-west aligned Slieve na Calliagh ridge which is the site of Loughcrew megalithic passage tomb cemetery (7, Plate 2).

An alternative method of viewing the topography is to construct a digital elevation model (DEM), which essentially produces a 3 dimensional view of the region, Plate 3. The Slieve Bloom Mountains and other upland regions in the south are seen to dominate this area with very little topographic variation in the northern half of the midlands. A close-up of the area north of the Slieve Bloom Mountains is shown in the lower part of Plate 3. At this detail, the trend of the glacial features, especially the linear eskers (left of centre) become apparent. Except in some of the higher regions, slopes within the Irish Midlands tend to be very shallow, generally less than 10 degrees often providing uninterrupted views extending tens of kilometres across the Irish Midlands. Such views can be obtained from various locations on the different itineraries as detailed in Section III.

Geological framework of the Irish Midlands

The present geographical arrangement of the continents on the Earth is not constant, their spatial relationships have changed through geological time and their evolution can be explained in terms of plate tectonics. The continents move slowly on lithospheric plates as oceans open up or close. Currently, the Atlantic Ocean is increasing in width as new oceanic crust is created at a mid-oceanic ridge, which is located at depth below the Atlantic Ocean. The Red Sea is also slowly opening as it too has a spreading ridge, but it is much narrower than the Atlantic because it has been opening for a much shorter time period. The Pacific Ocean also has a spreading ridge but it is also surrounded by subduction zones where oceanic crust is destroyed. As the oceanic crust is being destroyed quicker at the subduction zones than it is being created at the spreading ridge, the Pacific Ocean is slowly closing. When an ocean closes, eventually two continents will collide, and in this collision, which takes place over millions of years, a mountain belt will form. Thus today the Himalayas are being formed because the ocean that once existed between India and SE Asia has closed and the collision of the two land masses has compressed and crumpled the land producing the mountains. Such a mountain building process is called orogeny.

The oldest rocks in Ireland occur on the island of Inishtrahull off the coast of County Donegal and formed about 1770 million years ago (Ma). Very old rocks are also found near Rosslare, County Wexford. These rocks are less than 400 kilometres apart, but 500 million years (Ma) ago, during the Ordovician time period, they were separated by an ocean, thousands of kilometres wide. Northwest Ireland was part of the Laurentian plate

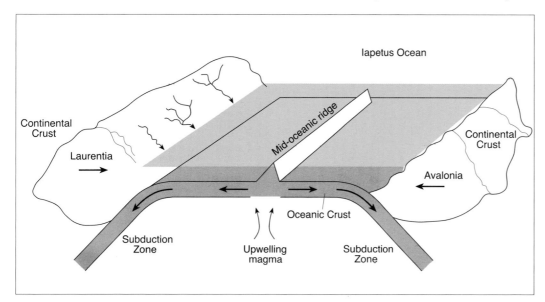

Figure 3:
Plate tectonic model for Ireland.

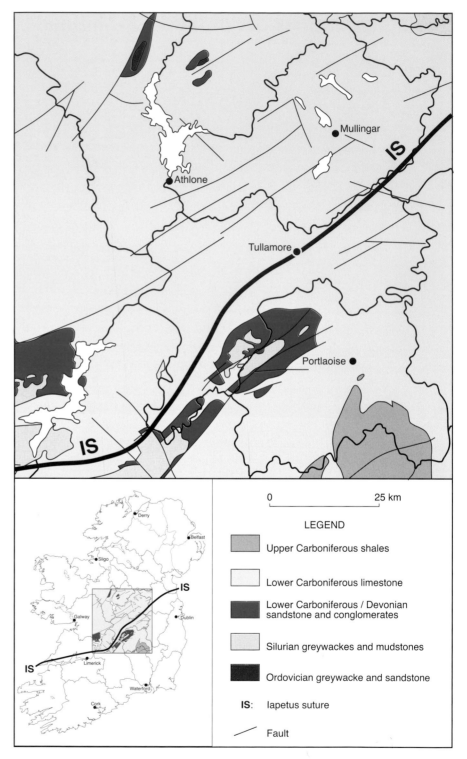

Figure 4:
Geological map of the Irish Midlands.

LEGEND

Upper Carboniferous shales

Lower Carboniferous limestone

Lower Carboniferous / Devonian sandstone and conglomerates

Silurian greywackes and mudstones

Ordovician greywacke and sandstone

IS: Iapetus suture

Fault

and Southeast Ireland was part of the Avalonian plate, Figure 3. This ocean was called the Iapetus Ocean (in Greek mythology Iapetus is the father of Atlas, the king of Atlantis after which the Atlantic Ocean is named) and for tens of millions of years vast amounts of sediments were deposited in the Iapetus Ocean. Interestingly, during this time period, both parts of Ireland were south of the equator. However, subduction zones developed on either side of the Iapetus Ocean and the two plates moved slowly towards each other and by about 400 million years ago (beginning of Devonian time period) they had fully collided. This collision, called the Caledonian Orogeny, resulted in extensive volcanism and the formation of a major mountain belt across Ireland, Britain and Scandinavia. The line (or more correctly zone) of collision between the Laurentian and Avalonian plates is known as the Iapetus suture, and it crosses the Irish Midlands at depth, running from the Shannon estuary in the west to Clogher Head, north of Drogheda, County Louth in the east, Figure 4. Two further points are worth making about this collision.

- Firstly, the rocks that occur at the surface in the Irish Midlands today are mostly much younger than the Caledonian Orogeny, so the Iapetus suture is not exposed. Phillips (2001) provides a discussion of various geophysical surveys on the suture stating that it appears to dip at a shallow angle (10 degrees) to the SE to a depth of around 6 kilometres.
- Secondly, a number of smaller plates were caught up in the collision process, possibly being moved larges distances along faults, and they have been amalgamated together to form distinct 'terranes' at depth.

Small outcrops of Ordovician rocks approximately 450 million years old occur just north of Lough Ree, either side of the River Shannon (Morris et al., 2003). Silurian rocks c. 420 million years old occur mainly in the core of the Slieve Bloom Mountains and south of Lough Derg, although there are further extensive outcrops northeast of the Irish Midlands. These were sediments that were deposited on the floor of the Iapetus Ocean and which today form mudstones and greywackes. Slate of Silurian age is also found near Lough Derg, Plate 4.

After the Caledonian orogeny, as we enter the Devonian period (400 million years ago), Ireland had been uplifted to a great height above sea level. Weathering started to wear the mountains down and the eroded debris and sediments were transported by fast flowing rivers running off the high ground and deposited in thick accumulations on flood plains. Over time these sediments were converted into rocks (mainly sandstones and conglomerates) and are known as the Old Red Sandstone. These rocks form the flanks of the Slieve Bloom Mountains and are also found near Lough Derg in Counties Tipperary and Clare, Plate 5. During this time Ireland still lay south of the equator but it was continuing to move north. At the beginning of the next time period, the Carboniferous, sandstones were initially deposited but following a marked change in the palaeo-geographical setting of Ireland, the types of sediments changed. The rocks that formed in

Plate 4:
Example of Silurian greywackes (top)
and slates (bottom) in the Irish
Midlands. Bottom image *c.* 4m high.

Plate 5:
Example of Devonian/Lower Carboniferous sandstone from the Irish Midlands. Bottom image shows cross-bedding (foresets) dipping to the left. Thus the river which deposited the sand flowed from right to left.

the Carboniferous period (approximately 355-290 million years ago) cover about one third of Ireland and over 80% of the Irish Midlands, Figure 4. There is a marked difference in the types of rocks that formed in the early (Lower) Carboniferous, generally called the Dinantian and the later (Upper) Carboniferous, called the Silesian. It should be noted that the Carboniferous has been intensively studied in Ireland, so has many sub-divisions. Thus for example, the Dinantian is further divided into two series, the Touraisian and the Viséan, with the latter further sub-divided into five stages. More details can be obtained from Sevastopulo (2001) and Sevastopulo and Wyse Jackson (2001). In the early (Lower) Carboniferous, the Old Red Sandstone continent had been eroded down so that a shallow sea transgressed most of Ireland. Ireland at this time was just north of the equator, and many plant and animals thrived in this warm shallow sea. They produced calcium carbonate and today the Lower Carboniferous rocks in the Irish Midlands comprise mainly limestone layers, which often contain fossils, Plate 6. Later on in the Upper Carboniferous, deeper water predominated. This, allied to the large input of carbonaceous material from the land, means that the rocks formed at this time did not consist of limestones, but shales and coal deposits. Such deposits can be seen in southern Laois and northern Kilkenny. There was some minor igneous activity during the Carboniferous and Croghan Hill in County Offaly is the site of an extinct volcano. This site is visited on Itinerary A.

Plate 6:
Example of fossils, mainly crinoids, found in limestone in the Irish Midlands. Image 20 cm across.

Following the deposition of the Carboniferous rocks, Ireland, especially the southern half, was affected by the Variscan Orogeny, which in the Irish Midlands produced some folding in the Slieve Bloom Mountains. The faults and fractures formed during the Caledonian and Variscan orogenies acted as conduits for the movement of mineralised fluids which, when they cooled, were able to form ore bodies. A number of important ore bodies formed mainly zinc and lead, occur near the southern edge of the Irish Midlands for example, Silvermines, Galmoy and Lisheen.

Presently there are no solid rocks younger than about 290 Ma in the Irish Midlands. Undoubtedly, many younger rocks were deposited, chalk (around 100 Ma old), for example, is found in northeast Ireland and across Britain, the Netherlands, France and Germany. However, erosion, most likely during the Tertiary time period (65-2 Million years ago), has removed all the younger rocks down to the Lower Carboniferous level except for some scattered outcrops of Upper Carboniferous rocks. The Devonian Old Red Sandstone and Silurian greywackes are hard resistant rocks so they form the mountainous area of the Slieve Blooms, Figure 4.

Although, as already stated, there are no solid rocks younger than about 290 Ma ago in the Irish Midlands, thick deposits of unconsolidated sediments presently overlie most of the rocks. To understand how they formed we must look at one of the most profound events to shape the landscape of the Irish Midlands – the coming of the glaciers.

Glaciation of the Irish Midlands

Today we are rightly concerned about global warming and the melting of the ice sheets in Antarctica and the Arctic. However, most people are unaware that the simultaneous presence of extensive ice at the North and South Poles, which we assume to be 'normal' is a relatively rare event in geological terms. There have been long times periods in the past, lasting tens of millions of years, during which the North and South Poles were free of ice. However, about 50 million years ago the global temperature of the Earth decreased which created the conditions conducive to the formation of glacial ice. During the Quaternary period (last 2 million years) the glacial ice sheets have waxed (increased their areal extent – glacial periods) and waned (decreased their extent – interglacials). Today glacial ice covers about 10% of the Earth's land surface and at its maximum extent it covered about 30%. It should be realised that for Ireland, a glacial period does not necessarily imply the presence of major onshore glaciers. For a glacial period lasting 100,000 years, significant amounts of glacial ice may only have existed for 20,000 years, with the other 80,000 years being represented by very cold tundra, northern latitude conditions. Also, even within a glacial period, temperatures can often increase for short time periods called interstadials.

Plate 7:
Glacial till deposits in the Slieve Bloom Mountains.

Coxon (2001) reports that oxygen isotope analysis from an ocean core suggests that Ireland has been affected by at least 5 glacial events in the last 750,000 years. The main difficulty with trying to determine evidence for glacial events using land-based sediments is that evidence for an early glacial event can be destroyed by a later one. Terrestrial records for Ireland have generally been interpreted as indicating that there have been 2 major glacial events in the last 2 million years, an older Munsterian one and a younger Midlandian one. Only the Midlandian glaciation is discussed here, as its effect on the landscape of the Irish Midlands has been enormous.

The Midlandian glacial period began about 120,000 years ago as conditions in Ireland became colder following the preceding interglacial. An ice axis extended from Galway Bay to Belfast and glaciers moved from this axis across the Irish Midlands in a south to southeast direction. There are essentially two zones in a glacial landscape, a zone of erosion and a zone of deposition. The zone of erosion in Ireland is most obvious in mountainous regions such as Donegal and Wicklow, where large U-shaped valleys have been carved by the movement of glaciers. The Irish Midlands are predominantly a zone of deposition. As a glacier moves across the landscape it picks up and transports large amount of boulders, sand, gravel, silt and cobbles. This material can eventually be extruded from the base of the glacier and plastered onto the underlying surface or if a glacier melts the material will also be deposited on the landscape. Sediment deposited

Plate 8:
Moraine near Abbeyleix, County Laois.
Inset shows detail.

Plate 9:
Glacial esker ridge, near Horseleap,
County Offaly.

directly from a glacier is known as till (formerly called boulder clay). Vast amounts of till were deposited on the Irish Midlands burying the underlying rocks in some places to depths of 50m. It consists of an unstratified non-homogeneous jumbled mass of sediment of various grain sizes, Plate 7.

Glaciers can either advance (when conditions get colder), retreat (when it warms up) or have a standstill phase (when the temperature remains constant). During a standstill phase, the unsorted sediments are dumped at the front of the glacier, which, when it retreats, are left in the landscape as linear undulating mounds of unsorted sediments known as moraines, Plate 8. A number of standstill phases are known to have occurred during the Midlandian glaciation, so a number of morainic ridges cross the Irish Midlands. Indeed, the northern part of the Irish Midlands has been interpreted as consisting of a 10 kilometres wide hummocky moraine zone, north of which are streamlined till deposits called drumlins (Mitchell and Delaney, 1997).

Tunnels form within the glaciers through which rivers flow allowing sediments to be deposited. When conditions warmed up, the glaciers retreated leaving behind these long winding ridges of sediment in the landscape, Plate 9. These are known as eskers (derived from the Gaelic eiskir) and the ones found in the Irish Midlands are some of the best examples in Europe. They vary in size and trend. The Tullamore esker in County Offaly is over 20 kilometres long, trends east-west in its western section and northeast-southwest in the eastern part, being paralleled by another 4 kilometres to the north. The Moate esker in County Westmeath is over 10 kilometres long and trends northwest-southeast in the west and east-west in the east. In County Laois, the Mountmellick to Portlaoise esker runs north-south. The glacial sediments deposited from water differ in character from those deposited directly from the glacier. A strong flowing river will transport sediment of varying sizes. However, as the strength of the river decreases, large stones will be deposited first but the finer material will continue to be moved by the glacier and deposited farther downstream. Thus, sorting of the sediment occurs, so that fluvio-glacial

Plate 10:
Sorted fluvio-glacial sediments showing layers
based on grain size, central County Offaly.
Image *c.* 10m high.

deposits are characterised by stratified layering according to grain size, Plate 10. The sediment type varies greatly both vertically and longitudinally even within the same esker system. Some indication of the size of these features is given by Plate 11 which shows a cross-section through an esker whose parent river carried boulders over 1 tonne in weight. Presently, eskers are exploited for their sand and gravel deposits and unfortunately in some places to such an extent that their destruction may alter the character of the landscape. Various Bronze Age burials have been placed on eskers presumably because of their prominent position in the landscape. Eskers form natural defensive sites and were often chosen for the sites of castles and mottes for example at Moate, Newtownlow, Athlone and Mount Temple. The steep sided eskers form natural territorial boundaries and they may delineate townland, farm or field boundaries. The eskers in the Irish Midlands provided routeways across the bogs, and even today many

minor roads continue to run along the crests of eskers. The Slighe Mor (one of the major routes from Tara) is believed to have utilised the Eiscir Riada (Royal Esker), which ran from Dublin to Galway (Geissel, 2006). Some early Christian monasteries were built near these eskers as they provided routes for scholars and pilgrims to travel between different monastic settlements.

When a river carrying sediment enters a lake, its velocity drops quickly and it deposits its load, so that 'foreset' layers are formed which dip in the direction in which the river was flowing. Similar events happened in the Irish Midlands as the glaciers melted. Today, these lakes are often gone, but the sediments they left behind allow us to reconstruct the landscape at the end of the glacial period, Plate 12. An analysis of the foresets in Plate 12 shows that the river that deposited the sediments flowed from right to left. As the glaciers melted, large blocks of ice were left in the landscape, often forming a hollow in the sediments. In situ mass wastage produced what are known as kettlehole lakes. Where the water drained away, kettleholes were left, Plate 13.

Scattered throughout former glaciated areas one often finds large boulders sitting isolated in the landscape, Plate 14. These are known as glacial erratics and are useful in helping to reconstruct the routes of the former glaciers that carried and deposited them. For example, erratics of Galway granite have been found in the Slieve Bloom Mountains indicating that a glacier must have moved eastwards across the Irish Midlands from the Galway region. They can also give information about the maximum extent of glaciers. By about 10,000 years ago, the glaciers in Ireland had fully melted and retreated to northern latitudes leaving the Irish Midlands to adapt to the new climatic regime.

Plate 12:
Dipping foreset beds in glacial sediments indicating that the
current was from right to left, central County Offaly.

Plate 13:
Kettlehole depression near Tyrrellspass,
County Westmeath.

Plate 14:
Sandstone glacial erratic, near Ballycumber,
County Offaly. Boulder approximately 1m high.

Formation of bogs in the Irish Midlands

Boglands are an ubiquitous feature of the Irish Midlands. As well as being a characteristic of the midland landscape in their own right, they have preserved, often for thousands of years, many historical and archaeological artefacts, which would have been destroyed. A satellite image from near Ferbane in County Offaly shows natural vegetation in green, whereas the areas exploited for peat extraction are shown as yellow or grey (Plate 15). At their peak, the bogs covered about 16% of Ireland's land surface, an area of 1.3 million hectares. The nomenclature regarding bogs can be confusing. Essentially there are two main types: blanket bog and raised bog. Blanket bog is itself further divided into lowland blanket bog and upland blanket bog. Blanket bog develops where the mean annual rainfall is greater than 125 cm, so it is concentrated along the western seaboard of Ireland, mainly in Counties Donegal, Mayo, Galway and Cork. Raised bogs form in drier conditions (mean annual rainfall of about 75-100 cm). Virtually all the bog in the midland counties is raised bog, so the discussion below concentrates on the formation of raised bogs.

Plate 15:
Satellite image showing areas of bog around Ferbane, County Offaly. Image *c.* 18 km wide.

Raised bogs originally covered approximately 300,000 hectares, 23% of the total area enveloped by bog (3.7% of the land surface of Ireland). By about 10,000 years ago the last vestiges of the ice associated with the previous glacial period had disappeared. However, the Irish landscape in the midlands appeared markedly different from its present form. Although the ice had melted away, evidence for its presence was everywhere. The melting glaciers had deposited vast amounts of sediments on the land, mostly directly onto the Carboniferous limestone. Some of these deposits were aligned in linear zones, such as the eskers referred to earlier, but there were also unsorted till deposits plastered onto the underlying land. Existing river systems had been destroyed by the glaciers or had been clogged up with sediments forcing new rivers to form and often cut new channels to the coast. The drainage was poor because of a combination of low gradients and low infiltration rates, so that the Shannon Basin consisted of much larger interconnecting lakes and other lakes in the midlands around Mullingar had merged into larger ones (Mitchell and Ryan, 1998). In addition, many small lakes would have developed in hollows within and between glacial sediments. The underlying rock and the glacial sediments derived from it were very calcareous (contained calcium carbonate) and as conditions ameliorated the lakes began to be populated by flora and fauna, which used the calcareous waters to produce shells. When they died their remains sank to the bottom of the lake floors to produce a fine-grained creamy white soft calcareous sediment called marl, Plate 16 and Figure 5(a).

The lakes were colonized relatively quickly by reeds, bulrushes, lilies, sedges and algae whose dead remains sank to the bottom of the lake. Low oxygen levels prevented full decomposition of this plant material which accumulated over time and was converted into fen peat, Figure 5(b). Fens continued to receive their nutrients from groundwater which was alkaline in composition. (Water can be considered acid, alkaline or neutral depending on the ions it contains. Water with a pH value from 1-6 is acid, pH 7 is neutral and between 8-14 is alkaline). The pH of fens is about 8.

Eventually the fen peat became so thick that the roots of the surface plants could no longer reach the groundwater and the only source of water then became nutrient-poor rainwater which is neutral to slightly acidic in nature. Plants, such as sphagnum mosses and heathers, which could survive in such conditions began to thrive. Other plants, such as sundews, which supplement their nutrient supply by trapping insects, also became established. Decay, compression and accumulation of these plants in acidic anaerobic (oxygen-poor) conditions led to the formation of bog peat, Plate 17 and Figure 5(c). This bog peat is typically 95% water and 5% compressed vegetable matter by weight. The average depth of the bog peat in the Irish Midlands is about 7m and the pH is about 4. Sphagnum moss can hold large amounts of water and locally can draw water up by capillary action to heights greater than the surrounding water level. This allowed the sphagnum mosses to continue to grow upward creating a domed appearance, hence the term 'raised bog', Figure 5(c). Fen peat began forming relatively quickly after conditions ameliorated at the end of the last glacial stage, probably by around 9,000 years ago and the change to peat bog was underway by 7500 years ago, although the exact timing varies

Figure 5:
Formation of a raised bog.

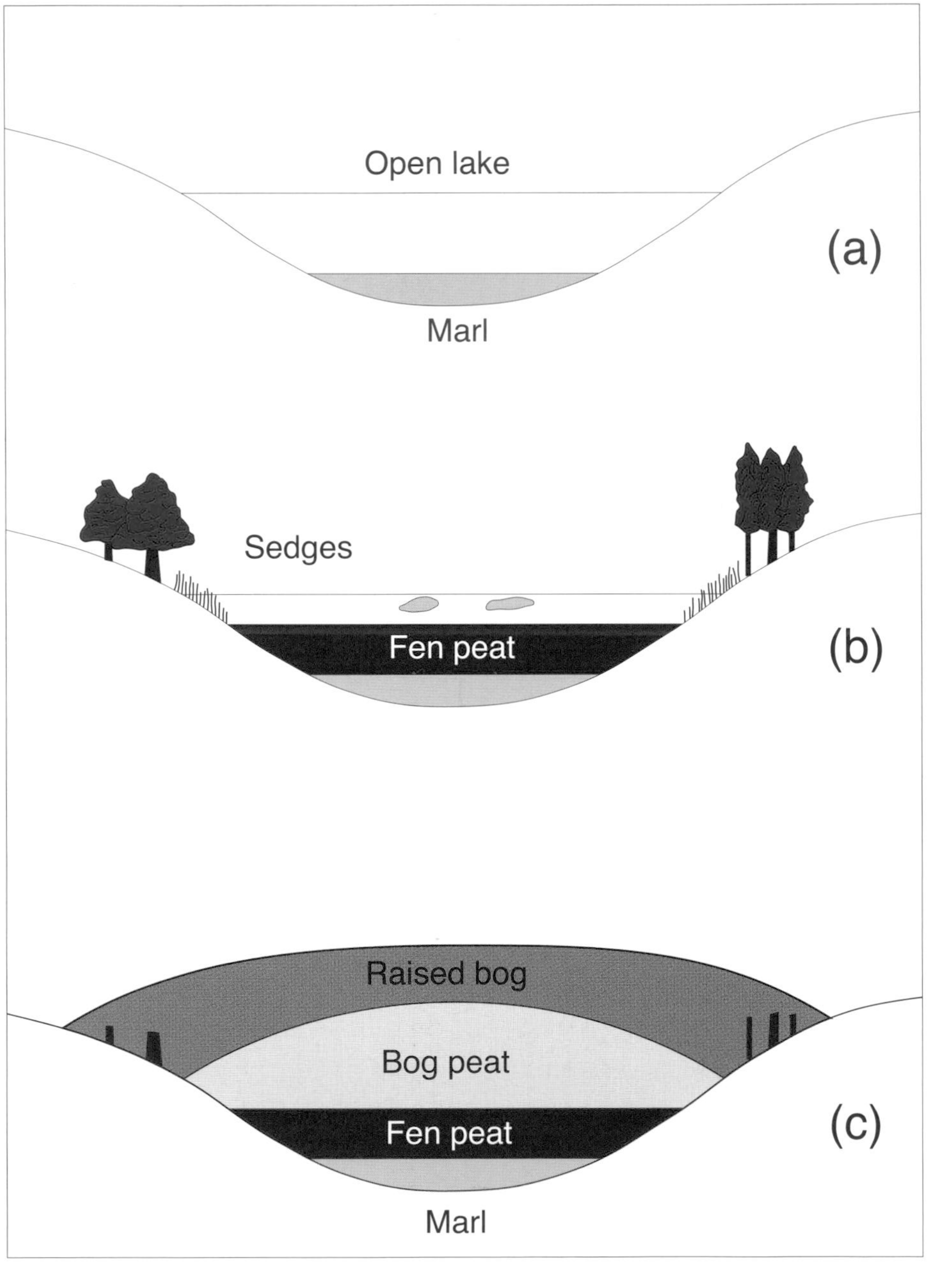

Open lake

Marl

(a)

Sedges

Fen peat

(b)

Raised bog

Bog peat

Fen peat

(c)

Marl

Plate 16:
Marl at base of peat, County Offaly.

with location. At the beginning of the Flandrian (Littletonian) warm phase, conditions were comparatively dry and cool (Boreal episode) though about 7500 years ago, Ireland became wetter (Atlantic episode) which favoured the growth of peat bog. As the raised bogs flourished and grew, they expanded into the surrounding areas eventually killing off any trees that surrounded the former lakes, Plate 18. The bogs were able to expand uphill to a certain extent, though some higher areas remained as islands surrounded by peat. Place-names such as Walsh Island, Troy's Island or Coyle's Island bear witness to the time that these were upland areas surrounded by bog and marshy ground.

Exploiting the boglands

Apart from a few scattered coalfields in the Upper Carboniferous rocks, the principal sources of fuel in Ireland up to the end of the 19th century were wood and peat. Peat was the preferred fuel for a number of reasons. The calorific value of a fuel is a measure of the amount of heat (energy) generated by a given mass. The calorific value of peat with 50% moisture content is about 10 MJ/kg whereas for wood with 50% moisture content it is 8 MJ/kg. Therefore, less peat than wood had to be collected in order to yield the same energy output. Also, it was relatively easy to cut and harvest the soft peat with the implements available at the time. The use of peat as an energy resource can readily be divided into small, medium and large-scale enterprises. Individuals or small groups of people have traditionally harvested peat by hand. Archaeological finds and historical records indicate that peat has been extracted in Ireland for millennia. Even today it is not

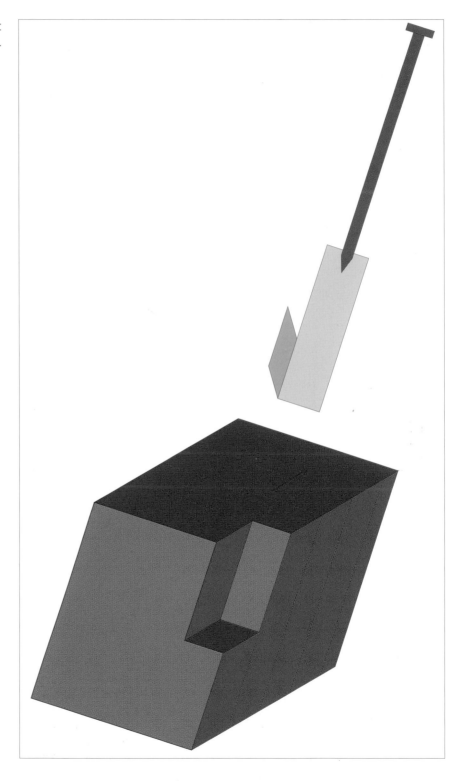

Figure 6:
Removal of peat by hand using a slane.

Plate 18:
In situ stump of tree in
peat bog, County Meath.

unusual to see peat being removed from family plots at the weekend and small (less than 0.5 hectares) plots of bogland are often sold. Peat is cut with a spade called a slane. Slane types vary in different parts of the country, but their general construction and use are similar. Typically a long wooden handle (about 1.5m long) is slotted into a metal spade end about 35 cm long and 15 cm wide. A metal flange is located along one of the long edges and at right angles to the main face of the metal blade. The slane is pushed into the top surface of the peat at a steep angle and when twisted removes a narrow slice of peat with a rectangular cross-section, Figure 6. This peat is heavily saturated with water and is left to partially dry and solidify for a few weeks. Subsequently, a number of the turves are grouped into small stacks known as footings in order that air can freely circulate and dry the peat more efficiently. It is difficult to estimate how much peat has been removed by hand-working over the centuries but Feehan and O'Donovan (1996) give an estimate of between 350,000 and 700,000 hectares.

Medium scale commercial peat enterprises have been greatly facilitated by the use of machinery and such an operation is illustrated in Plate 19. A chainsaw fitted to the back of a tractor cuts a narrow channel 15 cm wide and about 1.5m deep into the peat. The soft peat that is cut is carried into a compressor and extruded from multiple tubes producing long blocks with a rectangular cross-section. A drying process similar to that

Plate 19:
Tractor extracting peat and extruding blocks, County Meath.

described above then follows. This process is extremely efficient; a single operator could easily produce a 50 kilometres length block in a single day. The peat produced in such a fashion is usually bagged up and sold locally or in bulk in rural areas.

Bord na Móna was established in the mid 1940s to develop the peat resources of Ireland.

Bord na Móna owns 85,000 hectares of bogland, employs about 1800 people and produces peat from the boglands of central Ireland on an industrial scale. Peat extracted by Bord na Móna is used for agriculture and horticulture and as a fuel for producing electricity from peat-fired power stations. About 10% of the energy requirements in the Republic of Ireland are met by peat-fired power stations. The percentage of energy produced by peat has declined steadily from its peak in the 1960s, when about 36% of Ireland's energy was produced from peat-fired power stations. From an environmental point of view, this decline is to be welcomed because it helps preserve the bogs of central Ireland and the efficiency of producing energy from peat is very low (25%) compared with oil (36%) or gas (40%).

Plate 20:
Milling of peat near Kinnegad,
County Westmeath.

There are a number of stages in the production of peat in a Bord na Móna operation. The bog has to be partially drained in order to reduce the water content, so that the large heavy machinery can operate efficiently and safely. The drainage may take over a year. The top surface of the peat is milled, breaking it up and loosening it to a depth of about 10 cm, Plate 20, then harrowed resulting in long low linear mounds of peat. Next, these are amalgamated by a harvester into large linear mounds of peat, and are covered by plastic sheeting to dry.

Once the moisture content of the peat has reached about 55%, it is loaded into open topped carriages, which are pulled by small narrow gauge trains. Each carriage holds about 6 tonnes of peat and a typical train pulls a 100 tonne load, Plate 21. These trains travel up to 40 kilometres to the power station that they service. As one part of the bog is worked out, the tracks can be lifted, moved and re-used. The main areas within the Irish Midlands where extensive tracks remain are around Lanesborough north and west of Lough Ree, south of Athlone and around Ferbane and Rhode in County Offaly. (Ferbane power station has closed down and no peat is now used at Rhode).

Plate 21: Wagons of peat, Edenderry, County Offaly. Note approaching train in the background.

The carriages are emptied two at a time by being turned upside down (while still connected to the rest of the carriages by means of a coupling) allowing the peat to fall into an underground hopper. The peat is then transported by a conveyor belt into the power station and burnt. The 120 MW power station near Edenderry, County Offaly uses 3,000 tonnes of peat per day (just over a million tonnes per year). The amount of peat produced by Bord na Móna varies from year to year, but is typically of the order of 6-8 million tonnes.

Bord na Móna also produce peat briquettes for domestic heating purposes. In this process the peat is ground down to a fine particle size and dried until the moisture content is reduced to 10%. The peat is then compressed into moulds to produce the briquettes. Roughly twice as much energy is produced from a briquette than from an equivalent weight of milled peat that is used in a power station.

The extraction of peat to be used in agriculture or as a fuel is ultimately non-sustaining as it results in the destruction of the bogs and the unique ecosystems that exist on them. Of the 300,000 hectares of raised bog that was formed in Ireland, only about 24,000 hectares remain totally unmodified by humans, 8% of the original area. There has been an 80% reduction in blanket bogs. The use of the boglands as a tourist attraction has gained in popularity in recent years. The Irish Peatlands Conservation Council has developed the Bog of Allen Nature Centre at Lullymore, County Kildare where educational programmes and fieldtrips are offered on bog ecology, wildlife and conservation. The boglands around Lough Boora in County Offaly are now important wildlife habitats. Government initiatives in recent years have seen attempts to purchase boglands in order to protect them. However, it is not possible to maintain the integrity of a bog if adjacent areas are being drained, so large areas need to be purchased in order to create buffer zones around the bogs. Some progress has been made; over 30,000 hectares of bog are now protected (though this area is not all totally unmodified bog). Clara Bog in County Offaly, once owned by Bord na Móna, is now the largest raised bog protected site in Ireland encompassing 460 hectares. Coniferous forests were often planted once the peat extraction process was finished, but Coillte (the Irish Forestry Board) has, in recent years, removed over 500 hectares of trees and attempted to re-instate the raised bogs.

Karst in the Irish Midlands

The Karst Working Group of Ireland in their publication 'The Karst of Ireland' (2000) define karst as 'a term used world-wide to describe the distinctive landforms that develop on rock types that are readily dissolved by water'. Limestone is such a rock type as natural water containing carbon dioxide, forms a weak acid, which can dissolve the limestone. Such a process, operating over a long time period leads to the formation of a range of landforms, from some only a few centimetres in size to others that are kilometres long. Small-scale karstic features are termed karren and include the formation of small solution hollows on horizontal surfaces and channels etched in sloping limestone surfaces (Plate 22). The water is able to seep down through the cracks, joints and fissures in the limestone,

Plate 22:
Small-scale karstic features (channels) formed in limestone, Tuamgraney, County Clare. Channels are about 1m long.

widening them in the process and allowing a greater amount of water to flow underground. Entire rivers can disappear underground through swallow-holes. Here it is able to dissolve the limestone further producing subterranean passageways and caves, Plate 23. Collapse of the overlying limestone may occur when too much limestone is removed at depth. The greatest development of karst in Ireland is in the Burren in County Clare where a 15 kilometres long cave system (Pollnagollum) is known. It would be wrong to assume that the Irish Midlands are characterised by widespread karstic landforms because it is formed mainly of limestone (see the geological map of the midlands in Figure 4). Many of the limestones in the Irish Midlands are impure and contain mud which can greatly reduce the karstification process (Karst Working Group of Ireland, 2000). However, it is likely that there are unknown karstic features in the midlands which are hidden beneath the extensive glacial sediments. Karst features can be seen in Section III, on Itinerary C near Fore (swallow-hole and springs), caves and spring on Itinerary I near Tulsk, karren features near Scarriff on Itinerary H and what are believed to represent large-scale relict karstic hills near Portlaoise on Itinerary G.

Plate 23:
Cave formed by solution of limestone,
near Tulsk, County Roscommon.

Water in the Irish Midlands

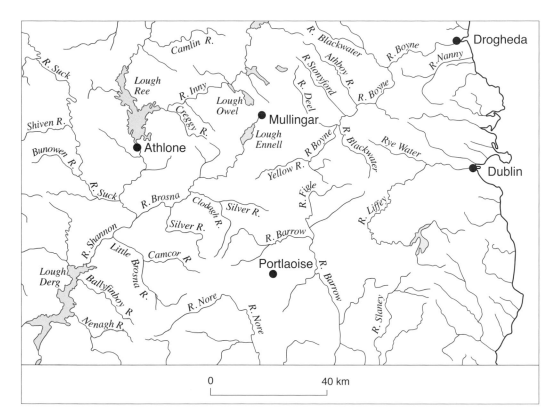

Many of the major rivers in Ireland either rise within the Irish Midlands or flow through the midlands for a considerable distance, Figure 7. The River Shannon is the longest river in Ireland and flows from the Cuilcagh Mountains in County Fermanagh to enter the sea at Limerick. From its source to the Atlantic Ocean at Loop Head, this is a distance of *c.* 340 kilometres. Its catchment area is around 13,000 km^2 and within the Irish Midlands, gradients tend to be very low. It is difficult to give flow rates for the Shannon as these vary seasonally and annually and are also affected by the opening and closing of sluices. Typically it is of the order of 200 m^3/s, which is about 17 million tonne of water per day. Low flow run-offs can be considerably lower, *c.* 12 m^3/s. During periods of flooding, sluice gates can be opened to alleviate flooding and the level of the loughs can be lowered in the late autumn in order to increase their storage capacity to accommodate the heavier winter rain. The Barrow and Nore Rivers both rise in the Irish Midlands, are the second and third longest in Ireland with catchment areas of *c.* 3060 km^2 and 2530 km^2 respectively. The Barrow is 190 kilometres in length, rises in the Slieve Bloom Mountains and flows east to Portarlington in County Laois then south to enter the sea at Waterford. The Nore is *c.* 140 kilometres in length, rises in the Devil's Bit Mountain in County Tipperary and flows through County Laois and County Tipperary to join up with the Barrow. The Boyne is *c.* 110 kilometres long and rises in the eastern part of the Irish Midlands, near Carbury in County Kildare and flows east through Trim, Navan, and Slane to enter the Irish Sea at Drogheda. Major topographic watersheds are absent in the Irish Midlands except for the Slieve Bloom Mountains.

There are a number of major loughs within the Irish Midlands, which can be broadly divided into 2 groups, those concentrated around Mullingar in County Westmeath and which are not associated with a major river and those on the River Shannon. Those around Mullingar include Loughs Derravaragh, Owel, Ennell and Lene. Such lakes can be important sources of drinking water. Westmeath County Council abstracts around 20 million litres of water per day from Lough Owel to meet the needs of the community. The loughs vary in size, Lough Derravaragh is *c.* 10 kilometres long and has an area of 1,000 hectares, Lough Ennell is 7 kilometres in length and covers an area of 1,300 hectares, Lough Owel is 6 kilometres in length and covers a area of 1,000 hectares, whereas Loughs Lene and Bane are much smaller (500 hectares and 125 hectares respectively). Although the loughs are of various sizes they are asymmetric in shape and most have a long axis which trends approximately northwest-southeast (NW-SE), Table 1. A satellite image of the Mullingar region illustrates that the glacial sediments and topography have the same trend. Movement of the glacial ice has gouged out depressions and moulded the hills in a northwest-southeast direction and the depressions have since filled with water to form the loughs, Plate 24.

Table 1:
Trend of loughs around
Mullingar, County Westmeath.

Name	Long/short axis ratio	Long axis trend
Lough Bane	3.4	WNW-ESE
Lough Ennell	2.6	NNE-WSW
Lough Adeel	4.2	NW-SE
Lough Lene	2.5	WNW-ESE
Lough Derravaragh	5.6	NW-SE
Lough Owel	2.7	NW-SE
Lough Iron	6.6	NW-SE
Lough Glen	3.3	WNW-ESE

Plate 24:
Satellite image showing lakes (black) around Mullingar, County Westmeath.

The largest lakes in the Irish Midlands and among the largest in Ireland are Loughs Ree and Derg on the River Shannon; see Figure 7 for location and Plate 1. Lough Derg is 35 kilometres in length, covers an area of *c*. 118 km^2 and reaches a depth of 36m in places. As the elevation of the lake surface is 30m, Ordnance Datum, some parts of the lough bottom are below present-day sea level. Lough Ree is smaller, being about 30 kilometres in length with depths generally less than 10m, though reaching *c*. 36m near Inchmore Island. Both loughs have very irregular shorelines, with changes in trend occurring over very short distances, Plate 25. The depressions they occupy were formed by glacial erosion but have since been modified by solution processes. The lakes were once larger and there are a number of 'mushroom stones' located around Lough Ree. (See Itinerary D for a discussion of such features). The southern part of Lough Derg has a very distinctive 'T' shape, and the lake goes from being 13 kilometres wide to 2 kilometres wide in a very short distance. An examination of Figure 4 shows that the narrowmost southerly part of the lough is surrounded by non-soluble greywackes and the wide part by soluble limestones with the sharp change in width occurring at the boundary.

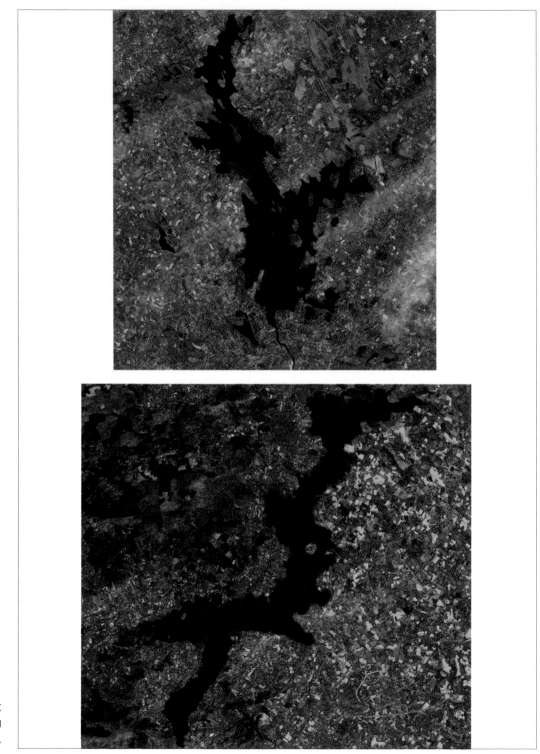

Plate 25:
Loughs Ree (top) and Derg (bottom) on the River Shannon. Both shown as black.

Therefore, solution of the limestone along the shore has allowed the lough to widen. Some have speculated as to why the River Shannon has apparently cut its way through the harder greywackes of the Arra and Slieve Bernagh Mountains to form a gorge rather than take an easier route through the Carboniferous and to leave the lough at Scarriff in County Clare. It is probable that glacial processes are responsible for its present course. Davies and Stephens (1978) have suggested that the harder rocks were 'breached' by glacial erosion and the Shannon then followed this course. It is also known in Ireland for rivers to have their courses altered by the deposition of glacial sediments in their path. The River Bush in County Antrim once flowed to Ballycastle. However the deposition of the Armoy moraine caused it to turn a right angle, abandon its former course, and seek a new route to the sea. The River Liffey, which rises in the Wicklow Mountains once flowed west to join the River Barrow but its course was totally altered by glacial sediments causing it to turn northeast to enter the sea at Dublin.

The loughs discussed above are all permanent lakes however there is a class of lake called a turlough (from the Gaelic 'tuar loch' meaning dry lake) which may contain water during part of the year and be dry at other times. Turloughs are inextricably linked with karst processes and tend to occur mainly in the west of the country in Counties Clare, Mayo Galway and Sligo. Within the Irish Midlands there is a concentration of turloughs in County Roscommon, to the west of Lough Ree (e.g. Corkip Lough, Loughs Glore and Nacreeva). The location of a turlough is indicated on Figure 11, Itinerary I. Turloughs remain dry while water is able to flow freely underground and the water table is low. However, if the subterranean passageways become clogged or the subsurface saturated with water, the water table can rise and when it reaches the surface, a lake forms.

Other water features which can be ephemeral are springs (though some may flow all year round with variable flow rates). Springs form when water which had been channelled underground re-emerges at the surface. The springs at Fore in County Westmeath are among the best known in the Irish Midlands (see Itinerary C) and many of the 'holy wells' in Ireland are natural springs.

Soils of the Irish Midlands

The types of soil that develop in any area depend to a large extent on the nature of the overlying vegetation, the character of the underlying non-organic material such as rock type, the climate under which the soil develops and the nature of the processes that occur within it. The situation in the Irish Midlands is complicated because of the large variation in the nature and thickness of the underlying glacial sediments and because the detailed distribution of the sediments is often not known. In some areas, well-drained, thick layered gravels may be deposited, whereas in others poorly drained till and clays may predominate. Even small changes in relief may alter the type of soil that develops. The soils in the Irish Midlands also developed under changing climatic and vegetational regimes. At the end of the last glacial period, the Irish Midlands were initially a vegetationless, poorly drained region, which later developed bogs and a deciduous forest cover. However, today a large proportion of the soils are developing under a grassland cover whose chemical composition has been artificially altered by the addition of fertiliser. Only the gross areal variations in soil type for the Irish Midlands are outlined here, Figure 8. Leaching and other

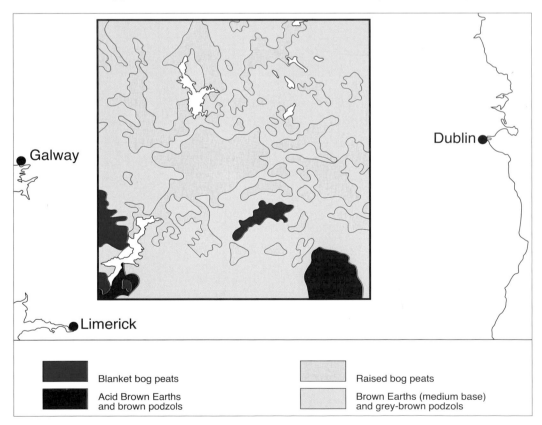

Figure 8:
Main soil groups in the Irish Midlands.

Blanket bog peats

Acid Brown Earths
and brown podzols

Raised bog peats

Brown Earths (medium base)
and grey-brown podzols

chemical and physical processes often result in the development of soil horizons where a section shows layers with different physical and/or chemical characteristics. This zonation may be employed in identifying various soil types, podzols; for example, are soils which have a pronounced leached upper horizon. Organic soils (of the soil order: histosols) have a very high organic content and are associated with raised bog and blanket peat deposits, Figure 8. In poorly-drained water logged areas, the oxidised form of iron (ferric) may be chemically reduced to the ferrous form resulting in a grey-blue gley. Gleying may occur locally in the Irish Midlands, but is most prevalent in the drumlin area to the north. Brown Earths do not show such distinct zonation as podzols and tend to be relatively free-draining. Much of the Irish Midlands can be characterised as a combination of grey-brown podzols and brown earths with medium to high base status (Orme, 1970). Acid brown earths are more common in southeast County Laois because the glacial sediments are less calcareous and contain more shale.

Climate of the Irish Midlands

Ireland lies on the eastern edge of a major ocean (Atlantic) at a mean latitude of 53° North and a mean longitude of 8° West. Its geographical position dictates the climate that affects the Irish Midlands. There are also meteorological variations within the county, for example the western seaboard receives more rain than the eastern side of the country. As well as spatial variations, there are also temporal variations, so some months are consistently wetter or windier than others. Also, some years show marked deviations from the mean and in order to obtain a representative value for a specific parameter it is necessary to take values averaged over a long time period. Met Éireann has acquired meteorological data at two Irish midland sites for many decades, at Birr in County Offaly and at Mullingar in County Westmeath. Data, collected over the 30-year time span 1961-1990, at these two recording sites have been averaged to produce values representative of the Irish Midlands. The resulting monthly values for temperature, rainfall, sunshine and wind speed are shown in graphical form in Figure 9. (Note, for this period, Birr was generally slightly warmer, drier and less windy than Mullingar but received less sunshine). The mean daily maximum and minimum temperatures for each month are shown in Figure 9(a). The mean maximum is around 6.6° Celsius (C) in January, which rises at a fairly constant rate to around 19°C in July. The pattern for the mean minimum temperature is similar, with the lowest values around 2°C and the highest 10.5°C. The difference between the maximum and minimum temperatures does not remain constant but also varies throughout the year, being lowest in the winter months (5.6°C) and highest April-August (greater than 8.5°C). The highest temperature recorded in the 20th century in Ireland was in the Irish Midlands (June 1976) near Lough Boora in County Offaly (32.5°C). The Irish Midlands on average receive 800-1,000 mm of rain per year, most of which falls during the winter months. The driest part of the year is usually April-May, Figure 9(b). The number of hours of sunshine is greatest in May (for both Birr and Mullingar) and least in December, Figure 9(c). Wind direction in the Irish Midlands is mainly from between the west and the south, with the average speeds being greater in January-March (around 16.4 kilometres/hr) than in June-August (12 kilometres/hr), Figure 9(d). The percentage change over the year for wind speed is less than the percentage change for rainfall, sunshine or temperature. The average wind speed maximum is 38% greater than the minimum wind speed, whereas the values for rainfall (59%), maximum temperature (170%) and sunshine (238%) are greater.

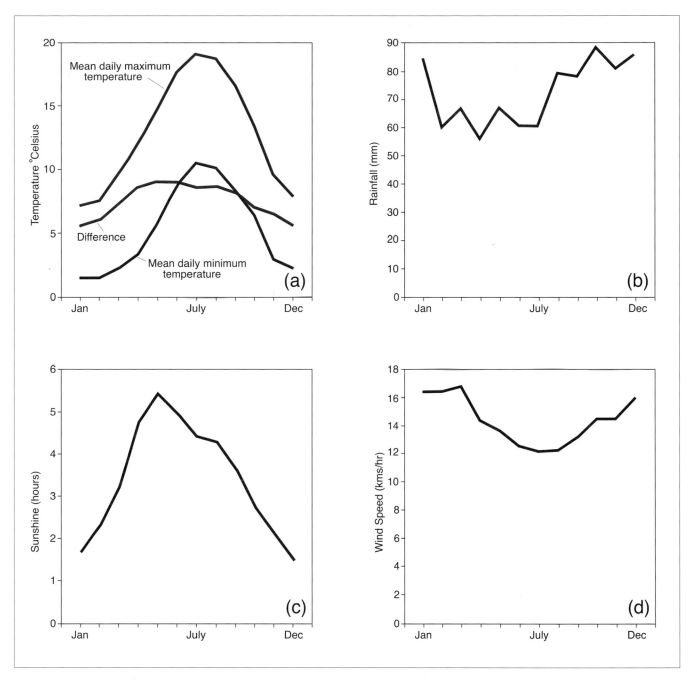

Figure 9:
Average climatic parameters for the Irish Midlands, 1961-1090. (a) Temperature; (b) Rainfall; (c) Sunshine; (d) Windspeed.

SECTION II

Archaeological and Historical Landscapes of the Irish Midlands

Introduction

Ireland's human occupation history extends over 9,000 years, a time span that was punctuated by significant events such as the arrival of Anglo-Normans which changed, often radically, the cultural practices and customs that existed at that time. Ireland's landscape bears witness to these changes as evidenced by the structures that were created at different times by different people. These structures include: Round Towers, High Crosses, mottes, castles, churches, megalithic tombs, souterrains, standing stones, crannogs, ringforts, tumuli and toghers. A generalised time line for human habitation in the Irish Midlands showing the major events and the major structures is given in Figure 10. Some of the features such as mottes or Round Towers were constructed over a relatively short time period. However, there are others, such as toghers, where dating evidence indicates that they have been built for thousands of years. A particularly difficult group to categorise is that of standing stones, some are prehistoric whereas others may be relatively recent.

Archaeologists and historians often divide the past into discrete time spans such as the Bronze Age, Iron Age or early medieval period. This is done for convenience and it should be realised that the boundaries between such discreet spans is not abrupt but much more transitional than may be realised simply by looking at dates. Thus, for example, iron implements were imported into Ireland before it had an indigenous iron-making capacity and bronze tools would continue to have been used in the Iron Age. Rather than provide a chronological discussion regarding human occupation, this section of the book deals with the major events that helped shape the landscape of the Irish Midlands:

- Prehistoric settlement in the Irish Midlands
- Arrival and development of Christianity
- Viking Ireland
- The Irish Church in the 12th Century
- Anglo-Norman Invasion and Aftermath
- 16th-17th century Confiscation, Plantation, Rebellion and War
- Suppression and Landlordism
- 19th century Famine
- Irish Midlands: Post Famine – Modern times

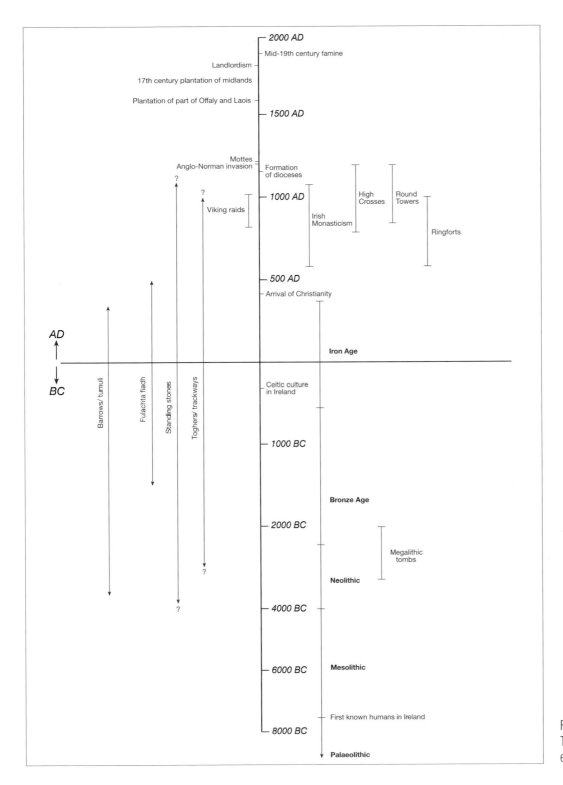

Figure 10:
Time line for the Irish Midlands. Note scale is not
even and some ranges are approximate.

Prehistoric settlement in the Irish Midlands

There are two main sources of information about the early human occupation of Ireland: archaeological excavation and the 'epic sagas', which were compiled much later than the times to which they refer. The sagas have generally been considered within four groupings: Mythological Cycle, Ulster Cycle, Kings' Cycle and Fenian Cycle. These legends have been recorded in a number of texts, such as the Book of Leinster, Yellow Book of Lecan or the Dinnshenchas, many of which date from the 12th century or later (Zaczek, 2000). One important episode in Irish lore is the Táin Bo Cuailgne, the Cattle Raid of Cooley (County Louth). This refers to an attempt by Queen Maeve (Maeb) of Connacht to capture the Brown Bull of Cuailgne, an attempt that was resisted by Cuchulainn. The Táin Trail can be followed through the Irish Midlands and is linked with Rathcroghan in County Roscommon, an important Celtic royal site, which forms part of Itinerary I. The sagas bring the Irish landscape to life populating it with kings and heroes, although they should not be taken literally. However, once the hyperbole has been stripped away, they may contain a core of truth. Archaeological excavation at the Hill of Uisneach in County Westmeath supports the legends about this site (see Itinerary E).

Once the ice had retreated from Ireland and conditions ameliorated about 10,000 years ago, it became suitable for sustained human occupation. There is no unequivocal evidence of humans in Ireland during the Palaeolithic. However, humans lived in Britain during the late upper Palaeolithic about 13,000 years ago at Creswell Crags in Derbyshire and Cheddar caves in Somerset (Smith, 1992). A large number of Mesolithic sites are known from northeast Ireland. This part of Ireland is the closest to Britain (which is visible from the north Antrim coast) and it is likely that the first humans used this route. In addition, abundant flint, from which tools could be manufactured, occurs in this area as layers within the Cretaceous chalk. A Mesolithic site at Mount Sandel near Coleraine, within which were found flint scrapers and other tools, has yielded radiocarbon dates of around 6900 BC (about 8,900 year before present, BP). After Lough Boora in County Offaly was drained, a Mesolithic site was discovered in 1977. Excavations revealed hearths, stone axeheads, scrapers and blades. The site was radiocarbon dated to around 7000-6500 BC (McDermott, 1998). Other Mesolithic sites have been uncovered in the Irish Midlands and there appears to be a large concentration around the northern shore of Lough Derravaragh in County Westmeath. It is likely that, within the Irish Midlands, other such lakeside sites are still to be uncovered.

Mesolithic people were to a large extent nomadic, Lough Boora has been interpreted as a summer camp (O'Brien and Sweetman, 1997). From about 4000 BC, during the

Plate 26:
Portal tomb, near Carlow, County Carlow.

Neolithic, there is evidence of farming and agricultural practices. Therefore, Neolithic people had a stake in the land that they cleared and worked and it was during the Neolithic that monuments began to be erected, the most significant of which are the megalithic tombs. Around 1500 such tombs have been discovered in Ireland, and they are generally categorized into four types based partly on their shape and style of construction: portal tombs, court tombs, passage tombs and wedge tombs. There is some evidence that wedge tombs are the latest that were built (after about 2500 BC whereas the others are pre-3000 BC), and some have been found to contain bronze objects. Stout and Stout (1997) state that radiocarbon dating indicates a considerable temporal overlap in some of the different tomb building styles.

Portal tombs (or dolmens) consist of two parallel upright stone slabs of rock (portals), which are joined by another slab at right angles, all of which are surmounted by a large capstone. Most tend to be concentrated in the northern part of the country, though groupings also occur in County Clare and County Waterford. They are rare in the Irish Midlands though one can be found near Carlow, Plate 26 (Itinerary G). Court tombs, which consist of a series of generally small stones set roughly parallel and forming a small courtyard through which one walks to reach the burial, occur almost exclusively in the northern part of Ireland. Wedge tombs usually consist of two rock slabs on which sits a capstone. The slabs are non-parallel, so have the appearance of a wedge shape. They are concentrated in County Clare, SW Ireland and northern Ireland. The portal, court and wedge tombs are all relatively small features measuring metres in size. However, the passage tombs are massive in comparison, up to 80m in diameter, the most widely known one being Newgrange and Knowth in County Meath. They consist of a passage, at the end of which there are one or more chambers, all of which are covered by a conical mound of stones, then usually grassed over, Plate 27. They are found mainly in the northern part of the country and occasionally occur in groups forming a passage grave cemetery. One such cemetery occurs southeast of Oldcastle, County Meath and is discussed in Itinerary C. The passage tombs are often faced around the perimeter with larger slabs, some of which exhibit rock art. This usually consists of geometric patterns such as parallel zigzags, spirals or radial lines. All types of tombs often contained cremated remains which may be accompanied by pottery.

Standing stones occur widely both spatially and temporally throughout the Irish Midlands, and they possess no unique identifying characteristic. Some are clearly associated with major prehistoric monuments or other less significant features such as barrows, whereas others do not appear to be associated with any other landscape feature. They are typically about 2m high and sometimes broader at the base tapering upwards. They are also often asymmetric, being much thinner (50 cm) than their width at the base

Plate 27:
Passage tomb at Loughcrew,
County Meath.

(1.2m). The direction of their alignment also varies, so they do not appear to conform to a set orientation. In general, they occur in isolation but a large group of about 300 (Timoney Stones) occurs southeast of Roscrea (Itinerary F). In rare instances they are arranged in a circle or in a line. Their purpose and age also vary greatly, some may be associated with burials or cremations. Others, due to their prominent hilltop positions may have acted as meeting places or the locations of some rituals or ceremonies, such as the inauguration of a leader. Others may simply have delineated different territories. Most stones are formed of the local bedrock and could also be erratics dumped from glaciers and later erected into an upright position. Their age can vary greatly and because they are rarely decorated, an exact determination is often impossible. Many are prehistoric, but others could be of relatively recent origin. Plate 28 shows a standing stone near Rhode, County Offaly. The Ballyburly stone is located adjacent to a mound and is positioned such that it can be seen from a great distance. Standing stones can be seen on Itineraries C, F, and I. Tumuli (singular tumulus) are artificial earthen mounds, believed to enclose prehistoric burials most likely dating to the Bronze-Iron Age, Plate 29.

The Bronze Age in Ireland (circa 2500-600 BC) is not characterised by large megalithic tombs but by small urn and 'cist' burials, in which the cremated remains or a body in the foetal position were placed in a small stone box. Such burials were sometimes located in prominent positions, but their small size and inconspicuous character means that many have been discovered by accident during road improvement schemes or by agricultural activity. Some burials contain the remains of one body whereas others contain several. A large concentration of such cist burials can be found in County Westmeath and Bronze

Plate 28:
Ballyburly standing stone near Rhode, County Offaly.

Plate 29:
Tumulus near Clonard, County Meath.
Width approximately 30m and height about 4m.

Age cemeteries have been found near Tulsk in County Roscommon and near Tullamore in County Offaly. Although one would tend to associate the introduction of metals during this period with the production of weapons such as swords or spears, the metals were also employed for decorative purposes. Gold twist torcs and lunulae (crescent-shaped neck ornaments) were manufactured during the Bronze Age (O'Kelly, 2005). Many of these objects are now housed in the National Museum of Ireland in Dublin and they have been discovered usually by accident such as the gold penannular bracelet found along with an amber bead necklace near Banagher, County Offaly.

Fulachta fiadh are low mounds (frequently over 10m across) consisting of piles of stones, which have been shattered by high temperatures, often in a matrix of charcoal-enriched soil, confirming these high temperatures. They are believed to represent cooking sites in which stones heated on a fire were placed in a trough of water within which meat was boiled. The rapid cooling of the stones, as they were placed in the water, caused contraction and resultant shattering. The discarded stones were then left in a nearby pile. They have been found at different locations in the Irish Midlands in Counties Roscommon, Laois and Offaly where a concentration of five are located at Garr, north of Rhode. A number of the fulachta fiadh have been dated and most dates group in the 3500-2500 BP range (Bronze Age) though they were probably used in later times as well (Brindley et al., 1989).

One of the most characteristic archaeological structures of the Irish Midlands is the togher or trackway. Figure 10 shows that they occur over an extremely long time span and cannot be easily fitted into any specific period. They are found in all the midland counties, although there is a particularly high concentration in County Longford. They vary in their construction method and in their sophistication. Most are formed of wood and may consist simply of bundles of brushwood, whereas others are formed of split oak logs pinned together to retain the integrity of the structure. There are two main reasons why there is such a concentration in the Irish Midlands. Firstly, the extensive bogs in the midlands greatly restricted movement, thus it was essential that trackways were made across them in order to facilitate trade and communication. Secondly, with constant use, the toghers would sink into the bog and be replenished by a new supply of wood placed on top. The chemistry of the bog waters was such that the timber did not decay but was preserved. Radiocarbon dating of 112 Irish trackways was carried out by Brindley and Lanting (1998). They show that some trackways are over 4500 years old (Corlea 10 in County Longford, 454040 BP) whereas others are around 1,000 years old. There is also evidence for the same trackways being used for long time periods, and they suggest that the Bloomhill one in County Offaly may have been in use for 450 years. Such trackways can be seen on Itineraries B and E.

The working of iron on mainland Europe can be traced back at least 1,000 years before the Iron Age began in Ireland (approximately 600 BC). The Iron Age on the continent is often described in terms of the artefacts produced, an older Hallstatt style and a later La Tène style (Zaczek 2000). The Hallstatt style is named after a site east of Salzburg, Austria and the La Tène style, which developed around 500 BC, after a site near Lake Neuchatel, Switzerland. The race of people associated with the La Tène style are inextricably linked with Ireland: the Celts. There was no 'Celtic invasion' by a warrior race into Ireland, but rather a diffusion of Celtic people, ideas, customs and practices around 300 BC. The Celts are associated with some of the major sites in Ireland today, such as Cruachain in County Roscommon, Navan Fort in County Armagh, Tara in County Meath and Dun Ailinne in County Kildare. A number of less well-known but impressive hillforts were also extensively used during the Iron Age. These are usually in the form of a circular embankment (or series of embankments) and fosse surrounding a hilltop. The Ballycurragh hillfort in County Offaly has a diameter of 140m whereas the Clopook hillfort in County Laois is 200m across.

Celtic society involved clans (tuath) and tribal alliances, which in turn led on to the concept of territories or kingdoms. Today, in Ireland we recognize four provinces, Ulster in the north, Connacht in the west, Munster in the southwest and Leinster in the southeast. Texts relating to this time often refer to five kingdoms. The fifth is Mide, which would encompass the present Counties Meath and Westmeath. The Gaelic word for province is coiceda, meaning one fifth. (Some writers believe that the 'fifth province' relates to Ireland as an entity).

Interestingly, we get some idea of the knowledge of Ireland in the latter half of the Iron Age from Greek sources. Ptolemy produced a map of Ireland (called Iwernia) around 150 AD. Many of the features shown relate to coastal sites such as islands or promontories but his Buvinda and Senos rivers have been correlated with the Boyne and Shannon Rivers respectively (Condit and Moore, 2003).

Arrival and development of Christianity

The first recorded evidence of Christianity associated with Ireland is in 431 AD when the pope appointed Palladius to be the bishop of the Irish who believed in Christ (Duffy, 2000). Early Christianity in Ireland is inextricably linked with St. Patrick. A difficulty in dealing with this important historic figure is the uncertainty about dates and the exaggeration that accompanies him and his works. There are a number of sites which are said to be where he is buried and many locations throughout Ireland which contain, for example, a 'St. Patrick's Well' or a specific site associated with a visit by the saint. It is likely that many may have been visited by a follower of St. Patrick, spreading his teachings, rather than Patrick himself. Patrick is believed to have been born in Britain, captured by the Irish and held captive for 6 years. After being released, his vocation to bring Christianity to the Irish led him into the religious life and his return to Ireland to convert the people. His works in Ireland are believed to have occurred around 450-470 AD and he is thought to have died around 493 AD.

Monasticism began to develop in Ireland from about the 6th century onwards. This tended to follow a general pattern. An individual would devote himself (and it was usually male, although some notable females such as St. Brigid are also known) to prayer, fasting and toil. Word would spread about this person and others would then join him to be trained for a religious life. A monastic community, consisting of small chapels, accommodation and kitchens, would then start to form. Often early Christian monasteries were enclosed within a circular earthen bank, separating the secular world outside from the religious world, within which the abbot's rules applied. Eventually, some of the disciples would move on to establish other communities in their own right, but still following the precepts of the original one, so forming a grouping of monastic settlements (paruchia) which followed the teaching of one person. A number of early monasteries were founded in the Irish Midlands, Figure 11. Parts of the earthen banks which formed their perimeter can still be seen at Killeigh (Itinerary A) and Rahan (Itinerary B) in County Offaly.

St. Finnian (Finian) founded a monastery at Clonard (County Meath) around 520 AD. He is known as the Master of the Saints of Ireland due to the large number of important bishops who studied under him at Clonard. Other important sites include Durrow and Kells founded by St. Columcille, Clonfert by St. Brendan and Clonmacnoise by St. Ciaran in the mid-6th century. In the following centuries, monasteries such as these would be associated with many of the iconic characteristics of Ireland's heritage such as illuminated manuscripts, High Crosses and Round Towers.

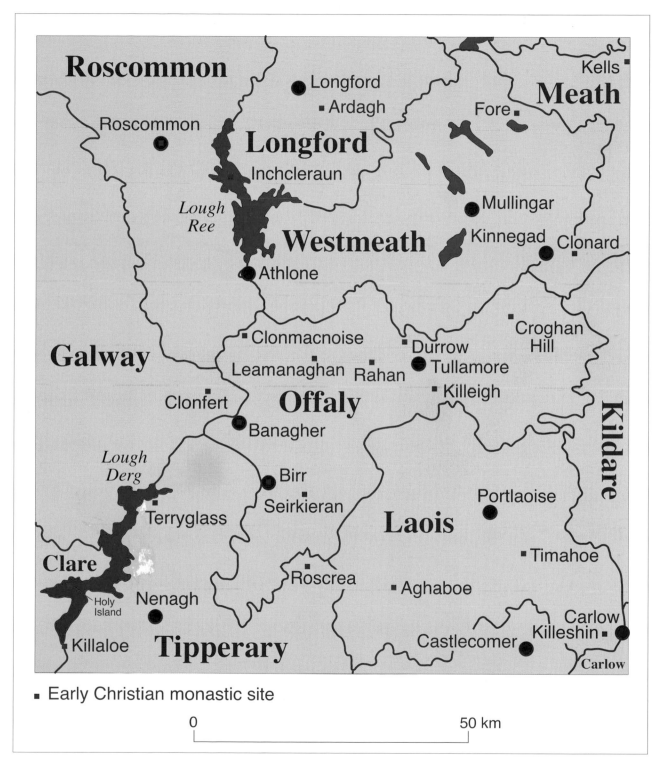

Figure 11:
Main early Christian monastic sites in the Irish Midlands.

Roscommon

Longford
▪ Ardagh

Roscommon

Meath

Kells ▪

Fore ▪

Longford

Inchcleraun

Lough Ree

Westmeath

Mullingar

Kinnegad   Clonard

Athlone

Galway

▪ Clonmacnoise

Croghan Hill

Durrow

▪ Leamanaghan   Rahan   Tullamore

Offaly

▪ Killeigh

Clonfert

Banagher

Lough Derg

▪ Birr

Seirkieran

Laois

Portlaoise

Terryglass

Clare

▪ Timahoe

Holy Island

Nenagh

▪ Roscrea

▪ Aghaboe

Carlow

Killeshin ▪

Killaloe   **Tipperary**

Castlecomer

Kildare

Carlow

▪ Early Christian monastic site

0   50 km

Plate 30:
High Cross at Kells, County Meath.

The Celtic Cross is one of the most enduring images of Irish Christianity and is today still widely used in cemeteries for headstones. Large Celtic Crosses made of stone termed High Crosses were constructed around the 9th-12th century and were associated with important monastic sites, such as Kells in County Meath, Plate 30. Their style changed over this time period (Richardson, 2005). They are typically about 3.5m to 4m tall and are divided into separate panels, within which various biblical scenes are shown such as the crucifixion or resurrection of Christ, It has been suggested that they represent the triumph of Christianity over paganism as the cross is usually seen to 'break' the circle, representing the sun which was worshiped by pagans. However, some of the crosses at Clonmacnoise do not conform to this convention. High Crosses and other early Christian crosses can be seen on many of the itineraries described later such as on Itinerary B at Clonmacnoise; Itinerary A at Tihilly and Durrow, Itinerary H at Killaloe, Itinerary F at Roscrea and Itinerary C at Kells.

Round Towers are tall (*c.* 25m) and narrow (6m in diameter), usually free standing stone structures and associated with some ecclesiastical centres such as Clonmacnoise (Itinerary B); Roscrea (Itinerary F); Timahoe (Itinerary G) and Kells (Itinerary C), Plate 31. They date from the 10th-12th century and around 60 still exist today, although many are incomplete.

Records show that they housed a bell, which was used, as today, to announce prayers. They are characterised by small windows and an entrance door that is about 3m above the ground. Monasteries contained important and valuable items such as relics, illuminated manuscripts and shrines that could be held in the Round Towers during attacks.

Associated with some of the ecclesiastical settlements are a number of smaller objects such as grave slabs or ballaun stones. The early Christian slabs are often relatively crude and generally show an incised cross on a thin slab of stone, Plate 32. The exact purpose of ballaun stones is not certain. They are typically medium-sized stones which contain a small basin on their upper surface, Plate 33. It has been suggested that they functioned as holy water fonts, although others suggest that they were employed in some grinding process.

Plate 31:
Round Tower at Kells, County Meath.

The majority of people living in Ireland at that time, while Christian, were not directly associated with monastic life and they too have left their mark on the landscape. Rural settlement in early Christian times was dominated by the ringfort, of which over 45,000 have been identified often by means of aerial survey (Stout and Stout, 1997). These are mainly circular to sub-circular features enclosing one or more farmsteads. Generally they consist of a fosse (annular ditch), the soil from which was thrown inward to form an enclosing bank. The term rath is also applied to a ringfort or cashel when the bank is formed of stone. There are concentrations in north Clare and in Counties Tipperary, Sligo, Roscommon, Westmeath and Longford, but all Irish midland counties contain many ringforts (County Offaly has about 200 known examples). No doubt there are many unknown examples in the landscape and over the centuries many may have been destroyed by agricultural activity.

Plate 32:
Cross slab at Leamonaghan,
County Offaly.

It should not be assumed that ringforts are all identical in character; there are variations in size, morphology, age and sophistication. Most ringforts date from 600-1000 AD (Stout 2000) and their diameters generally vary between 15m and 35m with an average diameter of about 30m (Edwards, 2005). The height of the ringfort interior is often raised up higher than the surrounding terrain possibly for defensive reasons but also to improve drainage. Plate 34 shows an example of such a platform ringfort near Clonard, County Meath where the platform is over 3m higher than the surroundings. The majority of ringforts, 80% according to Stout (2000), are univallate in character, that is they are surrounded by a single bank. A good example of a multivallate ringfort consisting of three encircling banks can be seen at Ballykilleen near Edenderry, County Offaly (Itinerary D).

Two other features, much less common than ringforts but broadly contemporaneous, can be seen in the Irish landscape: souterrains and crannogs. The name souterrain derives from the French 'sous terre' meaning 'under the ground'. They are underground chambers which are reached by means of narrow passageways which are often low and difficult to access. They are generally stone-lined, and may contain more than one chamber. Typically the chambers are a few metres wide and high and the connecting passages are mainly less than 20m in length. There are two general hypotheses regarding their function, which are not mutually exclusive. One is that they were convenient places to store food, being cool and dark (therefore, grain would not sprout too early) whereas the other view is that they were places of refuge where it was possible to hide in case of an attack. The morphology of the souterrains does indicate a defensive nature. If they were

used simply as storehouses, then entry to them, and movement within them, would have been made easier. However, some passageways are connected by 'creeps', very low areas where it is necessary to get down on your hands and knees to progress. Such a position leaves an attacker in a vulnerable position. Other passages contain hairpin bends around which an attacker, who does not know the layout, would venture with caution. One souterrain in County Meath (Fennor) consists of two passages at different levels running in different directions which are connected by means of a trap. Thus, refuge could be taken in the lower level unbeknown to any attackers who ventured into the upper level. There are considerably fewer souterrains than ringforts in Ireland (less than 4,000) and the concentration in the Irish Midlands is low. Oweynagat near Tulsk (Itinerary I) is a souterrain, which has partially exploited a natural cave.

Crannogs are small (30-40m in diameter) artificial islands created by pounding logs vertically into the lake mud to form a circular palisade. This is then infilled with brushwood and stones to form a stable platform above water level upon which a dwelling could be constructed. Access to the crannog was difficult, so they fulfilled a defensive role. They are broadly contemporaneous with ringforts though Ballinderry 2 crannog in County Offaly was itself built on a lakeside Bronze Age settlement. Around 1,000 crannogs are known in Ireland, mainly from Counties Roscommon, Leitrim, and Cavan. There are a numbers of crannogs in the small loughs around Strokestown in County Roscommon (Cloonfree Lough, Ardakillin Lough, Finn Lough). Crannogs can also be found at Loughs Ennell and Derravaragh in County Westmeath. Many crannogs have been found only relatively recently when the water level in a lake was lowered, thus there probably remain many undiscovered ones.

Plate 34:
Ringfort near Clonard, County Meath.

Viking Ireland

In the late 8th century, starting in 795 AD, a series of attacks by Norsemen from Scandinavia was carried out on a number of islands around the coast of Ireland (Rathlin Island and Inishmurray island). Similar Viking raids continued into the early 9th century and were limited forays mainly confined to coastal areas. Such attacks were difficult to counter because of their unexpected nature, the rapidity with which they were carried out and the speed of the withdrawal. However, around 837 AD a considerably larger force of Vikings reached Ireland and during this phase they began to penetrate farther inland along the rivers and overwintered on Lough Neagh in 840-841 AD (Larsen, 2001). Rivers, such as the Shannon, the Boyne and the Barrow allowed Viking penetration into the Irish Midlands and as a consequence many of the monastic settlements such as Clonmacnoise, Clonfert, Roscrea and Clonard were attacked and plundered, often more than once.

The Vikings settled in and helped to establish a number of major towns in Ireland, most notably Dublin, Carlow, Wexford and Waterford. The continued presence of Vikings throughout the year meant that indigenous Irish clans could often mount successful attacks against them. The Vikings were driven out of Dublin in 902 AD but returned in 917 AD. Brian Boru, King of Munster, was acknowledged as the High King of all Ireland by 1002 (Duffy, 2000) but died in 1014 at the Battle of Clontarf (Dublin) when his army defeated a combined army of Viking and indigenous Irish troops.

Silver was an important means of barter and it was only during the Viking era, from the beginning of the 10th century that Ireland began to use coinage (Kenny, 2005). Viking hoards that have been discovered sometimes consist only of silver ingots whereas others consist of silver ingots and coins.

The Irish Church in the 12th Century

The Irish Church for centuries had been mainly monastic in character allowing local abbots, often associated with or related to specific chiefs, to exercise their authority with a great degree of autonomy. The Bishop of Canterbury (Lanfranc) had claimed Ireland as part of his territory and had consecrated a bishop in Dublin by 1074. A number of synods were instigated in the early to mid-12th century to ensure that Irish ecclesiastical practices conformed to practices elsewhere in Europe and to regularise the position of bishoprics. The first synod was held by Muirchertach in Cashel, County Tipperary and was followed by later ones at Raith Bresail in 1111 and at Kells/Mellifont in County Meath in 1152. The end result of these synods was the formation of four ecclesiastical provinces in Ireland: Armagh in the north, which had primacy, Tuam in the west, Cashel in the southwest and Dublin in the southeast, Figure 12. All four provinces are represented in the Irish Midlands which also contained a number of important 'sees', Clonard, Kells and Ardagh in Armagh province, Roscommon and Clonfert in Tuam province and Roscrea and Killaloe in Cashel province (Duffy, 2000).

The term 'Romanesque' is used to describe a style of building, which developed in Europe in the 11th and 12th centuries (O'Keeffe, 2003). Fitzpatrick and O'Brien (1998) describe it, with regard to churches, as consisting of a succession of vaulted bays, composed of arcades with decorated arches, and columns with paired towers dominating the main façade. The Irish Romanesque style (also termed Hiberno-Romanesque) was different in that it borrowed from a number of sources (including Viking and early Irish styles) and consisted of abstract carved art on arches and portals often accompanied by scalloping and chevrons. Plate 35 shows the upper part of the single order Hiberno-Romanesque doorway at the small church at Rahan, County Offaly and Plate 36 shows details of the doorway at Clonfert, County Galway. The Rahan doorway is composed of a number of wedge-shaped chevron decorated blocks (voussoirs) with stops carved as the heads of animals. The earliest Hiberno-Romanesque style building in Ireland is believed to be Cormac's Chapel, built in 1134, on the Rock of Cashel, County Tipperary. Romanesque entrances were added to a number of existing churches and cathedrals in the 12th century and may have been related to the formation of an accepted diocesan system. Thus Killaloe Cathedral in County Clare and Clonfert Cathedral in County Galway (Itineraries H and B) have very elaborate portals. Other Hiberno-Romanesque features can be seen at Rahan and Clonmacnoise, County Offaly (Itinerary B) and Killeshin, County Laois (Itinerary G). This style was not only applied to churches as the Timahoe Round Tower in County Laois possesses a Hiberno-Romanesque doorway (Itinerary G).

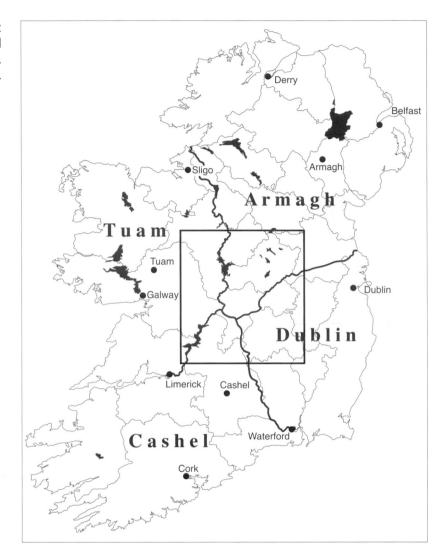

Figure 12:
Ecclesiastical Provinces in Ireland. Note, all four are represented in the Irish Midlands. Area covered by book shown in rectangle.

Plate 35:
Hiberno-Romanesque doorway at Rahan, County Offaly.

Many of the religious houses that had been formed on the continent, most notably the Franciscans, Augustinian canons, Cistercians and the Benedictines, established monasteries in Ireland from the 12th century onwards. Often these were constructed on the sites of early Christian monasteries such as at Durrow (Augustinian canons), Killeigh (Franciscans) or at Fore (Benedictines). The evidence for such monastic houses can be seen on all the itineraries.

Plate 36:
Hiberno-Romanesque detail on doorway at Clonfert, County Galway.

Anglo-Norman Invasion and Aftermath

Following the death of Brian Boru, a number of kings vied to claim the kingship of all Ireland. Muirchertach MacLochlainn from the north allied himself with Diarmait Mac Murchada (Dermot MacMurrough), king of Leinster. However, Ruaidri Úa Conchobair (O'Conor) king of Connacht, defeated Dermot, who fled abroad to obtain foreign assistance to reclaim his territory. Dermot obtained permission from Henry II, who was king of Britain and part of France, to raise an army. Dermot recruited the Anglo-Normans Richard FitzGilbert de Clare (known as Strongbow), Robert FitzStephen and Maurice FitzGerald and their followers to his cause (Roche, 1995). Dermot returned to Ireland and the Anglo-Normans landed in SW Ireland in 1169 and 1170. After subduing Waterford, Wexford and surrounding lands, they, along with the Irish allies, marched north and took Dublin. Soon after, Dermot died (1171) and, as Strongbow had married his daughter Aoife, he became king of Leinster. The Irish chieftains, along with Norsemen rallied, placed a siege on Dublin and retook Waterford and Wexford. However, the Anglo-Norman hold over Ireland was secured following a decisive battle at Castleknock.

Following Strongbow's successes in Ireland and wary of the possibility of a separate rival Anglo-Norman state, Henry II landed in Ireland in 1171. Most Irish kings acknowledged him as their ruler, and Strongbow duly submitted to him and was granted most of the kingdom of Leinster. Hugh de Lacy was granted the 'liberty' of Meath, a territory much large than the present day County Meath as it also encompassed County Westmeath and parts of Counties Longford and Offaly. He in turn granted parts of his territory to others,

Plate 37:
Anglo-Norman motte near
Loughcrew, County Meath.

so that Gilbert de Nugent controlled the area around Delvin and Richard Tuite controlled parts of present-day Counties Westmeath and Longford (Roche, 1995).

The initial defensive structures constructed by the Anglo-Normans were mottes. These are steep sided conical mounds of earth with a flat top, Plate 37. A wooden palisade would have surrounded the top perimeter, and an enclosed area at the base of the motte (a bailey) could be used for troops, animals and provisions. Good examples can be seen on Itineraries D, E, F and H. Around 350 are known in Ireland and they display a very distinctive distribution pattern. They occur mainly in two areas, a zone in northeast Ireland and in a broad arc from Waterford to Dundalk, Figure 13. Very few are located west of the River Shannon. Individual mottes were often built near important ecclesiastical centres such as Clonard or Aghaboe, or on top of pre-existing mounds, either natural (glacial sediment deposits) or man-made, as this increased the defensive capabilities of the structure and lessened the effort in their construction. Later, as the Anglo-Norman position became more permanent, stone castles were constructed, one of the most impressive being that at Trim (Plate 38), from which the liberty of Meath was administered by Hugh de Lacy (Potterton, 2005). Other stone fortifications constructed by the Anglo-Normans within the Irish Midlands are Lea Castle (Itinerary D); Dunamase Castle (Itinerary G), Rindown Castle (Itinerary I) and Delvin Castle (Itinerary C).

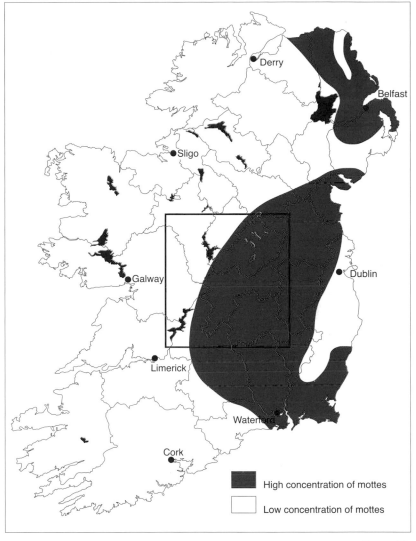

■	High concentration of mottes
□	Low concentration of mottes

Figure 13:
Location of Anglo-Norman 12th century mottes in Ireland. Area covered by book shown in rectangle.

Plate 38:
Anglo-Norman castle at Trim, County Meath.

The century following the invasion of the Anglo-Normans was one of consolidation and the formation of new towns such as Trim, Nenagh, Mullingar and Roscommon (Duffy, 2000, Simms, 2000). Irish families, such as the O'Conor Faly of County Offaly, the O'Farrells of County Longford and the O'Mores of County Laois continued to coexist with the newcomers. In the early 14th century (1315-1318), Edward Bruce invaded from Scotland and fought a number of battles in the midlands, although he was ultimately unsuccessful in his attempts to defeat the Anglo-Irish. (By this time, the term Anglo-Irish is more applicable than Anglo-Norman). Many Anglo-Irish lords coexisted relatively easily with the native Irish chieftains and assimilated many of their customs. This period is often referred to as the 'Gaelic Revival' because it represents a time when Irish culture flourished. Tower houses (tall rectangular fortifications) were used by both the Anglo-Irish and the native Irish lords from the 14th to 17th centuries, Plate 39. The settlers, who remained in towns, did not assimilate with the native Irish but continued their allegiance to England and constructed the Pale around Dublin, within which English rule prevailed. The Pale (which varied in its extent at different times) extended approximately as far westwards as Kells in County Meath or Kilcock in County Kildare, so the Irish Midlands were 'beyond the Pale'.

Plate 39:
Tower house near Kinnegad, County Westmeath.

16th-17th century Confiscation, Plantation, Rebellion and War

At the beginning of the 16th century, there were a large number of religious houses in Ireland of various orders (Dominicans, Augustinians and Franciscans). However, in the mid-16th century, Henry VIII of England ordered their dissolution, which involved the confiscation and transfer of their possessions, including land, to the King or one of his nominees. For example, Ballyboggan Priory on the Meath/Kildare border (see Itinerary D and Plate D11) ceded 5,000 acres to Sir William Bermingham. Therefore, throughout the Irish Midlands, land, which had been owned by the Church, was being transferred into English hands. English rule was extended in the 1550s when English settlers planted (i.e. settled in) parts of present-day Counties Offaly and Laois and an Elizabethan colony was established in County Roscommon towards the end of the 16th century (Cronin, 1980).

James I became King of England in 1603 and the first part of the 17th century in Ireland was characterised by a Jacobean plantation, mainly in Ulster, but also in parts of Counties Longford, Westmeath and the rest of County Offaly. Charles I became king in 1625 after the death of his father James and he appointed Thomas Wentworth as Lord Deputy of Ireland in 1633. Wentworth's administration alienated the indigenous Irish, the 'Old English' (those born in Ireland of English origin) and the 'New English', those who had recently come to Ireland from England. This eventually resulted in an uprising in 1641, which, in Ulster, was led by Phelim O'Neill and in the Irish Midlands by Rory O'More whose power base was in County Laois. The events that occurred around this time are often referred to as the 'Confederate Wars', because of the confederation that was established in 1642 at Kilkenny, one of the aims of which was to restore the rights of the Catholic Church (Duffy, 2000). Another major event took place in 1642, the start of the English Civil War between the royalists, those loyal to King Charles I, and the Parliamentarians. The success of the Parliamentarian forces and the execution of King Charles in 1649 allowed the English to concentrate fully on the Irish rebellion and in 1649, Oliver Cromwell landed in Ireland. In less than one year, most of the Irish resistance was ended after a series of battles at Drogheda, Wexford Town, New Ross and Kilkenny. The rebellion was completely crushed by 1652 when the Act of Settlement saw the widespread confiscation of the lands of those who had supported the rebellion. The lands of the Irish midland counties were allocated mainly to soldiers of the Parliamentarian army, with the Irish being expelled to Connacht. This had three main effects, it established a large number of settlers with allegiance to England who now had a stake in Ireland who could be called on to thwart any further rebellion and it removed Catholic 'gentry' from their historical power bases thus lessening the possibility of any such rebellion. It also involved a transfer of land from Catholic ownership to Protestant ownership (60% before 1641 and 20% after 1660).

The monarchy in England was restored soon after the death of Cromwell in 1658 and Charles II made an attempt to redress some of the injustices carried out under Cromwell. However, the accession of his Catholic brother, James, to the throne in 1685 and the arrival and coronation of William III (William of Orange) and Mary II in 1689 led to further conflict in Ireland. James fled to Ireland in 1689 and was followed by William in 1690. Williamite forces prevailed in the Battle of the Boyne in July 1690, when the Jacobites lost around 1,000 men, but the conflict continued into the following year. Jacobean resistance had moved to the west and the major conflicts occurred there. General Ginkel moved west from Mullingar and took the Jacobean outpost at Ballymore, 21 kilometres west of Mullingar, before taking Athlone (see Itinerary E). The most decisive battle took place at Aughrim, 6 kilometres southeast of Ballinasloe in east County Galway, where an estimated 7,000 troops loyal to James were killed. Soon after, Limerick was besieged and a peace treaty was signed with Patrick Sarsfield. Many of the defeated army fled to France in what became known as the 'Flight of the Wild Geese'.

Suppression and Landlordism

Following the Williamite victory at the end of the 17th century and into the 18th century under Queen Anne and George I and II, a number of anti-Catholic laws were enacted. These collectively are referred to as the Penal Laws. The degree and harshness of the enforcement of these laws varied both spatially and temporally. The laws included acts which prevented Catholics from possessing horses and firearms, removed voting rights and disallowed Catholics from becoming high constables and controlled inheritance rights. In addition, a series of draconian laws restricted or prevented free Catholic worship. The (Protestant) state decided which days were considered 'holy days', gatherings at holy wells or places of veneration were considered illegal assemblies and all priests were banished from Ireland being guilty of high treason if they returned. Mass would often be celebrated in relatively remote areas during these Penal times at 'Mass Rocks'.

The Irish landscape was also being transformed during the 18th and early 19th century. As the threat of rebellion decreased, the Protestant landlords began to build large country houses whose primary function was not defence but more an ostentatious show of their wealth, privilege and prestige. Such houses were built in the Palladian style (named after Andrea Palladia, 1508-1580) or later in the Gothic style (O'Brien and Guinness, 1992). Examples can be seen at Birr Castle and Charleville, County Offaly (Itinerary B); Emo Court, County Laois (Itinerary G); and Strokestown House, County Roscommon (Itinerary I). The houses stood within their large estates and long walls then enclosed these demesnes. Many of the demesnes were subsequently landscaped, new gardens laid out, water features created, new walks constructed and follies built. The Chapman family, for example, constructed a 12m tall obelisk in the early 19th century on their Westmeath estate to commemorate Sir Walter Raleigh and the introduction of the potato to Ireland, Plate 40. In addition, the landlord was often the driving force behind the laying out of the nearby village. The Countess of Belvedere (Jane) was responsible for the crescent in Tyrrellspass, County Westmeath (Itinerary A), Strokestown, County Roscommon was laid out for the Mahon family (Itinerary I) and the de Vesci family were responsible for the establishment of the new town of Abbeyleix, County Laois, in its present location (Itinerary G). Many buildings in towns such as Birr, County Offaly (Itinerary B) exhibit Georgian architectural characteristics. The large estates at this time needed to transport their goods to markets and as a consequence communication links were improved.

Communication links in the Irish Midlands – Roads

Crude tracks and paths have existed in Ireland for millennia especially when the main mode of movement would have been walking. The Gaelic word for road is 'bothair' and

Plate 40:
12m high 19th century obelisk to commemorate Sir Walter Raleigh and the introduction of the potato to Ireland, Clonmellon, County Westmeath.

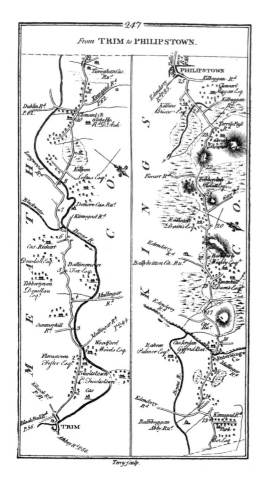

Figure 14:
Example of late 18th century Taylor
and Skinner road map.

is derived from 'bo' meaning cow. A bothair was a track, which was wide enough to allow two cows to walk beside each other. Today a little narrow lane is termed a boreen. Tara in County Meath has traditionally been seen as the royal capital of Ireland and five major roads (or slighe) are said to have radiated from it. The Slighe Assail extended to Rathcroghan in County Roscommon and the Slighe Mor went west to Galway (Doran, 2004). The military aspect of roads has been of major importance throughout Ireland over the centuries. The ability to communicate with outposts and allied strongholds and the capability to quickly move troops to quell rebellion were never far from the minds of chieftains, conquerors or settlers.

One of the most extensive mapping of Ireland's roads was carried out in 1777 by George Taylor and Andrew Skinner, the end result of which was the 'Maps of the Roads of Ireland' published in 1778. Over 250 pages of road maps are contained within the book, an example of which, map 247, is shown in Figure 14. Generally, the maps are in the form of 'strip-maps' showing a particular route such as the road from Dublin to Sligo via Longford or 'road from Philipstown to Naas by Kildare and through the Curragh'. Much of the funding for the mapping came from the landed gentry who wished to have the location of their various estates shown. Therefore, the maps contain the names of the various landowners and a special symbol is included in the key to the maps dedicated to 'Noblemen's and Gentlemen's Seats'. Various geographical features such as mountains and lakes are included in the maps, although it is clear from an examination of the maps that the features are often diagrammatic. Maps 244 and 245 show 3 small lakes to the north of Mullingar, which vary slightly in shape and size. However, the same lakes are shown on Map 250 where their spatial relationship is completely different. The road maps do however, highlight some interesting aspects of the roads in the Irish Midlands.

Many of the important routes in the mid-18th century can still be recognised in the main road networks even though today some of the towns are bypassed. Also, some of the towns of that time have retained their importance regarding communication links. Therefore, for example, Mullingar in County Westmeath is shown on 6 different maps (62, 66, 243, 244, 245 and 250) and today still forms an important communications hub. However, there are some important differences between roads in the mid-18th century and those of today. Some of the early important routes have no national significance now. A case in point is the road from Trim (County Meath) to Philipstown (now called Daingean) in County Offaly. Today, this route mainly consists of narrow winding lanes. In addition, Tullamore in County Offaly is now at the centre of a series of radiating nationally important roads (N52, N80, R420, R421), an attribute it did not possess in the mid-18th century. The Taylor and Skinner maps also show the position of turnpike roads in Ireland. These were roads of superior quality to the ordinary type of roads that existed in Ireland throughout most of the country in the 18th century. However, in order to finance the improvements, a toll was levied on any vehicles using the road. Turnpikes also existed on some bridges crossing rivers, such as Clonard Bridge, which crossed the Boyne. The old tollhouse is still in existence near the present-day Leinster Bridge. The introduction of the mail coach (which also carried passengers) in the latter part of the 18th century led to significant road improvement on the routes that they employed. To cater for the coaches, the roads had to be of specific width, the surface had to be sufficiently smooth for comfort on long journeys and the gradients had to be low enough so that the coaches could be pulled uphill by horses.

Communication links in the Irish Midlands – Waterways

From earliest days, communications in the Irish Midlands were difficult because of the large tracts of bog and forest that existed in the region. In such circumstances, the river and lake networks were extensively exploited for the movement of goods and transport. It is believed that some of the large stones weighing many tonnes, which are located at Newgrange, were transported from Clogher Head on the east coast to Newgrange in Neolithic times by means of the River Boyne. Many early monastic settlements (such as Clonmacnoise) are situated near major rivers or on islands within loughs, such as Holy Island on Lough Derg and again travel on boats would have facilitated communication between them. The rivers were also exploited in the 9th century as Viking raiders used them to gain access to Ireland's midlands. It was not until the 18th century that significant efforts were made to exploits Ireland's waterways. An Act was passed in 1715 to encourage work which would ease the inland carriage of goods. A Commission of Inland Navigation for the four provinces was formed in 1729 and eventually amalgamated into a single Corporation for Promoting and Carrying on Inland Navigation in 1751 (Delany, 1986). Initially, river systems, such as the Boyne, Shannon, Nore, Barrow and Suir, were improved in order to ease transport but this led on to the building of canals, the first of which (Newry Canal) was opened in the mid-18th century. A link between Dublin, the capital of Ireland and the River Shannon, the largest river in Ireland was believed to be important and two canals, the Grand Canal and the Royal Canal were built westward from Dublin across the Irish Midlands, Figure 15. The Grand Canal Company was established in 1772 and by 1780, Sallins in County Kildare was reached. The canal was extended to Monasterevin by 1786 and farther south navigation was via the River Barrow. The main canal route was extended westward across the Irish Midlands and reached Daingean and then Tullamore *c.* 1798. The Canal was continued to Shannon Harbour by 1804. The distance from Dublin to Shannon Harbour is about 128 kilometres. In addition, a number of branch lines were run off the main Grand Canal. The Edenderry branch opened in 1795 and was about 1.5 kilometres in length; the Kilbeggan branch opened in 1836 (13 kilometres in length); the Mountmellick branch opened in 1830 (19 kilometres in length); the Ballinasloe branch opened in 1827 (about 22 kilometres in length (D'Arcy, 1969).

The Royal Canal Company was formed in 1789 and a number of alternative routes were put forward (Clarke, 1992). John Brownrigg suggested that Edgeworthstown and Ardagh be included and that Mullingar be bypassed, although connected by a branch line whereas Thomas Page suggested that the canal go through Kinnegad. The eventual canal route took in Dublin, Maynooth, Longwood, Killucan, Mullingar, Ballymahon and Killashee and reached the Shannon at Clondara (Cloondara). It reached the Shannon in 1817 and an 8 kilometres long branch was extended to Longford in 1830.

Figure 15:
Location of Grand and Royal Canals across the Irish Midlands.

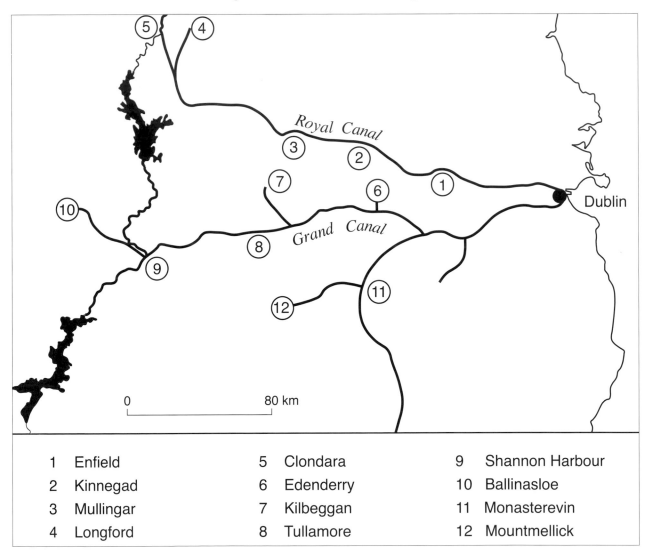

1	Enfield	5	Clondara	9	Shannon Harbour
2	Kinnegad	6	Edenderry	10	Ballinasloe
3	Mullingar	7	Kilbeggan	11	Monasterevin
4	Longford	8	Tullamore	12	Mountmellick

It is clear from Figure 15 that for a considerable portion of their routes the Grand Canal and the Royal Canal run parallel to each other and if relationships between the two companies had have been better, a connecting branch could have been run from the Grand Canal near Edenderry to connect up with the Royal Canal near Kinnegad. As well as providing a more integrated canal network, the Royal Canal east of Kinnegad to Dublin would not have been necessary and the Royal Canal could have been completed much sooner. The canals were used both for the transport of people and the transport of goods. The types and amount of goods varied at different times and for different sections of the canal. For example, whiskey was exported from Tullamore, a major distilling town on the Grand Canal. The main cargoes consisted of animal feed, sugar, alcohol, grain, cement, coal and turf. Tonnage carried varied greatly but was of the order of 150,000 tonnes in 1950. Passengers could also travel by barge along the canals. Prices also varied, depending on the distance travelled and the type of cabin. To travel from Dublin to the Shannon along the Grand Canal in the early 1800s cost around 10 shillings (less than 1 Euro). The Grand Canal Company was amalgamated with CIE in 1950 and the canals ceased to be used for the transport of cargo around 1960. Today, the canals and the inland waterways such as the River Shannon have again attained an economic importance. The canals are now seen as an important tourist amenity and have passed into the ownership of the Office of Public Works.

19th century Famine

The famine that occurred in Ireland in the mid-19th century is one of the most significant events to have impinged on the Irish psyche. In the Irish Midlands (Longford Town and Mullingar, for example) 'Famine Graveyards' are constant reminders of this. Large numbers of poor people died, then were buried in unmarked and often mass graves. Famine had affected Ireland in previous centuries, so why is the 19th century one so vividly remembered? The scale of the 19th century famine dwarfed previous ones and affected the rural poor the most. The perceived inaction or inadequate response from the English government helped fuel a sense of injustice, which various groups, agitating for Irish freedom tapped into. This sense of grievance was intensified by evictions that took place during the famine, when some landlords took the opportunity to reorganise their estates. The knowledge that food was being exported from Ireland while Irish people were dying from lack of food seems to us today an unbelievable concept.

Two main factors contributed to the scale of the famine: the size of the population and the over-dependence on one source of food; the potato. The population of Ireland throughout the 18th and early 19th century was increasing at a high rate and in the 1841 census it had reached just over 8 million. This increasing population, mostly rural, put immense pressure on the available land stock. Small farms were often themselves subdivided in order that each of the children would have their own plot. This pressure on land meant that increasingly poorer land was farmed, often high up on a steep hillside or in bogland. Potatoes are not indigenous to Ireland; they were brought from the Americas by Sir Walter Raleigh (who lived 1552-1618) but quickly became an important crop for a number of reasons. They are well suited to the wet Irish climate and could be easily grown on the marginalised land where many people were now living. Potatoes provide good nutritional value and can be stored, Mitchell and Ryan (2001) state that 1 acre of potatoes would provide sufficient food for a family of 6 for a year. Cultivation was relatively easy, could be performed by hand and the crop needed little attention. Initially, a line of manure was laid down on the ground, a parallel furrow dug and the upended sod placed upside down on the manure. Seed potatoes were then planted into the fertilized ridge of soil. Such cultivation ridges (often referred to as 'lazy beds') can be seen on Itinerary A (Plate A11) and on Itinerary C. In 1845, the potato crop was destroyed by the phytophthora infestans fungus, and again in 1846, 1848 and 1849. The combination of a large population depending on one crop, which was destroyed over a number of years, resulted in an estimated one million dead due to starvation and disease. The effects of the famine were not felt uniformly across Ireland; in general, the greatest number of deaths took place along the western seaboard. The famine death rate in the Irish midland counties of Laois, Longford, Westmeath and Offaly was about 20 people per 1,000. Westward this increased to 40-50 per 1,000 in Roscommon and Galway.

Irish Midlands: Post-Famine – Modern times

The mid-19th century famine had a devastating effect on the population of the Irish Midlands, an effect that extended into the 20th century. The results of the mass migration from the land can still be seen today in the landscape of the Irish Midlands, as evidenced by the large number of deserted cottages. The population of Westmeath before the famine (c. 141,000) had been reduced to c. 62,000 by 1901, a 56% reduction in population. Other midland counties saw similar reductions in the same period: Offaly (59%); Laois (62%); Longford (59%) and Roscommon (60%). The beginning of the 21st century has seen, for the first time in over a century, a sustained increase in population for the Irish Midlands, due in part to immigration from eastern European countries. As a result, the populations of midland counties such as Longford, Offaly, Westmeath and Laois at the beginning of the 21st century are similar to the populations of those counties at the beginning of the 20th century. In County Roscommon, however, the population in 2002 (c. 54,000) was still considerably less than that in 1901 (c. 102,000). Ironically, a means of distributing food quickly throughout Ireland became possible soon after the famine – railways.

Whereas the late 18th and early 19th centuries can be seen as the Age of Canals, the late 19th and early 20th centuries were the Age of Railways (Middlemass, 1981). Many railway companies were formed in Ireland in the 19th and 20th centuries – a full list is provided by Johnson (1997), the main source of the information presented here. Two companies predominated in the Irish Midlands: Great Southern & Western Railway and the Midland Great Western Railway, Figure 16. The Midland Great Western Railway runs alongside the Royal Canal (which it purchased) from Dublin to Mullingar, which was reached in 1848. The tracks diverge there, west towards Athlone, which was reached in 1851, and towards the northwest, through Longford (reached 1855) to Sligo (first temporary station opened in 1862). The Great Southern & Western Railway ran from Dublin to Portarlington (1847) then split to go northwest to Tullamore (1854) and Athlone (1859) or southwest to Portlaoise where it diverged again to go south to Waterford via Kilkenny or southwest to Limerick Junction, Mallow and Cork. The picture presented in Figure 16 gives a false impression of the railway structure as it exists today; it was far more extensive 100 years ago than it is now. For example, it was possible to get a passenger train from Mullingar to Athlone, a distance of 45 kilometres up until 1987 when the service was discontinued. To accomplish the same journey now by train, one has to go from Mullingar to Dublin, then from Dublin to Athlone, a distance of 150 kilometres. (At the time of going to press in 2007, there has been renewed interest in reopening this rail connection). The Clara to Streamstown line, opened in 1863, was finally closed in 1965;

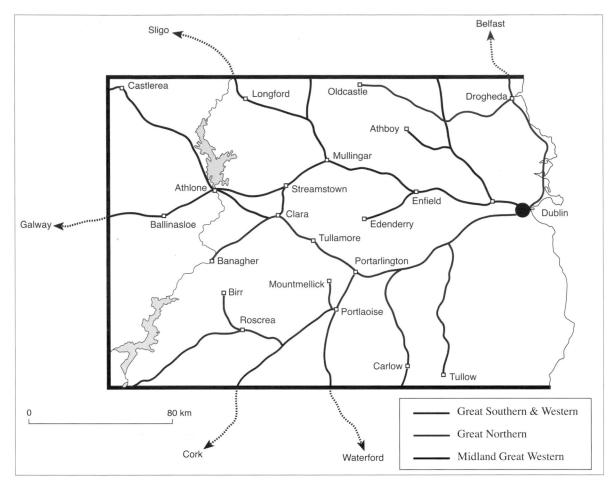

Figure 16:
Location of railways in the Irish Midlands in 19th and 20th centuries.

the Edenderry branch line to Enfield opened in 1877 was completely closed in 1963. Banagher's railway link to Clara which commenced in 1884, ended in 1963, and Oldcastle's connection through to Drogheda, via Kells and Navan, opened in 1863 and ended in 1958. (The dates given here are when all services ended; in some instances regular passenger transport ended up to 30 years earlier). The rest of Ireland has faired no better than the Irish Midlands. Much of the northwest (Donegal/Tyrone) and the southwest (Cork) have few or no train services whereas in the past most areas were relatively close to a railway.

Post-famine legislation and political changes also had their effects on the large, mainly Anglo-Irish, landowners. A series of Land Acts enacted from 1870 onwards initially by Prime Minister Gladstone reduced the power of the landlords and, in the words of Lydon (1998), began a process 'by which the old landlord ascendancy was ended and Ireland became a land of peasant proprietors'. These large landowners felt further alienated following the War of Independence and the formation of the Irish Free State in 1922. A combination of factors, such as some of the large houses falling into disrepair or destruction by fire has meant thatl whilst the demesnes' walls remain, many of the large houses are now gone. Examples from the Irish Midlands include Toberdaly in County Offaly, Loughcrew in County Meath and Heywood House in County Laois.

From the latter part of the 20th century and into the 21st century, the Irish Midlands have continued to evolve. Financial support is provided to many farmers in the midlands under the Common Agricultural Policy (CAP). A Rural Environmental Protection Scheme (REPS) was introduced in 1994 under which farmers, who managed their land in a manner which promoted wildlife habitats, minimised the effects of their activities on the environment and improved the visual appearance of the landscape, were rewarded financially. Over 30% of the farmers in the Irish Midlands have participated in this voluntary scheme (Lafferty et al., 1999). The increasing population in the Irish Midlands is only partly due to the increased immigration from abroad. The high house prices in Dublin have forced many people to live in the Irish Midlands and to commute to work in Dublin from places like Mullingar and Portlaoise. As the canals gave way to the railways, in turn the railways have given way to the roads as the main mode of transport for goods and people in the Irish Midlands. The concentration of the population in towns may increase further because it is considerably more difficult now to obtain permission to build one-off houses in the countryside and because the National Spatial Strategy for the Irish Midlands is to designate Mullingar, Athlone and Tullamore as 'gateway' towns around which economic development should be concentrated. This may bring major employers to the midlands, prevent economic leakage and ensure that those who live in the Irish Midlands are able to work in the Irish Midlands.

SECTION III

Driving Itineraries
in the
Irish Midlands

Introduction

Nine separate enclosed driving itineraries (Itinerary A to Itinerary I) are described in this section of the book, Figure 17. Collectively they cover *c.* 1,000 kilometres and each one includes a range of physical, archaeological and historical features in the landscape – see Table 2. A map, showing the main locations visited, is provided for each Itinerary, see

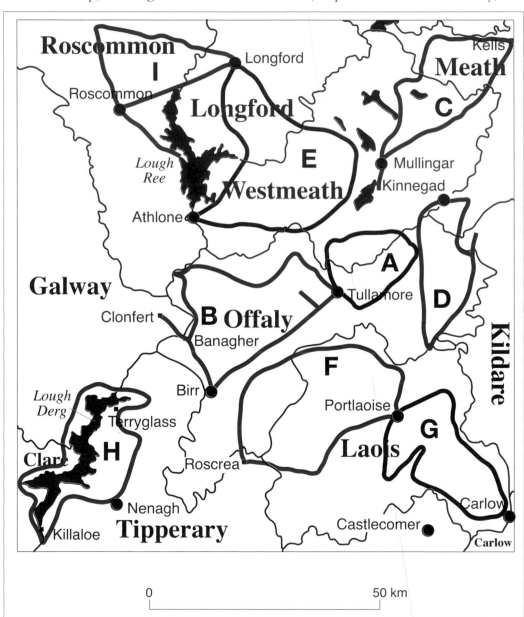

Figure 17:
Location of Itineraries A-I
in Irish Midlands.

Figure A1 for example. The 1:50,000 Ordnance Survey Discovery Series maps may prove useful and the relevant map numbers for the separate itineraries are given. The counties visited on each itinerary are given in Table 3, so that, for example, if one is located in County Westmeath, then itineraries A, C, D and E are all within easy reach. It is not necessary to confine your route to the separate itineraries given. Figure D1, for example, shows that you can leave Itinerary D to join up with Itineraries A, B, C, F or G. Alternatively, one can use Table 2 to visit specific structures, Round Towers, for example,

	Itinerary A	Itinerary B	Itinerary C	Itinerary D	Itinerary E	Itinerary F	Itinerary G	Itinerary H	Itinerary I
Prehistoric feature	÷	÷	÷	÷	÷	÷	÷		÷
Ogham stone							÷		÷
Early Christian settlement	÷	÷	÷	÷	÷	÷	÷	÷	÷
Standing stone		÷	÷		÷				÷
Togher/ trackway/ pilgrim's way	÷	÷			÷				
High Cross/ early Christian Cross	÷	÷	÷		÷	÷	÷	÷	
Ecclesiastical objects (grave slab, ballaun stone, font etc.)	÷	÷	÷	÷	÷	÷	÷	÷	÷
Round Tower		÷	÷			÷	÷		
Anglo-Norman motte	÷		÷	÷	÷	÷	÷	÷	
Castle/ tower house	÷	÷	÷	÷	÷	÷	÷	÷	÷
Ecclesiastical buildings (church, priory etc.)	÷	÷	÷	÷	÷	÷	÷	÷	÷
Historic buildings/ structures	÷	÷	÷	÷	÷	÷	÷	÷	÷
Cultivation ridges (lazy beds)	÷		÷						÷
Geological features	÷	÷	÷	÷	÷	÷	÷	÷	÷
Glacial features	÷	÷	÷	÷	÷	÷	÷	÷	÷
Karst features		÷	÷	÷			÷	÷	÷

Table 2:
Features observed on various itineraries.

can be seen on Itineraries B, C, F and G. The itinerary maps are up to date at time of production (early 2007) but major road building projects are currently underway across the Irish Midlands and some roads are being renamed. These new motorways and national roads are not included, as they are not completed. Most of the sites are readily accessible but some are on private land, which should not be entered without the permission of the landowner. Neither the author nor the publisher accept any responsibility for injury to any person nor damage to property caused by or to persons who follow the itineraries.

COUNTIES	ITINERARY								
	A	B	C	D	E	F	G	H	I
Carlow							÷		
Offaly	÷	÷		÷	÷	÷			
Galway		÷						÷	
Laois				÷		÷	÷		
Longford					÷				÷
Kildare				÷					
Meath			÷	÷					
Roscommon		÷							÷
Tipperary						÷		÷	
Westmeath	÷		÷	÷	÷				
Clare								÷	

Table 3:
Counties included on various itineraries.

Itinerary A: East Central Irish Midlands

Approximate Distance: 55 kilometres
Ordnance Survey 1:50,000 Discovery Series Maps: 48 and 54.

This circular route takes in Tullamore, Killeigh, Daingean, Croghan Hill, Tyrrellspass, Kilbeggan and Durrow – see Figure A1. For the purpose of this discussion, Itinerary A commences in Tullamore, County Offaly. Most sites are relatively accessible, although the climb to Croghan Hill may be difficult and the driveway up to Durrow is quite long.

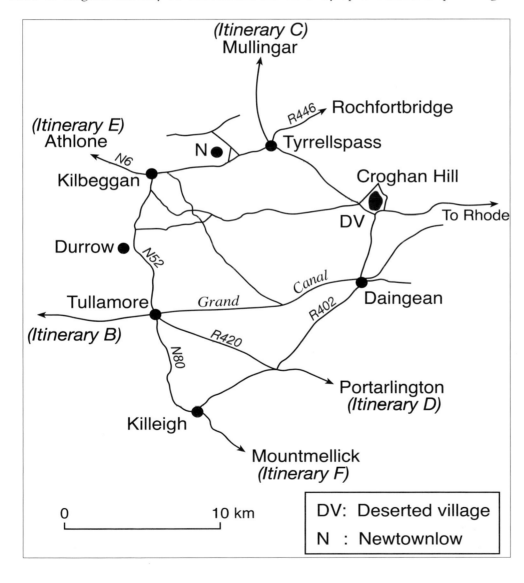

Figure A1:
Location map for Itinerary A.

Tullamore (from the Irish Tulach Mhor meaning large hill) is the largest town and county town of County Offaly though it did not always enjoy this status. Birr, 35 kilometres to the southwest, was larger in the 17th century and Daingean, 14 kilometres to the east, was the county town until 1833. Most of the street names in Tullamore fall into one of two categories, they are either named after an important family (e.g. William Street or O'Moore Street) or named after some function that was carried out there (Harbour Street, Chapel Street or Store Street). The following section provides an introduction to some of the localities in Tullamore.

Plate A1:
Moore Hall, Tullamore,
County Offaly.

Commencing at the new Tullamore Court Hotel walk up O'Moore Street. Approximately 150 metres from the hotel on the opposite side of the road is Moore Hall. This was initially built in the 1750s but was remodelled about 100 years later, Plate A1. Continuing onwards to the roundabout at the top of the street, the scene is dominated by a newly refurbished limestone building constructed by Thomas Acres in the 1780s, which is now used by the Urban District Council of Tullamore. Located behind Acres Hall is Acres Folly constructed around the same time, although it is now in a poor state of repair.

Turn left at the top of O'Moore Street into Cormac Street and you pass a number of houses before coming to the courthouse, one of the largest buildings in Tullamore and the county jail, Plate A2. The jail was opened in 1830 and prisoners, who had previously been held in Daingean jail, were transferred to Tullamore. The courthouse was built beside it in 1835. Even though the jail and courthouse are beside each other they were connected by a tunnel, a not uncommon practice, to reduce the possibility of escape.

What remains now of the jail is simply a façade, one can now enter it, the inside having been removed, now houses business premises. The courthouse was occupied during the Irish Civil War by Republican forces and it and the jail were set on fire in 1922. The obelisk, which is now positioned within the courthouse grounds, is to commemorate Republicans from Offaly who were killed in action.

The large limestone plaque situated above the main entrance to the jail provides some information about its commissioning. The first two lines read, 'The first stone of this prison was laid by Dr. Charles William Baron Tullamoore'. Note the spelling 'Tullamoore'. This was essentially an attempt by the powerful Moore family who had substantial holdings in the locality to rename the town after their family name.

Cross the road and return back into town, one comes to the town park before reaching Acres Hall. The old Kilcruttin graveyard is located within this park. Most graves date from the mid-1700s to the late 19th century when it was closed due to the large numbers of poor people who were being buried here in unmarked graves. The most striking feature in this graveyard is the limestone column. This was erected to commemorate the members of the First German Dragoons Regiment, part of the British Army in the late 1700s/ early 1800s who are buried in this graveyard. The inscription refers to a Captain Frederick Oldershausen from Hanover who died in 1808.

Return to Cormac Street and continue past Acres Hall and the Presbyterian Church, then on down High Street. This is relatively narrow and its most obvious characteristics are the two tall limestone buildings nearly opposite each other, both of which are presently occupied by solicitors. Hoey and Dennings building was formerly the Bank of Ireland, and its upper façade is still relatively untouched since it was built in the late 19th century. The Georgian door and general architecture of the building opposite indicates a late 18th century origin.

Continuing along High Street, one comes to O'Connor Square where many of the buildings date back to the mid to late 1700s. Before entering the Square you should now be standing near the Brewery Tap public house. This was built in the 1780s and once housed a brewery, hence the name. The most striking building in the Square is the present Irish Nationwide building with the small coat of arms and the clock tower. This was formerly the Market House. Many of the doorways in O'Connor Square are Georgian. The old Post Office has had a later elaborate limestone canopy added to the entrance. The date in Roman numerals (MCMIX) is for 1909.

Leave the Square and turn right into Bridge Street, which as its name suggests is where the street crosses the River Tullamore. The most imposing building here is the Bridge

Plate A2:
Tullamore prison, County Offaly.

House Hotel on the far side of the road. The present frontage dates from 1910 (note the dates 1852-1910 located near the top), although it replaces earlier buildings on this site. At the next crossroads, the road to the right is Church Road and the street off to your left on the same side of the road as the hotel is Patrick Street, which was practically destroyed in a fire in 1785 when a hot air balloon crashed. One of the few buildings not burnt down is the limestone fronted building halfway down the street on the right hand side. This was built in 1760 and is now called D. E. Williams House (after an important distillery owner in the town in the late 19th century).

Walk along Church Road past the Methodist Church (1889) and the houses with distinctive arched fanlights over the doors dating to the late 18th/early 19th century. About 100m past the church, a large wide street continues to the left (O'Carroll Street) with a very prominent set of limestone buildings at the corner. The buildings and school were constructed in the 19th century by the Earl of Charleville. Continue along O'Carroll Street, past the entrance to the Market Square as far as the roundabout. The large building on the corner of Harbour Street was initially a distillery built in the 1820s for P & H Egan Malsters. Today it is used by a number of small premises but note the large arched windows, which were initially archways, used for the movement of material into and out of the building. Continue on straight through the roundabout and walk along the top of the grassy ridge on your left. This waterway is the canal harbour and connects with the Grand Canal at the top of the street. This canal reached Tullamore *c.* 1798 as discussed in Section II of the book.

Walk to the canal (Bury) bridge constructed in 1799. Examine the corners of the bridge at a height of about 1m. There are a number of very deep horizontal grooves cut into the corners over a long period of time. The barges in the Grand Canal would have been initially pulled into the canal harbour by horses and the deep grooves have been caused by the ropes cutting into the stone. Return to the road, turn left over Bury Bridge and walk along Convent Road. Off to the left down a side street, you will see the Catholic Church of the Assumption built in 1906 on the site of an earlier one. Continue on to the next road where Kelly's Bar is situated on the corner and the canal is crossed by the Kilbeggan Bridge. This building dates from the 1790s. (A stone set into the bar around the corner is inscribed 'Charles Berry AD 1792'). Continue across the street parallel to the canal for 200m along Bury Quay to the Tullamore Dew Heritage Centre. This was formerly a bonded warehouse built in 1897 by Daniel E. Williams. Its location by the canal made export to Dublin relatively easy. Return to Kelly's Bar, turn right into William Street (also called Columcille Street) and continue along this street back to your starting point at the Tullamore Court Hotel.

By car, drive along O'Moore Street (opposite direction to which you walked) through the traffic lights and take the N80 road signposted for Mountmellick. After 8 kilometres you

Plate A3:
Wall at site of Augustinian Priory, Killeigh.
Inset shows various building styles.

come to the village of Killeigh. As you drive into Killeigh, a good place to park is in front of the hall on the left side of the road just after the Killeigh sign. The name Killeigh comes from the Irish 'Cill Achaidh Droma Fada', which is translated as the 'church of the field of the long ridge'. The long ridge refers to a nearby esker, which you may have noticed on your right as you were driving into the village. Killeigh represents a good example of a phenomenon relatively common in Ireland whereby a small village, which today seems small and unimportant, was, in the past, an important ecclesiastical centre. Clonard, in County Meath is another example – see itinerary D. Records and archaeological remains show that Killeigh possessed an early Christian monastery, castle, Augustinian priory, Augustinian nunnery, Franciscan priory and a number of mills. Evidence for some of these structures still exist; however, extensive ecclesiastical remains are few here, as in many other parts of Ireland, for a number of historical reasons. Ireland's history of repeated conquest, occupation and rebellion has resulted in the destruction of many important buildings. A monastery, which might have had an English patron, would be seized by local Gaelic lords and either destroyed or occupied only to be later destroyed when being retaken. The dissolution of the monasteries in the 16th century by Henry VIII was also a major contributory factor in their rapid decline. The remains of the buildings' walls were often robbed out, then and re-used to construct later structures. However, the tradition of a location being 'holy' has often persisted down the centuries and resulted in a continuation of places of worship being built on or close to known but now no longer major ecclesiastical centres. Such a tradition has persisted in Killeigh.

The short length of wall in the field beside the hall where you have parked is marked on old maps as 'Abbey in ruins'. This is believed to mark the location of the Augustinian priory, which was founded, in the latter half of the 12th century. The wall shown at this location is too late for this priory (Plate A3) but it shows evidence of different stages of building and could have been built with robbed out material. Some skeletons, related to an unknown graveyard, have been uncovered in this region. An Augustinian nunnery was

Plate A4:
13th century Chapter House at
Abbey Farm, Killeigh.

founded around the same time in Killeigh possibly to the east of the priory. A female stone head of medieval age was discovered in this locality and is referred to locally as the 'Nun's head'. Little of archaeological interest can be observed in the field behind the wall but in 2005 a geophysical survey was undertaken, by the Environmental, Geophysics Unit from the national University of Ireland, Maynooth, to ascertain if any features were present beneath the ground. The results of this survey revealed a wealth of information about hidden archeological structures. The present wall is seen to be parallel to an unknown linear feature which turns a right angle and appears, with the existing wall, to form a rectangular building, 40-50m in length (east-west) and up to 20m wide (north-south direction). The orientation and size of this feature are consistent with what one would expect for a priory church. A number of major arcuate linear features are also apparent on the geophysical plot, mainly in the northeast part of the field along with a 60m wide rectangular enclosure.

To visit other sites in Killeigh, proceed down the lane on the opposite side of the road (signposted for the Seven Blessed Wells of Killeigh) and stop outside Abbey Farm which is beside the Church of Ireland Church. This is believed to be the site of the Franciscan friary, which was founded sometime before 1303 (FitzPatrick and O'Brien, 1998). A good example of a 13th century barrel-vaulted Chapter House still exists in the courtyard of Abbey Farm, Plate A4. It is approximately 12m x 5m in size and shows various phases of building and alteration. Detailed architectural investigations, based on building styles, have indicated that it was constructed around 1250, although it was altered in the late 14th or early 15th century (FitzPatrick and O'Brien, 1998). The courtyard that it is situated within is also believed to have been a former cloister. The main house of

Abbey Farm is dated to late 16th to early 17th century. It has a prominent base-batter and has two blocked up decorated windows uncharacteristic of the rest of the house. Many architectural fragments have been discovered in the fields surrounding the abbey site, which are presently housed within the Chapter House. These include stones decorated with carved crosses, parts of decorated window fragments and statues, Plate A5.

Proceed now to the front of the Church of Ireland Church and look out over the field in front of it. The church itself has been extensively modified over the years, mainly in 1830 and 1889, though the doorway is dated to the early 18th century. To the far right of the field a path leads down to the 'Seven Blessed Wells of Killeigh', beside which is a 'holy tree', where the tradition of tying pieces of cloth to the tree as an offering still persists (the path is shown as St. Senchall's Way). St. Senchall founded the first monastery in Killeigh in the 6th century and the Annals of Killeigh list the abbots over the following centuries (Kearney, 1992). Early Christian monasteries were often enclosed within an earthen bank. The main purpose of this was probably not defensive but more a statement of the extent of the area where the monastic rules held sway and a delineation of sacred ground as distinct from the secular area outside the boundary. The hedge in the field opposite (about 200m from the road) is the outer boundary of the early Killeigh monastic site. It consists of two concentric banks of earth separated by a ditch (fosse). It has been suggested that such monastic sites may contain a series of concentric enclosures with the more inner ones being more important. A geophysical survey was also carried out in this field by the Environmental Geophysics Unit, National University of Ireland, Maynooth and it located the outer boundary banks and fosse – even where there is no visible evidence for them – but it also revealed the presence of an inner one which would encompass the church and Abbey Farm, the centre of the monastic settlement. Go back to your car and drive on through Killeigh. Note the large horseshoe shaped window in a house on your left, the site of an early 19th century blacksmith. Turn left at the staggered crossroads (Doyle's public house is on the corner) and note the graveyard on your left as you drive by St. Patrick's Catholic Church on your right built in 1971. The former Catholic Church was through the cemetery and its foundation stone which records that the land for the chapel was provided by Lord Digby dated 1808 can be seen as one enters the graveyard. Proceed along this road for 7 kilometres until you intercept the main Tullamore – Portarlington road (R420). Turn right and then after 50m turn left towards Daingean.

Drive along this road for about 1.5km, until a narrow road is seen to the left. At the end of this road (1 kilometre), through some, fields is an old cemetery (Annagharvey graveyard) within which is located an Anglo-Norman (12th century) motte. The motte is very overgrown and difficult to access. Continuing toward Daingean the road clearly dips in the direction that you are driving and this is because you are coming off a ridge

Plate A5:
Carved stones relating to former ecclesiastical buildings in Killeigh.

composed of fluvio-glacial sands and gravels. Continue through Ballinagar for 4 kilometres and enter Daingean from the south.

Daingean consists of one main street bounded on its northern edge by the Grand Canal. It was the county town of County Offaly until Tullamore superseded it in 1833. The town enjoyed fairly prosperous times when the canal was extended to reach it, but its significance waned when the canal was extended on to Tullamore. Entering Daingean from the south, there are a number of clues, which attest to its military connections. The word 'daingean' means impenetrable or not being able to be overcome. The small bridge which one crosses at the southern part of the town is called Footbarrack Bridge and the street to the right is named Fortfield Drive. The actual street nameplate is set into a small, stylised military sentry tower.

Daingean was the location from which the O'Conor (O'Connor) clan exerted their influence in the surrounding areas and in order to curtail their activities Fort Governor was constructed by Sir William Brabazon in 1546. County Offaly was called King's County in 1556 in honour of King Philip of Spain who was the husband of Queen Mary of England (hence Queen's County for County Laois). At this time, Fort Governor was renamed Philipstown, a name still preserved for the Philipstown River to the east of Daingean.

Fort Governor was located in the small field at the end of Fortfield Drive. The central portion of this field (approximately 80m x 80m) is 2m higher than its perimeter and the remains of the walls can be seen at many localities. A number of internal walls can be seen within the fort itself (i.e. in the central raised portion of the field). Most of the fort was broken up for stones and two armorial stones were discovered, Plate A6. Both stones are very similar in style showing a coat of arms surrounded by a garter and surmounted by a crown. The French words 'Honi soit qui mal y pense' are inscribed on both, which is roughly translated as 'shame on him who thinks this evil'. This is the motto of 'The Most Noble Order of the Garter', an order of knighthood founded in 1348 by King Edward III. The date 1566 has later been carved into one of the stones. One of the stones bears the Arms of Thomas Ratcliffe who was the Lord Deputy of Ireland and the other, those of Mary Tudor, Queen of England. (One of the armorial stones is stored in Daingean library and the other at the clubhouse of the golf course in Daingean).

Continuing along the main street, the remains of the Church of Ireland Church come into view on your right. It was closed due to a declining congregation and, apart from its belfry, was demolished in 1961. The centre of the town is dominated by the early 19th century courthouse, which is now the Town Hall. It was designed by James Gandon (1743-1823) who was also the architect for some of Dublin's most imposing buildings (Kearney, 2003). He designed the King's Inns, the Four Courts, the Customs House and made alterations to Parliament House. The Catholic Church in Daingean (Church of Mary

Mother of God) is a short distance along the street between the Town Hall and the Protestant Church. This arrangement of the Protestant Church on the main street (or in a prominent location in the village square) while the Catholic Church is off the main street is one which can be seen in many Irish towns. The majority of landlords were English Protestants who were often instrumental in the layout of the towns, hence the prime location for such churches whereas the Catholic Churches were often built much later (after Penal times) and by then most main streets had already their full complement of buildings. If one continues to drive past the Catholic Church for 2 kilometres out of the town, you come to a wide expanse of Bord na Móna peat working from which peat is removed and transported by small trains to Edenderry power station.

Return to the main street, turn right, drive to the northern edge of the town and cross over the canal (Molesworth) bridge. A disused building adjacent to the canal is a former store for canal traffic. The towpath to the right leads to Castle Barna Golf Club where the Mary Tudor armorial stone is on display. There is a rock exposure on the second tee, which is totally different from the vast majority of the rocks in the Irish Midlands. It is an igneous rock which cooled from a lava and points to a time when isolated parts of Ireland were affected by volcanic activity. Return to the main road from the golf club road and turn right

On the left near the canal bridge, a long wall accessed by a gate with substantial stone posts over 5m high is evident. This was initially an 18th century cavalry barracks, which also housed a jail. In the late 19th century it became a boys' reformatory (St. Conleth's). Continue northwards past St. Conleth's and remain on the main road that is signposted to Croghan.

Continue northwards on this road and after about 4 kilometres the road narrows where the remains of late 18th/early 19th century corn mills and kilns can be seen. Shortly afterwards you will pass St. Brigid's Catholic Church (built in 1827) on your left. The view in front of you is dominated by Croghan Hill (cruachan in Gaelic means round or piled hill), Plate A7. Most volcanic activity in Ireland took place either around 500 million years ago and was associated with the Caledonian Orogeny, or about 56 million years ago when the Atlantic Ocean was opening. However, volcanism occurred at other times in a few scattered locations in Ireland. Croghan is the site of an extinct volcano than erupted during the Carboniferous time period about 250 million years ago. The Carboniferous time period in most of Ireland was volcanically quiet, except for a few other isolated locations, such as in County Limerick. The basaltic volcanic rock that formed at this time was a hard resistant rock, which has eroded much slower than the surrounding limestone and hence Croghan stands as a prominent 234m high hill, which overlooks a large part of the Irish Midlands.

Continue on the main road, which turns to the right at Croghan Stores, drive past St. Brigid's school for 1 kilometre and park in the lay-by beside the modern graveyard.

Plate A6:
16th century carved armorial shields relating to Fort Governor, Daingean, County Offaly.

Plate A7:
Croghan Hill in County Offaly, an extinct Carboniferous volcano, also an important site in prehistoric times. Note tumulus at the top.

Plate A8:
Vertically folded limestone layers on flank of Croghan Hill overlain by glacial sediments forming a geological unconformity. Height of image approximately 6m.

(There is a small road around Croghan hill though it is not suitable for driving). Walk back from the modern graveyard for about 100m and take the road to your right (signposted for St. Patrick's Well). Walk up the road for a distance of about 500m. Extensive peat workings can be seen in the lowlands to your right. Most of the area to the left is grass covered but about 5m from the road a 3m high horizontal limestone outcrop can be seen with a thinner layer of underlying shale amongst some trees. Continue on the path for a further 300m until you come to a small quarry on your left. This quarry contains a number of interesting geological features. The limestone rocks at this locality are much thinner than farther back along the path, contain thin bands of black chert and have been folded into a nearly vertical orientation, Plate A8. This upturning of the sedimentary rocks may have been caused by the formation of the volcano, as the magma forced its way up, some of the limestone beds near the volcano were buckled by the pressure. The volcano formed in an island environment and the main core of Croghan Hill is formed of basaltic magma and is surrounded to a large extent by ash that was blasted out of the vent. Immediately above the limestone rocks in the quarry there are soft sediments of glacial origin, the contact between the two is known as a geological unconformity because of the large time gap separating the rocks (250 million years old) and the sediments (about 10,000 years old). The sediments show evidence of some very crude layering suggesting some small degree of fluvial transport. Most of the rock material within the sediments is limestone and is often scratched due to the rocks being scraped on each other as they were transported by ice (Plate A9).

Plate A9:
Scratches on limestone caused by glacial transport of material.

Plate A10:
Views from top of Croghan Hill showing
cemetery on the flank and the flat peatlands
of County Offaly.

At this locality, it is possible to climb the hill and to make your way towards the trigonometric pillar at the summit. As you climb higher, the rocks you are walking over were once molten magma which are now solidified into igneous rocks which are much darker than the limestone.

Croghan Hill because of its dominance over the landscape has had a long history of religious importance. It is crowned by a prehistoric tumulus and St. Brigid, a 5th century Irish saint is believed to have received her veil here. Just below the summit, one encounters an old graveyard which was in use up to about 50 years ago. Traditionally it marks the site of the 5th century Bishop MacCaille's Church. The views from the summit are excellent and one can see over much of the midlands in all directions, Plate A10. The long low ridge to the southwest is the Slieve Bloom Mountains and to the southeast the Wicklow mountains can be seen. It has been suggested that the Bealtine fires on the Hill of Uisneach (see Itinerary E) would have been easily visible from Croghan Hill and that similar fires would have been lit here. To this day, fires are lit on Croghan Hill on St. Patrick's Day. The tumulus (prehistoric burial mound) at the summit is described in an ancient poem as the 'monument of Conga on the Hill of Bri Eile' (O'Brien, 2006). An Iron Age male torso (dating from around 2300 years ago) was found in the bog at the base of Croghan Hill in 2003. He was an estimated 1.98m tall (6 foot 6 inches) and died violently with some evidence of torture. Interestingly his body (and others found in similar circumstances) was deposited at a clan boundary and it has been postulated that bodies were placed at these locations to delineate territories. An important routeway or togher ran along the base of the hill towards Durrow, an important ecclesiastical site near Tullamore.

Plate A11:
Cultivation ridges ('lazy beds') on Croghan Hill.
The red line shows their orientation.

Return back down the hill to the lane and continue walking along it past the quarry for a few hundred metres to St. Patrick's Well where people still make offerings. Other wells are known higher up the hill. If, from the well, one looks back along the path towards the small quarry, one can see horizontal terraces on the slope. Theses are purely natural and are caused by soil creep as the soil moves down slope due to gravity. However, if you look up Croghan Hill, a landscape feature which was once very common in Ireland but which now is considerably rarer can just be discerned. Running down the slope is a field of cultivation ridges often referred to as 'lazy beds', Plate A11. Evidence for these features has now been largely removed from the Irish landscape by modern agricultural activities except in a few localities where it is difficult to operate agricultural machinery.

Extensive sand and gravel quarries are located farther along the path past the well, Plate A12. Again they provide important information for interpreting the landscape. At the end of the last glacial period, the lowland around Croghan Hill would have been covered with glacial ice pressed up against the hill. As the glaciers melted, streams would have deposited the sand and gravel layers on the flanks of the hill. Once the ice melted, the water in the streams escaped leaving the sediments where they are today.

Return to your car, head back towards Daingean, but after 800m at Croghan Stores take the road to the right towards Tyrrellspass. Continue along this road for about 700m and stop where the road comes in from the left. If one looks west (i.e. away from Croghan Hill, a farm can be seen about 200m away in

Plate A12:
Sand and gravel layers on flank of
Croghan Hill deposited by meltwater steams.
Height approximately 10m, inset shows details.

Plate A13:
Two views of buildings incorporating parts of fortified house known as O'Conor Faly's Castle.

the lower ground. This is the site of the former O'Conor Faly's Castle (fortified house) and was once an area of significant settlement. Parts of the castle still remain and have been incorporated into the present-day house and buildings, Plate A13. The field beside the road where you have stopped is the site of Cannakill deserted medieval village and one can see linear banks in the field marking the outlines of houses and buildings. The church and graveyard beside the village have also been removed and are no longer standing. Return to your car and continue driving the 6 kilometres to Tyrrellspass.

As you approach Tyrrellspass, just after passing over the motorway bridge, a cemetery can be seen on your right. The grave of James Daly is behind and to the left of the main Celtic Cross in the centre of the cemetery. (Note that the inscription is in Gaelic: Sheamuis Uí Dálaigh) He was a Connacht Ranger, who was executed in India in 1920 after he took part in a mutiny in protest at the actions of the Black and Tans in Ireland. His body was returned to Tyrrellspass in 1970 (Egan, 1986). Proceeding into the town, one comes to Tyrrellspass Castle, one of the distinctive landmarks of the midlands, Plate A14.

Tyrrellspass gets its name from the Tyrrells who were an important Norman family who took part in the Anglo-Norman invasion of Ireland in 1169. The present castle dates from around 1411 and controlled an important route through the bogs of central Ireland which were much more extensive than today. Its location was of strategic importance, a factor which has led to it being occupied by various military commanders down the centuries. The most celebrated military engagement in this region occurred in 1597 a few kilometres north of Tyrrellspass. An English force led by the son of Lord Barnwall moved from Mullingar to Tyrrellspass to intercept Richard Tyrrell who was supporting the northern O'Neill chieftain. The English force was ambushed and around 1,000 soldiers are believed to have been slain.

Proceed into the centre of Tyrrellspass and park near the Village Hotel. This looks out over the village green, which is dominated by the Georgian (early 1800s) crescent of limestone buildings at the centre of which is the church, Plate A15. The appearance of this crescent owes much to the Countess of Belvedere (Jane) who was married to George Rochfort and then on his

Plate A14:
15th century Tyrrellspass Castle, County Westmeath.

death to Arthur Boyd. Three memorials are located within the church (St. Sinian's), two erected by her to her two husbands and one erected for her on her death in 1836. The story of Belvedere and an earlier generation of Rochforts is considered further on Itinerary C. Other buildings in the crescent were once used as a school, barracks, dispensary and courthouse.

Return to your car, drive back the way you came, then past the castle on the old N6 road (now called the R446) west towards Kilbeggan, see Figure A1. About 1.5 kilometers past the castle take the narrow road on your right, signposted for Rahinmore. As you drive along this narrow road it rises up because the road is built along the crest of an esker. This was a common practice as the eskers provided dry route-ways across the midland bogs. Continue along this road for 2 kilometres, until the T-junction, where there are excellent sections through the esker exposed in a quarry. Return the way you came but after about 1 kilometre take the narrow road to your right and stop 400m along this road at the old church and cemetery on your left. This is Newtownlow and the present ruined church was probably built in the 1700s, although records of earlier churches on this site exist. The oldest grave that can be observed in the cemetery is dated 1776, and the use of small stone enclosures to delineate some burials is unusual. The vault on the west side of the church has been damaged, although the armorial plaque to the Pilkington family is still intact. The Pilkingtons settled in this area in the late 1600s, until the early 1920s, when their home, Tore House, was burned down.

The small castle in the adjacent field is sometimes called MacGeoghegan's or Low Castle. The MacGeoghegans, who were a component of the Southern O'Neill clan, were an important Gaelic family in the midlands region, where they had a series of castles in the region (Castletown Geoghegan, west of Lough Ennell in County Westmeath is named after them). They lost their territory after supporting an alliance against the English when forces loyal to Oliver Cromwell secured the region in about 1650. The land was taken from the native Irish and given to sympathetic 'planters'. The castle and lands around Newtownlow were taken over by William Lowe, who fought on the Cromwellian side. The Lowe family, over the following generations, was renowned for its animosity toward the native Irish people. Continue on down the lane back to the main road and turn right. Almost immediately you will cut through another esker and continue for 4 kilometres to Kilbeggan where you turn left at the roundabout and take the Tullamore Road. Kilbeggan (from the Irish Cill Bheagain, Church of Becan) contained an early Christian monastery and a later 13th century Cistercian abbey. The most noteworthy building complex in the town is Locke's whiskey distillery, reputedly Ireland's oldest licensed pot distillery, Plate A16. It was established in 1757 and still contains much of its 18th and 19th century features including a steam engine and water wheel.

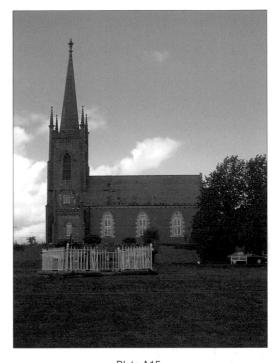

Plate A15:
Village green at Tyrrellspass, showing St. Sinian's Church of Ireland Church.

Proceed south towards Tullamore on the N52 and after about 4 kilometres the road crosses another east-west aligned esker. Shortly after, the entrance to Durrow demesne and Durrow Church can be seen on the right. Durrow has a long ecclesiastical history stretching back to early Christian times. It is the site of St. Colum Cille's (Columba or Columbkille) Abbey founded around 556 AD and many early Christian (8th-10th century) grave slabs are presently housed within St. Columba's Church, a late medieval church rebuilt around 1802. A nearby well (St. Columbkille's Well) may also be visited. Surrounding this well is a large mound of natural stones but incorporated within it are a number of dressed stones which have been found locally and represent parts of former ecclesiastical structures. An Augustinian priory (St. Mary's) was founded here in the mid-12th century. The Book of Durrow, a 7th century illuminated manuscript similar to the Book of Kells, was reputedly produced here and is presently housed in Trinity College Dublin. Still situated within Durrow demesne, but now located within St. Columba's Church is the 9th century 3m tall High Cross decorated with biblical images. Interestingly, the cross and the grave slabs are formed of sandstone which is not the natural underlying bedrock, as the nearest sandstone bedrock is 14 kilometres away. Either the sandstone was moved to the site or glacial erratics were employed.

After leaving Durrow, continue on the N52 road towards Tullamore. After about 2.5 kilometres, one crosses Gormagh B ridge, over the Silver River. A Bronze Age burial, containing cremated remains, food vessels and a female skeleton, was discovered approximately 600m upstream of the bridge. Continue along the road, through another esker and back into Tullamore.

Plate A16:
Locke's whiskey distillery,
Kilbeggan, County Westmeath.

Itinerary B: Central Irish Midlands

Approximate Distance: 150 kilometres
Ordnance Survey 1:50,000 Discovery Series Maps: 48, 54. 53 and 47.

This itinerary encompasses parts of three counties: Offaly, Roscommon and Galway. It starts in Tullamore, see Itinerary A for discussion of the town. Take the N52 road towards Birr out of Tullamore, see Figure B1. Shortly after passing the courthouse, you will come to Charleville demesne on your right. Although there is evidence for a large house here

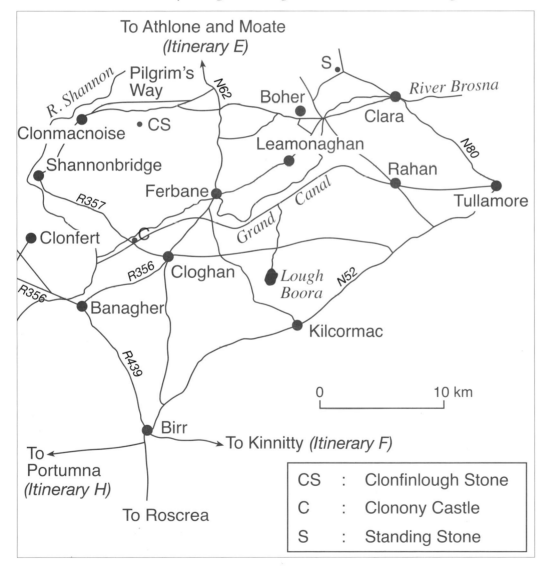

Figure B1:
Location map for Itinerary B.

Plate B2:
Details of window surround and arch at Rahan, note the small sculpted heads at the edge of surround.

since *c.* 1641, built by Sir Robert Forth, brother-in-law of Thomas Moore, the present building, which is in the Gothic style, and associated landscape features were built *c.* 1812 by the Earl of Charleville (Byrne, 1998).

Take the road to your right about 4 kilometres past Charleville demesne signposted for Rahan Churches. As you drive along there are two things to look out for. Firstly, you will get excellent views over the lowlands to your right. whereas to your left, the ground is much higher. The higher ground is composed of glacial sediments formed as deltas as the meltwater deposited sediments on the edge of a glacial lake which would have stretched out into the lowlands on your right. (There would have been up to 1 kilometre of ice above your head during the last glacial period). Once all the ice had melted, the water in the lake was able to drain away, leaving only the sediments. Secondly, there is a sign for a 'Mass Rock' (beside which is St. Anthony's Well) on your right. These were used as locations to celebrate mass during Penal times when it was not possible for Catholics to worship openly. Continue along this road for 5 kilometres, then, after passing over the Grand Canal, stop in the lay-by on your right (signed Rahan Churches). As you approach the main church look off to your left at the field boundary. This consists of an embankment and ditch which both formed part of the original boundary enclosure for the monastery founded here in the 6th century by St. Carthach (Carthage). There are three churches on this site, though one is only a small ruin in the cemetery. The largest is dated 1732 but has been built onto a 12th century church, substantial parts of which remain. The most prominent features are the excellently preserved 12th century Hiberno-Romanesque arch surmounted by a large round quarter-foil window on the east end of the church, Plates B1 and B2. FitzPatrick and O'Brien (1998) record that only two such windows exist in Ireland, with the one at Rahan being the largest and most elaborately decorated. It is believed that such important architectural features have been moved from their original position and incorporated into their present position during the latest renovation phase of the church. A small church (15th century) is situated about 150m east of the largest one. It too incorporates earlier 12th century Hiberno-Romanesque features, in this case a doorway. Some of the window surrounds of this church are elaborately decorated. Note the small carved head on the outside window jamb on the eastern gable wall end of the church.

Return to the main N52 road, turn right and continue towards Birr. As you drive along, you will see on your right at different locations an esker ridge, often tree lined. To the left you may notice a low set of hills in the distance, these are the Slieve Bloom Mountains. Lough Boora, the first Mesolithic habitation site discovered in the Irish Midlands is located north of the N52 road, see Figure B1. Continue through Kilcormac into Birr, Figure B1.

Birr, like so many other towns in the Irish Midlands, is associated with an early Christian settlement; in this instance St. Brendan founded a monastery here in the mid-6th century. The surrounding territory is known as Ely O'Carroll after the ruling Gaelic clan, the O'Carrolls. Their castle at Birr and lands were confiscated in 1621 and given to Sir. Laurence Parsons. He arrived from England with his brother William at the end of the 16th century (Malcomson, 1998). Thus commenced a link with the Parsons family that continues to this day and on some old maps 'Birr' is shown as 'Parsonstown'. The town and castle were virtually destroyed in 1642 by Confederate forces, then were rebuilt (O'Brien and Sweetman, 1997). By the 18th century, the title of Earl of Rosse had been inherited by the Parsons family (Earl of Rosse, 1982). It was during the late 18th – early 19th century that many of the well-preserved buildings associated with Birr were constructed.

Plate B3:
Birr Castle, Birr, County Offaly.

As you drive into Birr the first major building you will see is the courthouse on your right. Just past it, again on the right you come to a large church. Turn right here and park the car as Birr is best seen on foot. (Note that there is a one-way traffic flow system in operation either side of the church). This is Oxmantown Mall laid out by the Second Earl of Rosse in the early 1800s, one end of which is dominated by St. Brendan's church built *c.* 1815 whereas the other end of the street is dominated by the entrance and wall of Birr Castle. Much of this road is Georgian except for the building half way down on the left. This building with its carved wooden gables is the Victorian Oxmantown Hall. At the end of the Mall, turn left and follow the wall of the castle to its entrance. It is possible to visit the grounds of the castle (Plate B3). One of the most dominant features within the

Plate B4:
19th century telescope in Birr Castle grounds.

demesne is the great telescope, its housing and the mechanisms used to move it (Plate B4). This was built by the Third Earl of Rosse in the 1840s and its tube is about 2m wide and 16m long, making it the largest telescope in the world for about 70 years. When leaving the castle, turn left and after about 100m turn right and walk towards Emmet Square past the Masonic Lodge, built in 1747. Emmet Square was formerly known as Cumberland Square but was renamed Emmet Square in honour of Robert Emmet who was executed in 1803 for a failed rebellion. A statue of the Duke of Cumberland originally topped the tall column in the centre of the Square. He was the son of George II and he developed a military strategy to thwart the Highland Charge at the Battle of Culloden in Scotland in April 1746. His subsequent treatment of the Scots resulted in him being known as the 'Bloody Duke' or the 'Butcher'. It was erected in 1747, although the statue has since been removed as it was in a dangerous condition. The Square contains buildings with a range of ages from Dooly's Hotel, a coach inn since the 1740s to the red brick post office dated 1903. The entrance to this post office is surmounted by a limestone canopy similar to that seen over the old Tullamore post office in O'Connor Square (Itinerary A). Walk through Emmet Square to Johns Mall on your left, signposted for Kinnitty. This street contains Johns Hall built in 1833 in a Greek temple style with Ionic columns near the statue of the Third Earl of Rosse (Hogan and Short, 1994). Within the grounds of Johns Hall is a limestone block known as the Seffin stone, said to have crosses carved on it, although none can be seen presently, and a cannon captured during the Crimean war in the mid-19th century that was presented to the town in 1858. Facing the hall is the small Presbyterian church, built in 1855 and currently housing the town library. Return to your car, drive down Oxmantown Mall, turn right at the end and take the R349 road to Banagher.

Parts of the road to Banagher are undulating as it cuts through glacial sediments. A few kilometres from Banagher, set back 100m on your left is Garrycastle. The remains of a mid-15th century tower house, occupied by the MacCoghlan clan, can be seen behind a 17th century fortified house. Banagher gets its name from the Gaelic 'Bann Char' which is translated as 'pointed rocks'. It is the site of a convent founded in the 6th century by Rynagh, sister of St. Finnian of Clonard (see Itinerary D). As you drive down the main street, two buildings stand out, both on the left hand side. One is the red brick Bank of Ireland built c. 1874 and the other farther down the street is known as the Crank House. This bow-fronted house dates from around 1750 and now houses a number of small premises, including the tourist office. Proceed past the Crank House and park near the bridge. Banagher undoubtedly owes its existence to its strategic position on the River Shannon. This is reflected in the number of military installations that have been erected here in the past. The Shannon not only separates Counties Offaly and Galway at Banagher but also the Provinces of Leinster and Connacht. A military settlement here could not only

Plate B5:
Napoleonic fortification (known as Cromwell's Castle, on the River Shannon, County Galway.

control movement across the Shannon but also along it. The present bridge dates from the mid-19th century though records of a bridge at this location go back to the 11th century. Sir Arthur Blundell built Fort Falkland to the left of the present bridge on the Offaly side in 1624 in an attempt to plant the territory (Delvin) controlled by the MacCoghlans. Also situated on the Offaly side of the Shannon is Fort Eliza (also known as the Sal Battery) a small gun emplacement, which still preserves its guardhouse and powder room. This can be reached by driving along Crank Road (beside Crank House) for about 1 kilometre. The battery is on your right. The steep sided moat surrounding it is still in place and care should be taken if walking around it. It is possible to get down to the Shannon in front of Fort Eliza. This area floods easily because of the very low gradients around the river.

As you cross over the bridge spanning the Shannon, two further fortifications are apparent, Cromwell's Castle (Plate B5) to the left and the Martello tower to the right. The castle is located on the site of an earlier 17th century castle (hence the name) but both fortifications are associated with the Napoleonic wars in the early 1800s. Martello towers were equipped with cannon and were built as a defence against a possible French invasion. For this reason, most were built around the coast of Ireland; however, the one at Banagher and also 7 kilometres farther down the Shannon at Meelick are rare examples of inland ones. It was feared that the French might land on the west coast and march east across Ireland, thus they were constructed in order to thwart such an attack. The towers often tend to be slightly oval with thicker walls facing the expected direction of attack.

Continue driving into Galway for 1.5 kilometres along the R356 and take the road on your right at the limestone block 1858 school signposted for Clonfert. Clonfert is derived from the Gaelic 'cluain ferta' meaning 'meadow of the grave'. Clonfert was the location of a meeting between Brian Boru and Mael Sechnaill in 997AD where they agreed which parts of Ireland each would control (Ó'Corráin, 2000). Follow the signposts for Clonfert (you will turn right at crossroads about 5 kilometres along this road signposted for Clonfert Cathedral) and stop outside St. Brendan's Cathedral. A monastery was founded here in the mid-6th century by St. Brendan (the navigator). The west doorway of Clonfert Cathedral displays one of the best examples of Hiberno-Romanesque architecture in Ireland, Plate B6. The cathedral dates from around the 10th century but the doorway itself

Plate B6:
12th century Hiberno-Romanesque doorway
at Clonfert Cathedral, County Galway.

Plate B7:
Detail of Hiberno-Romanesque doorway at Clonfert Cathedral.

was constructed in the latter part of the 12th century (O'Keeffe, 2000). It was attacked and burned on a number of occasions over the centuries, in 842 AD, 1016 AD, 1045 AD and 1179 AD. The doorway has seven orders formed of sandstone all dating to the late 12th century and a later inner one constructed of limestone probably in the 15th century. The doorway contains a range of carved motifs including beast' heads, figures and ornamentation some exhibiting a Scandinavian or French style, Plate B7. The key to the cathedral can be obtained from a nearby house. Housed within the cathedral are a number of grave slabs, dating back to early Christian times. Various carvings can be seen on the chancel arch within the cathedral, the most noted one being a small mermaid whom St. Brendan supposedly encountered on a journey. In the forest adjacent to the cathedral is a 'rag tree' tied to which are various offerings by those seeking cures or help. Follow the road around the cathedral for 200m and you come to a derelict house which is known as the Bishop's Palace. This had been home to the Trench family but was used also as a residence for various bishops over the centuries. It was accidentally burned down in 1954. Return to Banagher (note as you drive back from the cathedral you will see a tower house in front of you as you approach the first crossroads). Apart from the monastic and military aspects of Banagher and its environs, two Englishmen are also associated with the area. The Bishop's Palace near the cathedral at Clonfert was also the Irish home of Sir Oswald Mosley who in the early 20th century founded the fascist 'blackshirts'. Anthony Trollope, who is best known for his many novels, worked as the deputy postal surveyor in Banagher in the mid-19th century.

Drive back up the main street of Banagher and take the R356 road on your left (signposted for Tullamore). Continue on this road for *c* . 8 kilometres to Cloghan and turn left and take the R357 for 12 kilometres to Shannonbridge. 3 kilometres along this road, you pass over the Grand Canal which terminates at Shannon Harbour. Shortly after passing over the canal you come to Clonony Castle (tower house) on your right, Plate B8. This castle, built around the 15th century, was a MacCoghlan stronghold, although it was confiscated by Matthew de Renzy when the region was being planted. There are two additional points of interest for this site. The castle is built on a natural limestone outcrop, which exhibits good examples of small solutional karst features, such as hollows and runnels. To the left of the castle doorway (as you look at it from the road) a large grave slab is located at the base of a bush. This is dedicated to Mary and Elizabeth Bullyn the second cousins of Queen Elizabeth I, who was the daughter of Anne Boleyn, second wife of Henry VIII, who was executed by him in 1536 (Friel,1997). Drive into Shannonbridge through the Main Street and across the bridge over the Shannon. As you drive over the bridge into County Roscommon, you will see that the far bank is dominated by a large Napoleonic fortification now used as a restaurant. This fortification and its associated

Plate B8:
Clonony Castle, County Offaly.

battery positions form the largest such Napoleonic site in Ireland. It was built around 1810 and, like those farther south at Banagher, its purpose was to defend against a possible French invasion coming from the west. Compare the wall of the fort facing the west with that facing the Shannon (east). The latter contains doors and many windows, whereas the former has only a few windows because any attack was expected to come from this direction. The battery was equipped with 18 pounder cannons and howitzers. A military camp capable of housing over 2,000 soldiers was constructed at the same time opposite Clonony Castle which was passed on the way to Shannonbridge (Kerrigan, 1998). Return back through Shannonbridge and take the R444 road to your left signposted to Clonmacnoise. As you drive towards Clonmacnoise, you will get good views of the Shannon floodplain to your left, whereas the higher ground on your right is composed of esker ridges of glacial sediment. Park in the car-park provided at Clonmacnoise.

Plate B9:
12th century Round Tower at Clonmacnoise, County Offaly. River Shannon and its floodpain visible in the background.

Plate B10:
Round Tower (Temple Finghin) at
Clonmacnoise, County Offaly.

Clonmacnoise is one of the most important ecclesiastical centres in Ireland. The Archaeological Inventory of Ireland for County Offaly records 13 churches, 2 Round Towers, a number of High Crosses or fragments, an ogham stone and over 600 grave slabs. St. Ciaran founded Clonmacnoise in the mid-6th century. As with other monastic sites, nothing remains of the early wooden buildings; the present stone buildings date to later periods. The two Round Towers are arguably the most prominent architectural features at Clonmacnoise, Plates B9 and B10. The tallest unroofed one (sometimes referred to as O'Rourke's tower) is 19m high, is believed to have been built in 1124 by Ua Maoleoin and its top was destroyed by a lightning strike in 1135. The 8 small windows at the top were added long after the original tower was constructed. The other Round Tower is the bell tower for Temple Finghin (Templefineen or McCarthy's Church). This is a 12th century church with Hiberno-Romanesque features including a doorway with 3 orders and a window (Manning, 1994). The largest building in the complex is known as Temple McDermot or the cathedral, Plate B11. This possibly dates back to 909 AD and has been associated with the High King Flann. The sidewalls (antae) project slightly, a feature common in early churches. The doorway on the north wall is a later 15th century addition, with the small statues representing St. Dominic, St. Patrick and St. Francis. Other smaller churches in the vicinity include Temple Ri (the King's Church or Temple Melaghlin) with two thin round-headed 13th century windows and the connected

Plate B11:
Doorway on Cathedral at Clonmacnoise.

Plate B12:
12th century Nun's Church,
Clonmacnoise, inset shows detail.

churches Temple Dowling and Temple Hurpan, the former being partly pre-Anglo-Norman in date whereas the latter is late medieval (O'Brien and Sweetman, 1997).

Proceed through the modern day cemetery, exit via the small gate in the wall, walk along the road (with the Shannon on your left) for a distance of around 500m and on your right you will come to the Nun's Church, Plate B12. This is a small 12th century Hiberno-Romanesque church of which the chancel arch and doorway still remain (though have been rebuilt somewhat). It is associated with Dearbhforgaill (Derbforgaill), the wife of O'Rourke, the King of Breifne, who had it constructed in 1167. Both the chancel arch and the doorway are associated with abstract carvings, beasts and human heads. The road connecting the Nun's Church to Clonmacnoise is known as the Pilgrim's Way and has been in use for more that 1,000 years. It continues on past the church for a number of kilometres and it is built on the flanks or the top of the eskers. These, as stated earlier in the book, represented dry routes through the bogs. Excellent views of the Shannon callows and the eskers can be seen from this road. Creep processes in the esker slopes have resulted in small 'steps' in the hillside.

Return to the Visitor Centre at Clonmacnoise. The High Crosses located among the churches are replicas of the originals, which are housed within the Interpretative Centre to prevent deterioration from the weather. The Cross of the Scriptures is decorated with panels many of which depict biblical scenes such as the crucifixion or last judgement, Plate B13. An inscription on the cross base relating to Flann Sinna, High King of Ireland

Plate B13:
10th century High Cross at Clonmacnoise
(Cross of the Scriptures).

suggests an early 10th century date for its construction. The Southern Cross is of a completely different style, consisting to a large extent of abstract linear, spiral and rounded patterns. It is mid-9th century, so is earlier in date than the Cross of the Scriptures, and is attributed to the father of Flann Sinna. A number of early grave slabs, most dating from the 8th-12th centuries, are also housed in the Interpretative Centre (Plate B14). The importance of such a major monastic settlement at Clonmacnoise meant that over the centuries it was raided and plundered many times. Lucas (1967) records over 55 attacks from 722 AD to 1552 AD. Conflict could also occur between different monasteries, resulting in Clonmacnoise battling Birr in 759 AD and Durrow in 763 AD.

The remains of an Anglo-Norman stone castle are located adjacent to Clonmacnoise. It was built *c*. 1200 and investigations within the Shannon showed that a wooden bridge crossed the river at this location. Many wooden timbers have been located, some in situ, and have been dated to 804 AD (O'Brien and Sweetman, 1997).

Plate B14: Example of early Christian grave slabs discovered at Clonmacnoise.

Leave the car-park and turn left onto the R444, noting the esker in front of you. (You will pass a road to your left in 500m, this leads to the Pilgrim's Way, where you visited the Nun's Church and along which you can drive, if you wish, though the road is narrow). Continue on the R444 road for 3 kilometres and take the road to your right signposted for the Clonfinlough Stone. Stop at Clonfinlough Church and walk the 250m along the signposted path. A slab of irregularly shaped limestone (a glacial erratic deposited by glacial activity) is a short distance into the field at the end of the path. Examination of this stone in the 19th century led to the conclusion that, although many of the hollows and grooves on its surface were natural, that there was some evidence for humans having carved some of the stick-like figures and patterns, Plate B15. The stone is reported as the only example of 'rock art' in the Archaeological Inventory of Ireland for County Offaly. Jackson (1967) performed a detailed geological investigation of the stone and compared the natural joint patterns with the direction of the arms and bodies of the figures. He came

Plate B15:
Clonfinlough Stone showing markings. Photograph copyright and courtesy of Thomond Archaeological and Historical Society.

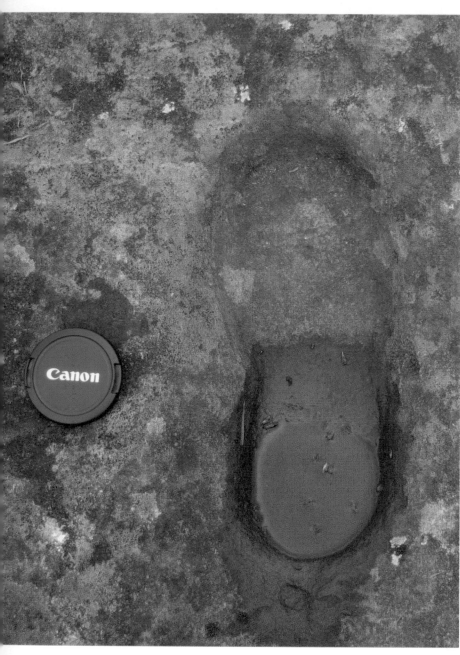

Plate B16:
'Footprint' hollow in Clonfinlough Stone.

to the conclusion that most of the figures could be explained by natural processes except what he termed 'group 3 (d) arms akimbo figures', where artificially inscribed grooves appear to have been added. Today, due to a combination of weathering and lichen growth, little detail of the figures is evident, the most prominent observable feature is the 'footprint', which may also represent a natural hollow, Plate B16. The carving has been tentatively assigned to the Bronze Age, on stylistic grounds, and Fin Lough, 500m west, is the site of a Bronze Age lake settlement dating to *c*. 900 BC (McDermott, 1998).

Return to the main R444 road, turn right and drive on for 7 kilometres to Ballynahown where you should turn right onto the N62 road. (Note turning left at this junction would take you to the old N6 road where, a right turn, would take you to Moate on Itinerary E). After a few kilometres you come to Doon Crossroads, near which are the remains of two tower houses (Esker/Doon Castle and Togher Castle), one of which is located in a very commanding position on a mound of glacial sediments.

Continue on the N62 and drive the 7 kilometres to Ferbane. The ruling family in the Ferbane area were also the MacCoghlans. They forfeited their lands including the area around Ferbane after the 1641 rebellion. Parts of the land then passed through various ownerships, Baldwin Crowe, Thomas Jessop, John King and John Henry (Ryan, 2003). Drive straight through the Main Street and a few hundred metres after you pass the Gardai station, you will see a sign on your left for the monastic site of St. Canoc and Gallen Priory Nursing and Retirement Home. Turn left and drive to the end of the lane then proceed on foot through the gate to the signposted building remains. St. Canoc founded a monastery here at Gallen in the late 5th century and a later 12th century Augustinian priory was established at the same location. (St. Mary of Gallen). During excavations in the 20th century over 200 early Christian grave slabs (many 8th-11th century) were uncovered indicating the presence of a long-lived major cemetery. Some of these grave slabs are presently positioned on a wall at the site (Plate B17), in front of which is a

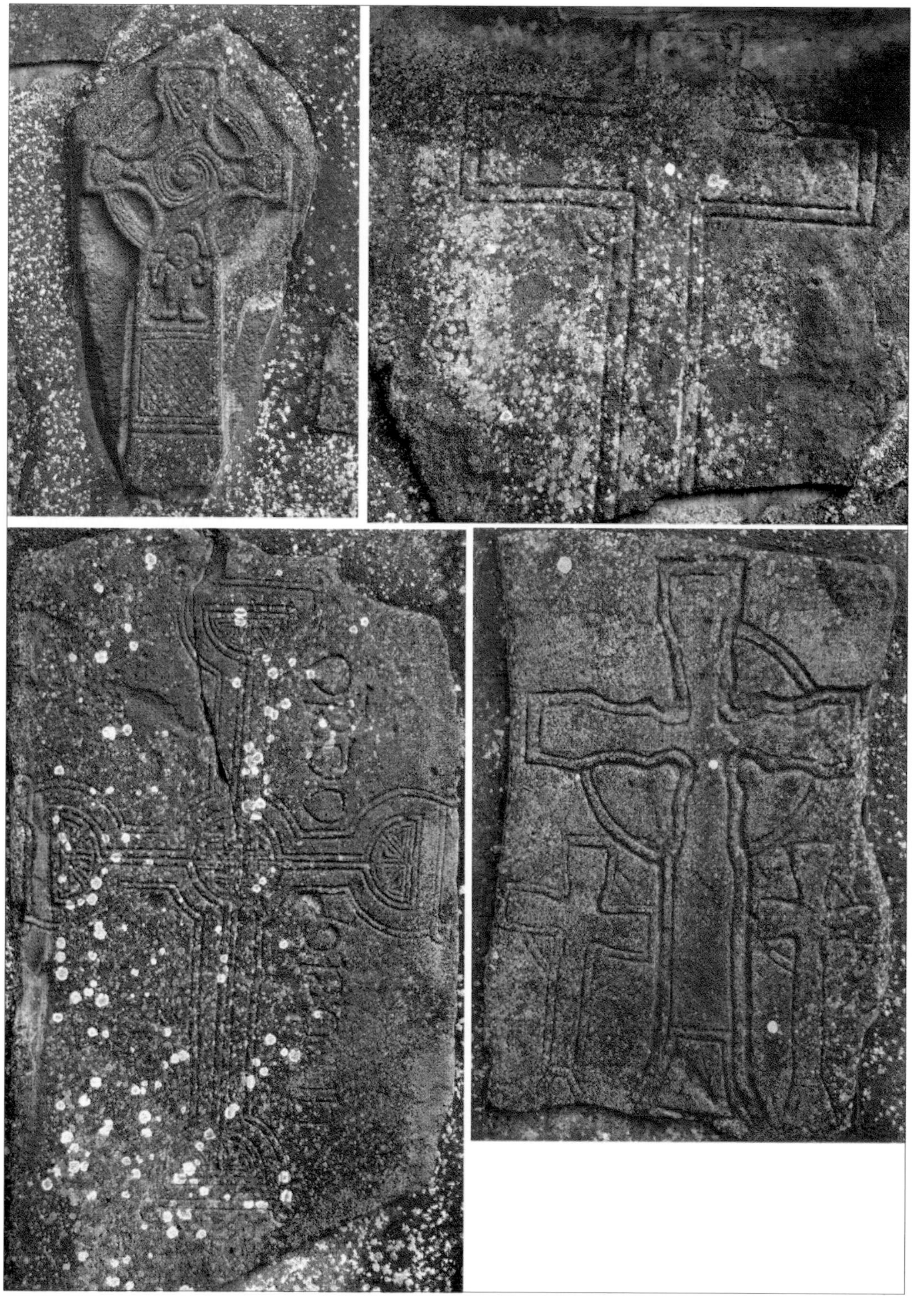

Plate B17:
Example of early Christian grave slabs discovered at Gallen Priory, Ferbane, County Offaly.

hollowed out stone basin (ballaun) and a pillar carved with scenes reminiscent of those seen on High Crosses. If you walk to the high ground with the modern cross you will see a nearby graveyard within which are the remains of a medieval church. Drive back to the main street of Ferbane and turn right onto the R436 road for Clara and Ballycumber just past the Gardai station. (This road has a narrow entrance and is easily missed!).

After about 6 kilometres, you come to Leamonaghan, which is located at a crossroads with a school to your left and the remains of a church across the road to your right. (Parking is difficult but you may be able to park behind the disused school or in the small lane down the side of the church). St. Manchan founded a monastery here in the mid-7th century, although the present abandoned church is much later. However, within the church there are two early Christian grave slabs, secured to the walls and the small school

Plate B18:
Decorated stone at Leamonaghan monastic site, County Offaly.

houses a number of others that have been found in the vicinity. Early Christian sites were often characterised by an enclosure bank and ditch, such as can still be seen at Rahan or at Killeigh. There is no surface evidence for such an enclosure at Leamonaghan but geophysical work carried out by the Environmental Geophysics Unit at the National University of Maynooth in 2004 revealed the presence of such an enclosure at this site. The present church is multi-phase; parts of it date from the 12th century and parts from the 15th/16th century (O'Brien, personal communication). Various building periods can be deduced because of the different window styles. Note that one, has a small carved head, similar to that seen on the window border at Rahan. Both limestone and sandstone have been used in the church's construction. Stand at the front of the church and look back along the road you travelled, this is west. There is part of the enclosure in the field across the road which has no surface expression. To your left (about 15m distance), roughly in line with the front of the church among the modern grave markers is a 0.6 m high stone slab. The slab is tapered and an intricate swirling maze pattern is repeated across its surface, Plate B18. Its origin and age is unknown but it has been commented on that the motifs are similar to early Christian illuminated manuscripts. Leave the churchyard by the small stile which leads you into the lane east of the church. Follow the roadway and shortly, on your left, you will come to a holy well in front of which there is a ballaun stone (see Plate 33 from Section II of the book). Note also the 'rag tree' where offering, mainly concerning children, have been left. The trackway is

350m in length, and leads from the church at Leamonaghan through a field to a stone enclosure within which is a small stone oratory. This is called St. Mella's Cell (St. Mella was the mother of St. Manchan). The oratory, trackway and enclosure are believed to be contemporaneous and date from about the 11th century.

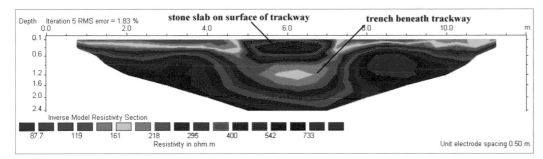

Plate B19:
Resistivity plot across c. 11th century trackway at Leamonaghan, County Offaly.

The trackway between the cell and the church is paved with slabs of sandstone rock. Some large erratics of sandstone can be seen around the edge of the field through which you walked and it is possible that such erratics were used in the construction though sandstone does outcrop nearby. The trackway however, has not been built simply by

Plate B20:
St. Manchan's Shrine, Boher Church, County Offaly.

laying slabs of rock onto the surface. Plate B19 shows a geophysical section through the trackway carried out by the Environmental Geophysics Unit at the National University of Maynooth. The section shows that resistivity values are relatively low in the top 30 cm with values of 100-200 ohm metres except where the traverse crosses the trackway. This is generally associated with a regular zone of high resistivity values of 600-700 ohm metres caused by the slab of rock on the surface. Generally, the slabs do not extend right across the full width of the trackway but tend to occur in the middle. The resistivity values are high either side of the trackway (600-1,000 ohm metres) below depths of around 60 cm. However, this pattern does not extend across it. A deeper, low resistivity zone, shown mainly in blues and greens on Plate B19, replaces the high resistivity surface signature of the trackway indicating that it was not produced simply by laying stepping stones across the field but that that a trench was excavated and back-filled before being capped by stones. Return to your car, continue driving along the R436 for 3 kilometres, then take the first road to your left. At the next junction turn left, drive the few hundred metres and stop outside the church at Boher. The shrine of St. Manchan is located within the church to the left as you enter, Plates B20 and B21. The shrine is in the form of a gabled box formed of yew wood, on which is an intricately worked metal cross, dividing it into 4 segments, within which are metal human figures. Originally 50 such figures would have been on the shrine, but only 11 now remain. One, carrying an axe is believed to represent St. Olaf of Norway. Fine interlaced patterns can be seen on the edges of the shrine. This is the largest (60cm x 50m) such 12th century shrine in Ireland. Rings at the 4 corners allowed the reliquary to be processed using poles and analysis of the bones within it showed that they were human. Its existence was not documented, until the mid-19th century, when it was exhibited in Dublin; until then, the local Buckley family had protected it over the centuries. Return now to the main R436 road and continue to Ballycumber which was developed by the Armstrong family in the 18th century. At the eastern end of Ballycumber main street (where the statue of a cowled monk is located), the road to the right leads on to Clara. However take the road to the left (for Moate) and after 500m take the road to the right for 4 kilometres. A small road comes in from the left and 50m up this road on the left (behind a bungalow), is a good example of a tall standing stone (townland of Bolart North). Return to Ballycumber and drive to Clara. Clara's development especially from the mid-18th century onwards, was based to a great extent on the textile industry. The Goodbody family ran various industrial enterprises in the 19th century such as a gasworks and flourmills. However, their most important industrial work, which employed hundreds of people, involved the spinning and weaving of products for which imported jute was the raw material. Clara is also the site of Clara Bog which is the largest (460 hectares) protected raised bog in Ireland. Take the N80 to Tullamore out of Clara and note the small building on your right near Clara Bridge which was the Quaker Meeting House.

Six kilometres along the N80 road you come to the townland of Loughaun which contains the remains of a small church at Tihilly beside which is a poorly preserved 9th century High Cross and an early Christian grave slab. The site is on the left near a 19th century mill backs onto a mound (a possible prehistoric tumulus). Continue along the road into Tullamore noting as you do that the road rises over an esker, which crosses the road.

Itinerary C: Northeast Irish Midlands

Approximate Distance: 130 kilometres
Ordnance Survey 1:50,000 Discovery Series Maps: 41 and 42.

This itinerary takes in parts of Counties Meath and Westmeath and commences in Mullingar, Figure C1. Mullingar, the administrative capital of County Westmeath, is located between Loughs Owel and Ennell. The town is surrounded on three sides (north, east and west) by the Royal Canal, which loops around the town. Mullingar gets its name from the

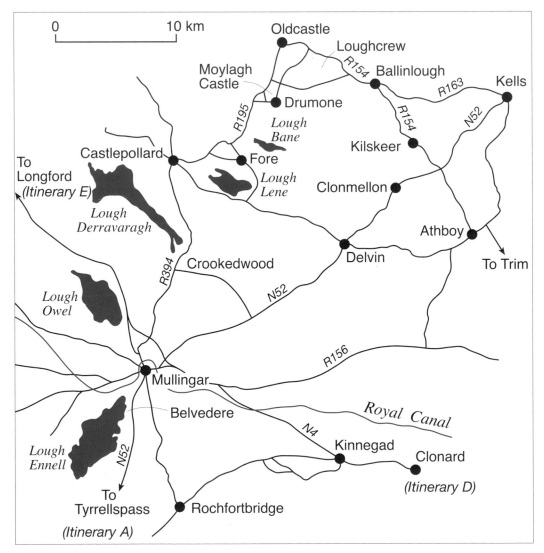

Figure C1:
Location map for Itinerary C.

Gaelic 'An Muileann gCearr' which loosely translated means 'the wry or left handed mill' and refers to a legend in which St. Colman caused a mill wheel to change direction. Confusion can arise when describing various locations in Mullingar as many of the street names have changed. As a result, Linen Street, Main Street, Bridge Street and Gaol Street from the 19th century are now respectively Dominick Street, Oliver Plunkett/Pearse Street, Austin Friars' Street and Mount Street in the 21st century. Some of these streets had other names at other times.

Today the centre of Mullingar can conveniently be taken as the Market House at the junction of Pearse and Mount Street, Plate C1. The present Market House was built in 1867 on the site of an older one. Proceed down Mount Street and part way down on the left-hand side; a narrow laneway leads to All Saints Church at the end of Church Avenue. The present church was built around 1814 and later modified, though memorials around and within it, date back to 1670 (Winckworth, no date). However, Mullingar has a much longer ecclesiastical history. The Anglo-Norman Hugh de Lacy granted what is now known as the Barony of Magheradernan to William Petit who adopted Mullingar as his

Plate C1:
Market House, Mullingar,
County Westmeath.

centre of power. A church was built and put into the care of the Augustinian prior of Llanthony, Gwent, in Wales around 1200 (Daly, no date). The brother of William, Ralph Petit, who became bishop, established St. Mary's Priory (also known as the House of God) under the auspices of the Canons Regular of St. Augustine around 1227 (Andrews and Davies 1992). The sites of these establishments are not known, but, based on tradition and some archaeological finds, are believed to be between All Saints Church and Cross Keys, 150m northwest of the church. Also, in Church Avenue are the Masonic Lodge, built 1869 and the Parochial Hall.

Return to Mount Street and turn left. In front of you across the road are the county buildings of Westmeath Council. This was the site of the old jail and some maps show it as the location of Petit's castle and motte, with the former being dismantled in 1828 to accommodate the jail. On your left as you near the County Buildings is the courthouse built in the 1820s. Return to the top of Mount Street, turn left and walk along Oliver Plunkett/Pearse Street to the roundabout at the junction with Dominick Street. There is a very abrupt widening of the street at this location and it has been suggested that this is the site of a medieval gateway (Andrews and Davies 1992). Walk up the street at right angles to Dominick Street (Mary Street) and proceed to the Catholic Cathedral, Christ the King, which dominates the town. This twin-towered edifice was built in 1936 replacing an older church on the site. It houses an ecclesiastical museum, which contains 18th century penal crosses and vestments. The nearby parochial house was constructed *c.* 1871.

To continue the itinerary return to your car, drive past the Market House and the Greville Arms Hotel (the site of a hotel since *c.* 1750), both on your right, then turn left into Castle Street. Continue along this road until you come to the roundabout at Mullingar General Hospital, where you turn right, signposted for Castlepollard and Sligo. Continue to the flyover roundabout over the N4 and take the R394 road out of Mullingar to Castlepollard, Figure C1.

A few kilometres out of Mullingar, the main gates of Knockdrin Castle can be seen on your right. Continue on this road for a further 5 kilometres until you will come to Crookedwood. Several Bronze Age skeletons and food vessels were found here in 1933, when the road was being straightened (O'Riordain, 1935). Take the road to your right, signposted for Delvin and after about 1.5 kilometres, you come to Taghmon Church (from the Irish Teach Munna, meaning Munna's House), on your right (Plate C2). The present day church was built as a parish church in the 15th century on the site of the 6th century monastery of St. Fintan (Munna). It has a vaulted stone roof and the four-storey tower at the western end of the church would have been used as living quarters for the residing priest. A number of carved figures can be observed on its exterior, a carved head can be seen over the door and a grotesque figure (sheela-na-gig) surmounts one of the windows.

Plate C2:
15th century Taghmon Church (St. Munna's)
at Crookedwood, County Westmeath.

Return to the main road, turn right and continue towards Castlepollard. In about 1 kilometre, a lake can be seen on the left, sandwiched between 2 hills, Knockbody and Knockoyon. This is Lough Derravaragh (lough of the oak wood in Gaelic) and the next turning on the left (a further 1 kilometre) takes you down to it. Lough Derravaragh features in one of the most famous legends in the Irish Midlands, the Children of Lir. Lir, a local chieftain, had 4 children and he married Aoife after the death of their mother Eva. However, in a fit of jealousy she turned them into swans and they were forced to live on the lough for 300 years. They were eventually returned to human form by a follower of St. Patrick. Continue on to Castlepollard (a further 6 kilometres).

The Irish name for Castlepollard is 'Baile na gCros'- Town of the Crosses, as a number of crosses were once sited on its outskirts. A number of demesnes were located in this area, such as the de Bourghs of Galstown, the Pakenhams of Tullynally (Earls of Longford) and the Pollards of Kinturk. The Pollards came to Ireland from Devonshire, England in the 1500s (Captain Nicholas Pollard) and were granted land and a castle in this part of Westmeath. The lands were constituted by a Charles II charter into the town of Castlepollard with permission to hold fairs and a weekly market. The present buildings around the Square are mainly 19th century, including St. Michael's Church of Ireland Church which is on your right as you enter the Square. The land for this was donated by the Pollard family and memorial plaques within the church reflect the importance of this family. The most ornate one is to Walter William Dutton Pollard-Urquhart, who died in 1872. (The Urquhart family were from Craigston Castle in Aberdeenshire, Scotland). The Square is dominated by the Town Hall and a recent monument to the Children of Lir.

Take the road signposted for Oldcastle and Fore (R195). As you drive out of Castlepollard, you will see (on your right) typical undulating topography caused by the deposition of glacial sediments. Continue on for 3.5 kilometres and turn right onto the road signposted for Fore Village and monastic site.

As you drive into Fore, stop at the car-park on your left. Fore was the location of a monastery founded by St. Fechin around 630 AD, and continued as a site of worship in the following centuries. Across the road from the car-park is St. Fechin's Church, which you can enter through the graveyard by going up a short flight of steps. St. Fechin's Church is a multiphase structure, Plate C3. The western part is about 10th century in date, whereas additions at the eastern end date from the 1200s or later. The lintel over the western doorway is formed of a single massive stone on which is carved a cross enclosed by a circle. Similar Greek crosses have been found in the same position on churches from the Middle East from the 6th century. There are a number of early Christian grave slabs (some made of sandstone which is not the local rock) located within the church and a small carved figure of a seated monk can be seen on the northern edge of the archway. Return to the car-park across the road. There are two rag trees near the car-park (near springs or wells) one of which has the remains of a tree into which coins have been hammered as offerings. The main ecclesiastical focus of Fore is the large Benedictine Priory which can be seen in front of you, Plate C4. This was founded by the de Lacy family in the 13th century but was added to later, mainly in the 15th century. Follow the path over to the

Plate C3:
Inside of St.Fechin's Church, Fore, County Westmeath. Construction commenced in the 10th century.

Plate C4:
Benedictine Priory at Fore.

priory and walk around its exterior and interior. The ground floor would have been arranged around the cloister, Plate C5 and contained a refectory, nave, choir and chapel. Upstairs would have been the living quarters, most likely a large dormitory for the monks with smaller rooms for the more important monks or abbot. Near the priory is part of a building, the interior of which is composed of small compartments like pigeonholes, Plate C5. Literally that is what they are. This is a columbarium, and the circular building would once have been roofed and each compartment would have contained a pigeon nest. The monks would have used the pigeons for food or to obtain eggs.

Plate C5:
Part of cloister (top) and columbarium (bottom) at Fore Priory.

As you make your way back towards the car-park, the small building on the far side of the road with the backdrop of the vertical cliff face is very prominent, Plate C6. This is the Greville-Nugent mausoleum. The tower on the eastern side is older than the rest of the small chapel, and is believed to date from about the 15th/16th century. It was restored around 1680 and again in 1874 and adopted as a mausoleum. A number of memorial slabs are contained within this building, one to Richard Nugent, Earl of Westmeath dated 1680. The story of Fore has been one of repeated attacks over the centuries, mainly because monastic communities were often relatively wealthy. It was attacked repeatedly in the 15th century and a defensive wall was built around the town. Entry to the town was via gates, two of which still partially exist, one just 100m back along the road towards Castlepollard and one at the other (east) side of the town opposite St. Fechin's Catholic Church.

Various legends are associated with St. Fechin, which collectively are called the Seven Wonders of Fore. They are:

- The monastery in a bog. The land around the car-park near the priory is very marshy and contains many flag irises which thrive in boggy ground.
- The mill without a race. This relates to a mill supposedly built here, which was to employ a water wheel to provide the energy for grinding, but the mill was built where there was no river to power the wheel.
- The water that flows uphill. A number of natural springs emerge at Fore near the car-park (holy wells), and, as the water emerges from the ground, it can be viewed as water flowing uphill. The author has visited Fore a number of times, sometimes there is virtually no water emerging, while at other times vast quantities are flowing. This wonder will be considered further shortly.

- The tree that doesn't burn. If you look carefully at the remains of an old tree near the well you will see coins hammered into the stump as offerings.
- The water that will not boil. Tradition has it that water from St. Fechin's well cannot be boiled and bad fortune will afflict anyone who tries.
- The stone raised by St. Fechin's prayers. Legend has it that the large cross-inscribed stone comprising the lintel of St. Fechin's Church could not be lifted into place but was raised by a miracle performed by St. Fechin.
- The anchorite (hermit) in a stone. This is believed to refer to the anchorite Patrick Beglen (or Begley) who lived in a small cell in 1616 in the oldest part of the structure that is now the Greville-Nugent mausoleum.

Plate C6:
Greville-Nugent mausoleum at Fore backed by limestone cliff.

The water that issues from the springs at Fore comes via underground channels from Lough Lene which is on the other side of the high cliff behind the mausoleum. To visit this lake, return to your car and drive through Fore. As you pass the road on your left note, the small roadside cross, medieval in age, one of several which occur in the general vicinity. Drive on past the modern Catholic Church on your left and the school on your right. Take the road to your right after the school signposted for Drumcree. After 500m take the road to your right (cul-de sac), then 50m farther on take the narrow road to your right. Follow this lane up around the bend and stop at the first gate past the small forest on your left. Walk down this field to Lough Lene. Once you reach the lakeshore turn left (southeast) and walk along the shore edge for a few hundred metres. Rock outcrops here show that the rocks have been tilted up and are dipping quite steeply. At a number of locations, narrow channels have been cut and the water flows from the lake along the channels, disappearing underground through what are known as swallow holes, Plate C7. The slightly acidic water has dissolved away some of the limestone forming subterranean tunnels through which the water can flow. At certain times of the year, you can hear the underground water flowing through the channels. This water flows underground to emerge as springs at Fore. Return to your car, drive back into the centre of Fore, then take

Plate C7:
Swallow-hole in limestone rock at Lough Lene near Fore through which water flows underground. Width of image is 1.5m.

Plate C8:
Motte and remains of castle at
Moylagh (top) and tower (bottom).

the road to your right near the small cross. As you drive out of Fore, note the general geographical context within which the village is situated. It is in a narrow valley containing springs and high limestone hills towering over 100m above it to the southwest (Windtown) and to the northeast (Ben Knockcurreen). These would once have formed a continuous upland limestone area. However, the subterranean movement of water in this karst area would have produced subsurface channels, which would have eventually weakened the limestone, leading to a collapse thus forming the valley. The high steep hills also aided the defence of Fore as any attack on the town had to be mounted along the valley. Continue on this road until you meet the R195 Castlepollard-Oldcastle road, and then turn right.

Drive towards Oldcastle for 7 kilometres, passing some sand and gravel pits on your left until you come to Millbrook where you should turn right onto the road signposted for Loughcrew and Kells (Boyne Drive). There are the remains of a seven-storey mill at this road junction. Extensive flour milling commenced at this location when John Henry built the first mill in the 1770s (hence the name Millbrook). A number of small limestone houses and a forge, built around 1868 in the vicinity of the mill, are believed to be labourers' cottages. The Naper family were granted vast tracts of land in this area during the time of Elizabeth I, and were the main landowners in the following centuries. Drive along this road for about 1 kilometre (during which time you will pass other small cottages) and turn right, taking the road signposted Drumone. In Drumone, turn right at the crossroads, drive 1.5 kilometres, take the road to your right near the Catholic Church and stop at the ruins on your right (Moylagh Castle). There is a long history of human habitation at this location partly due to its physical characteristics. The site offers a good vantage point to view the surrounding terrain (and any approaching enemy), as it is located on a high mound of glacial sediment. Note the nature of the uneven hummocky glacial sediments in the vicinity. A 12th century Norman motte was built on the glacial mound and a later castle built onto it, Plate C8. Beside the motte is an old graveyard and the remains of a church. The church was probably built around the 15th century and the best preserved part of it is the tower in the southwest corner. The site is surrounded by 3 hectares of field systems consisting of banks and a road.

Return to the main Loughcrew road by retracing your route, turn right and continue to Loughcrew Historic gardens which you can enter shortly after passing a long wall on your right. This land was in the possession of the Plunkett family who arrived in Ireland after the Anglo-Norman invasion and whose most famous member was St. Oliver Plunkett. Oliver Plunkett was born in 1629 and travelled to Rome in 1645 to train as a Catholic priest. He was appointed primate of Armagh in 1669 and returned to Ireland. Persecution of Catholics was widespread and he was arrested, tried in England and executed at Tyburn in 1681. He was canonised as a saint in 1975. The family church can still be seen within Loughcrew Historic Gardens. The Naper family were influential in Ireland from the latter half 16th century and dispossessed the Plunketts. They built a large house and gardens in the grounds in the 1670s and incorporated a 12th century Norman motte as a viewing platform. The house was later demolished and a large Grecian style mansion fronted by Ionic columns with associated landscaped gardens and parkland was built in the 1820s. This house suffered fires in 1888 and 1959 and was finally destroyed by fire in 1964. All that now remains is essentially a massive 'garden feature' formed from the columns, Plate C9.

Return to the main road and turn right as you leave the gardens. Shortly on your left you will see a gate lodge to this estate which was built c. 1821 and modelled on the mansion, complete with Ionic columns, Plate C9. Continue

Plate C9:
(Top) remains of Naper family house and (bottom) surviving gate lodge built in the same style as the house.

driving for about 2 kilometres, noting the long high ridge to your left, which is formed of greywacke rocks that are hundreds of millions of years older than the limestone which forms most of the Irish Midlands. Turn left at the signpost for Loughcrew, drive up the narrow steep road and park in the car-park after about 1 kilometre. The ridge you are on is called Slieve na Calliagh which translates as the hills of the witch (or hag) who in mythology is believed to have dropped the megalithic tombs onto the summits of the hills. The Loughcrew cairns comprise a passage tomb cemetery and were built in the Neolithic period about 5,000 years ago (3000 BC). They were constructed at the same time as the Carrowmore and Carrowkeel passage tomb cemeteries in County Sligo to the northwest and the Boyne Valley complex including Newgrange and Knowth, to the east. Whilst the individual tombs are not as large as those at Newgrange or Knowth, their spectacular setting, located on the top of the three highest hills in the area, means that they would have formed an impressive sight and were intended to be seen from afar. In all, there are over 30 cairns in the vicinity, most grouped on three hills, twelve on Carnbane West, seven on Carnbane East and three on Patrickstown Hill.

The steps and the path from the car-park lead up towards Carnbane East, which is possibly the focal point of the entire cemetery complex. The ascent is steep for about 500m. (It is possible to climb up to Carnbane West, across the road, but there is no well-defined path and the route, for a distance of about 1.5 kilometres, is very steep in places).

Proceed up the steps, through the gate and follow the path to the left. Note the blocks of limestone lying around. These are glacial erratics carried to this height and dumped by the glaciers, which covered this area 12,000 years ago. Many of these limestone blocks (which do not form the natural underlying bedrock of Slieve na Calliagh) have been used in the construction of the tombs.

Plate C10:
Cairn T passage tomb on Carnbane East,
Slieve na Calliagh, County Meath.

Follow the path until you reach the main passage tomb, Plate C10. This is known as Cairn T. All the cairns (tombs) were allocated a letter by Eugene Conwell who mapped them in 1863. Cairn T is about 35m in diameter, although it does not form a perfect circle, being flattened on its eastern (entrance) side. Arranged around its base, are large stones and slabs, partially acting as a retaining wall for the large internal stones and the mound of small loose stones that cover the cairn. The passage is low and narrow, requiring one to crouch down on entering, Plate C11. The passage tombs do not have a uniform shape. Some have a simple linear entrance, whereas others, like Cairn T are cruciform in shape, which in essence produces three chambers at the end of the passage. Often these alcoves contain cremated remains or bone fragments. Cairn L on Carnbane West has seven alcoves, one of which contains a large shallow basin stone, similar to one found at Knowth. A special feature of Cairn T is the carvings on the stones both along the passage and in the chambers, Plate C11. The name Carnbane means in Gaelic 'white cairn' and lumps of white quartz have been found around Cairn T. Similar white quartz is found around Newgrange which is now included on its façade and is believed to have come from the Wicklow Mountains. If the quartz found on Slieve na Calliagh had the same origin, it would have had to have been transported a distance of 75 kilometres.

If you move to the northern edge of Cairn T (the direction in which you first approached it) there is a very large prominent kerbstone called the Hag's Chair. Various hypotheses have been put forward as to its purpose; for example, it was sat on by Queen Maeve to pass laws or that it was used as a Mass Rock, where Mass was celebrated during Penal times. A crude cross is inscribed on its upper part. From the chair one gets superb views out over the northern part of Ireland. The other cairns on Carnbane East have all been unroofed, one Cairn U (which is to the right of the Hag's Chair as you face north) also contains carved stones. Although the cairns were built in the Neolithic period, there is also evidence of much later Iron Age (approximately 300 BC) activity at one of the monuments (Cairn H) on Carnbane West as evidenced by the La Tène ornamentation style.

Cairn T is not the largest of the Cairns on Slieve na Calliagh; Cairn L is 40m in diameter and Cairn D is 55m across but no passage has ever been found in the latter. However, Cairn T is believed to be the centre of the tomb complex for a number of reasons. It is situated on top of Carnbane East (276m) which is higher than Carnbane West (254m) or Patrickstown Hill (267m) where the other cairns are located. Most of the other cairns in the complex have passages that point towards Cairn T. The passage for Cairn T, like that at Newgrange, has an alignment which is of astronomical significance. The passage at Newgrange is lit by the rising sun at dawn on the shortest day of the year (c. 22nd of December). The number of hours of daylight on the shortest day is at a minimum, which gradually increases until the longest day (c. 22nd of June) from which it decreases again

Plate C11:
Passage (top) of Cairn T and
rock art (bottom) on sandstone
slab along passage.

until the following winter solstice. However, there are two other dates, the 21st of March and the 22nd of September, when there are 12 hours of sunlight and 12 hours of darkness, not only in Ireland but also everywhere on the earth. These are the Spring and Autumnal Equinoxes. Shortly after dawn on both equinoxes, the rising sun illuminates only Cairn T's passage.

As you make your way back down towards your car, you should be able to make out the cultivation ridges ('lazy beds') running down the slope of Carnbane West. Continue driving in the same direction (off the northern flank of Slieve na Calliagh) and turn right at the T-junction after about 1.5 kilometres. Continue on this road to the next T-junction with the main Oldcastle-Kells road.

Turning left at this junction takes you towards Oldcastle. As you drive into Oldcastle the grey, limestone Gilson endowed school on your right is most striking, Plate C12. Lawrence Gilson, who died in 1810, left, the sum of £35,000, in his will, for building and maintaining schools in the Oldcastle district. The present school was built in 1828 on land provided by the Naper family and was for children of both sexes and of all religions. Gilson also explicitly stated in his will that the Master of the school could be either a Roman Catholic or a Protestant but must be appointed solely on merit. Driving into Oldcastle, you come to the Market Square upon which all roads converge. The former Market House has now been converted into a shop, but note the arched windows. In its original form, these were open arches from which trade could be conducted. There is little information about Oldcastle before the 16th century, although there have been reports of old castles in the vicinity. The first detailed map of Oldcastle was produced in 1778 for the Naper family (who owned the town). On it, apart from the Market House,

Plate C12:
Gilson endowed school at Oldcastle, County Meath.

Plate C13:
Spire of Loyd (Lloyd) 'Lighthouse' folly built in 1791 near Kells.

virtually every other building mentioned was called a cabin. Most of the main buildings in Oldcastle centre have been built in the 19th century (the present Market House was built in 1821). A church is shown on this map on the site of the present St. Bride's Church of Ireland Church which itself was built in the early 19th century. There is a small medieval cross at the door of the church similar to those located at Fore and at other locations in the vicinity. Many of the buildings exhibit fine detail in their upper stories especially Gibney's with its arched windows and Mullens, just off the Square. Its upper storey is composed of red brick, itself unusual but its façade has 8 large panels each composed of 9 decorated tiles. Retrace your route out of Oldcastle, and continue towards Kells (20 kilometres distance), see Figure C1. You pass a viewing point on your left about 9 kilometres from Oldcastle and 200 m farther on you should take the road to your left towards Kells. Note, near this junction are some outcrops of the greywacke rock that forms Slieve na Calliagh. Shortly you pass through Ballinlough noted for its church built in the 1830s. A stained glass window was erected over the doorway dedicated to Patrick Aranyas, who was killed in the Twin Towers attack in New York on the 11th September 2001. Nearer to Kells, you will soon see a tower, which looks like a lighthouse, close to the road (Plate C13). This is located on the Hill of Loyd (Lloyd), within the People's Park, where you can stop. It is known as the Spire of Loyd and is a monument, erected in 1791, by the First Earl of Bective to the memory of his father Sir Thomas Taylor. It was used as a viewing platform from which to watch nearby races and the hunt. There are excellent views from this position and the Slieve na Calliagh hills are particularly prominent. Return to the main road and continue into the town of Kells. Stop beside the remains of a 10th century Round Tower, which is situated on the left hand side of the street. The town of Kells has a rich ecclesiastical history and is closely associated with the 9th century illuminated Book of Kells, presently housed in Trinity College Dublin. The Book of Kells was possibly produced on Iona, a Scottish island where a community of monks lived in a monastery founded by St. Columba (Colum Cille or Columbkille) in the 6th century. Viking raids resulted in the monks leaving Iona and founding a monastery at Kells in the early 9th century (804 AD). This Columban centre of learning persisted in Kells for the following 300 years even though it was periodically raided and sacked. The early monastery encompassed the Round Tower and the present St. Columba's Church. The Round Tower in Kells is 30m tall, but its roof is missing. Near the very top you can discern 5 windows, each looking out over one of the five ancient roads that led into the town. Kells was given the status of a diocese in 1152, although it was later merged with the Diocese of Meath. The present-day church on the site was constructed in the late 18th century though beside it is the bell tower, built in 1578 by Bishop Brady, and the steeple erected on it in 1783 by the Earl of Bective. There are three High Crosses within the graveyard, plus the base of a fourth (the North Cross), adjacent to the bell tower. The most complete one is the early 9th century South Cross (named the Cross of Patrick and Columba because of an inscription), Plate C14. Only the shaft of the West cross remains and the East Cross is referred to as the unfinished cross as the panels are undecorated, Plate C15. Various biblical figures and representations are shown in various panels

Plate C14:
9th century High Cross (South Cross) in Kells, County Meath.

Plate C15:
Round Tower and the unfinished High Cross in Kells.

Plate C16:
10th century oratory (St. Columciles's
or St. Columba's house) in Kells.

Plate C17:
13th century grave slab
of robed abbess, Kells.

around the crosses such as Noah's Ark. Particularly striking is the figure of Christ crucified on the unfinished cross. None of the crosses are made from the local limestone rock, but from sandstone, possibly because it was easier to carve the figures. Also located within the church or its grounds are a stone sundial, a font, possibly pre-Norman in date and a medieval memorial slab.

Leave the grounds of the church, turn left and walk up Church Lane/ Market Street for 200m. On your right (beside the Gardai station) is a 10th century stone-roofed oratory known as St. Columba's House, Plate C16. Now retrace your steps but continue on downhill past the church along John Street into Headfort Place. This is named after the important Headfort family, who owned buildings in this locality. Note the width of the street, its Georgian houses and the two primary schools on your right, which were built in 1840, using an endowment given by Catherine Dempsey. At the end of Headfort Place, where the road splits is the old courthouse, built in 1801, which now houses Kells Heritage Centre. The Market High Cross of Kells now stands in front of the centre under a canopy to protect it from the elements. It was moved to its present position to prevent any accidental damage. From the Heritage Centre look back up Headfort Place and on your right, there is a small cemetery behind a modern limestone fronted wall. This was the site of the Priory of the Hospitallers of St. John which was founded here in the late 12th century. Enter by the small gate and follow the path in front of you around the perimeter of the cemetery. A well-carved *c.* 13th century grave slab depicting a robed abbess is located beside the wall, Plate C17.

Return to your car, drive past the Round Tower and take the road to the right signposted for Mullingar (N52). After a few hundred metres, near the Railway Bar, take the N52 to the right, still signposted Mullingar. After 8 kilometres you may wish to make a short diversion to Kilskeer (Kilskyre) by turning right onto the R154 for Oldcastle. Kilskeer is a small village dominated by the Catholic Church. Across the road from the church, there is an old cemetery which is believed to have been the site of a monastery founded by St. Sciria in the 6th century. Records of the names of the abbots exist from the 8th century onwards as well as the dates of Viking raids. There are the remains of an ivy-clad tower (part of a tower house) along with an old church in the graveyard. The most elaborate tomb is that of the Plunkett-O'Reilly family (dated 1686), enclosed by a wall and metal railings, bearing the coats of arms of both families. The oldest grave also has carved figures along its side, Plate C18. The field within which the graveyard stands is characterised by buried boundaries indicating the presence of a number of large enclosures.

Return to the main N52 road, turn right and continue on to Clonmellon and then Delvin. Clonmellon's main street was laid out by the Chapman family who lived in nearby Killua Castle. (You may have seen the ruin on your left, near which is the large obelisk shown in Plate 40). Much of present-day Meath and Westmeath was ceded to Hugh de Lacy by Henry II in the late 12th century. The de Lacy stronghold was in Trim 20 kilometres east of Delvin and outside the scope of this book. However, it is well worth a visit because it contains the largest Anglo-Norman castle in Ireland as well as a 13th century abbey and a 14th century bell tower. The de Lacy's gave the lands around Delvin to the Nugents. Part of their lands also included Fore and some of the abbots in Fore were Nugents, hence the location for their family mausoleum (see Plate C6). The Nugents built the castle in the centre of Delvin in the late 12th to early 13th century. Initially it had 4 towers of which only 2 now remain, Plate C19. Beside it is the remains of St. Mary's, a 13th century Norman church which has been extensively altered over the centuries as evidenced by its blocked up archways and redesigned windows.

The Nugents later built a castle at Clonyn nearby but it was destroyed in the mid-1600s to prevent it falling into Cromwell's hands though it was later rebuilt around 1680. A later castle was built on the site in the 19th century by which times the family had become the Greville-Nugents after marriage into the Greville family from Mullingar. Continue through Delvin remaining on the N52 road back to Mullingar. A few hundred metres past the Norman castle if you look along the street to your right you can see the 19th century castle, Plate C20. Eight kilometres past Delvin, you come to the staggered Turin crossroads.

Plate C18:
Coats of arms for the Plunkett and O'Reilly families and grave plaque within old cemetery at Kilskeer (Kilskyre), County Meath.

Plate C19:
Late 12th to early 13th Anglo-Norman castle at Delvin, County Westmeath, built by the Nugent family.

Approximately 150m up the left hand road, set back on the left about 200m into the field is a 1.8m high standing stone.

Drive into Mullingar and remain on the N52 to Tyrrellspass (following the signs for Belvedere House) and after 6 kilometres, turn right into the grounds. Belvedere House was built in the 18th century and overlooks Lough Ennell. Belvedere is associated with the Rochfort family, after whom the nearby town of Rochfortbridge is named. Belvedere House is most well known for two interlocking stories. The First Earl of Belvedere, Robert Rochfort along with his brother George accused their other brother Arthur of having an affair with Robert's wife Mary whom he married in 1736. Arthur was bankrupted and imprisoned while she was imprisoned in nearby Gaulstown House for 30 years, only being released when Robert died in 1774. Meanwhile, George had built Rochfort (later called Tudenham) House near Belvedere. In order that he might not look upon his brother's grander house, Robert had a large intervening folly built, called the 'jealous wall'. Note, the Countess of Belvedere (Jane) discussed in Itinerary A, was married to George Rochfort, the *Second* Earl of Belvedere (who was the son of Robert the First Earl and Mary) Return to the main road where you can turn left, and return to Mullingar, or turn right and travel to Tyrrellspass, which is on Itinerary A.

Plate C20:
Clonyn Castle built in the 19th century at Delvin by the Greville-Nugent family.

Itinerary D: East Irish Midlands

Approximate Distance: 100 kilometres
Ordnance Survey 1:50,000 Discovery Series Maps: 55, 49 and 48.

Figure D1:
Location map for Itinerary D.

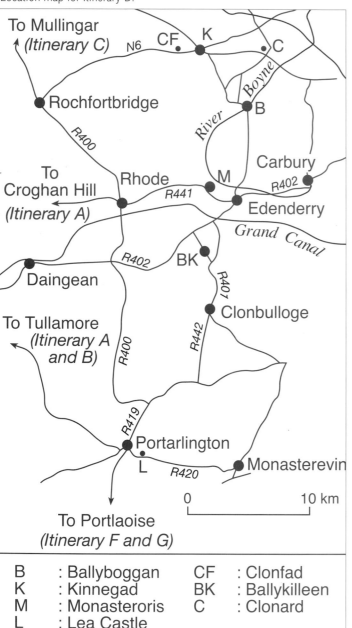

B	: Ballyboggan	CF	: Clonfad
K	: Kinnegad	BK	: Ballykilleen
M	: Monasteroris	C	: Clonard
L	: Lea Castle		

This route takes in parts of five counties, starting in Portarlington in the south (Co. Laois), through Clonbulloge and Edenderry in Co. Offaly, on to Carbury in Co. Kildare and Clonard in Co. Meath and returning via Kinnegad and Rochfortbridge in Co. Westmeath, Figure D1. Portarlington owes its existence to Sir Henry Bennet (who also had the title of Lord Arlington) who, in the 1660s, was granted the lands of Lewis O'Dempsey (Viscount Clanmalier) by Charles II. A late 17th century map shows that Portarlington was established in a meander of the River Barrow, which formed a natural defence on its western, northern and eastern sides. The town initially consisted of four major streets laid out as a 'cross' pattern with a Market Square and Market House located at their intersection. The streets, clockwise from north, were named Bennet Street, James Street, Queene Street and King Street, although these are now called Spa Street, Church Lane, Main Street and French Church Street respectively.

Proceed to the Square at the top of Main Street. The garage in the centre of the Square is a later Market House built around 200 years ago. The main building in the Square is St. Paul's French Church (Plate D1) and accompanying graveyard beside which is the Celtic Cross commemorating United Irishmen who were executed in the Square in 1798. The church

Plate D1:
St. Paul's
'French Church',
Portarlington,
County Laois.

owes its existence to French Huguenots (Powell, 1996). The Huguenots were Protestants who lived in France and followed the teaching of John Calvin from the mid-16th century. Their religion was not acceptable to the French Catholic monarchy and massacres of Huguenots took place periodically in the late 16th to early 17th century. Many Huguenots fled from France to escape the persecution; most going to neighbouring countries but an estimated 50,000 went to Britain and 10,000 to Ireland. The Marquis de Ruvigny (Henri de Massue) who fought against James on the side of King William was granted lands for his support of the king and settled about 500 Huguenots in the Portarlington area around 1700 (Hylton, 1999). The new settlers established French schools and the French Church (1696), though the present building is a later one on the site of the earlier one and dates to the mid-19th century. The register was written in French until about 1816, and the names of the clergy from the late 17th century (Jacques Gillet and Benjamin de Dallion) to the mid-19th century (Jean and Charles Vignoles) all indicate the important French connection. A visit to the graveyard is well worthwhile. (The key can be obtained from Fletcher's newsagents at the top of Main Street). Many French names are shown on the gravestones (Blanc, Champagne, Despard, Lacombre) and just behind the church is a horizontal grave slab dedicated to Antoine Fleury dated 1801 with the inscription written in French, Plate D2.

Plate D2:
Graveslab inscription in French at St. Paul's 'French Church', Portarlington.

Plate D3:
Early 18th century bell in St. Paul's
'French Church', Portarlington.

Plate D4:
Lea Castle, Portarlington.

There are two main points of interest within the church. The bell that hung in the original French Church and which was donated in 1715 by Wilhelmena, wife of George, Prince of Wales, daughter-in-law of King George of Britain is located beside the pulpit, Plate D3. The cross on the altar, which was donated by the Odlum family, has set within it the Huguenot Cross. This consists of what is often referred to as a Maltese cross surmounting a descending dove. The Huguenot Cross is full of symbolism. The 4 arms of the cross represent the 4 gospels and the 8 circles at the end of the arms represent the 8 beatitudes. The dove is the 'sainted spirit', which guides the Church.

There were English 'planters' settling in Portarlington as well as French Huguenots and their religious needs were catered for by St. Michael's, the 'English Church'. This was located at the northeast corner of the Square where a later church was built. Today it is used as a parochial hall. The square structure on the front of the building at roof level was once the base of a narrow spire, which was removed in the 1920s.

From Portarlington take the R420 road (east) towards Monasterevin for 3 kilometres. Just after passing a road on your right signposted for Killenard, a small lane on the left leads to Lea Castle one of only two Anglo-Norman stone castles in County Laois. Lea castle is built adjacent to and on the south bank of the River Barrow, Plate D4. Originally, it was quite a large structure, although even today, its ruins are impressive, consisting of a keep, corner tower, inner and outer ward and gatehouse. The castle dates from the 13th century and shows different phases of building. O'Conor (1999) discusses the castle in some detail and believes that the earliest phase was built around 1220 and that it was a Geraldine castle (Fitzgerald family), but the keep was possibly built by Sir William Marshall. Various forces periodically attacked Lea Castle in the centuries following its completion before it was finally destroyed around 1650 on the orders of Oliver Cromwell.

Return to the Market Square in Portarlington and take the R419 road north (Spa Street) for Clonbulloge. Once across the bridge over the River Barrow, the terrain either side of the road is very flat, except for occasional mounds of glacial sediment, one of which on the left side of the road is being worked. The glacial sediments often show evidence of slumping and are extremely fine-grained suggesting deposition by slow moving streams, Plate D5. Drive on to Bracknagh (7 kilometres distance) and take the road to the left, signposted for Clonbulloge (R442). Clonbulloge gets its name from the Gaelic 'Cluain Bolg'. Cluain means field or meadow in Gaelic and Bolg is the name of the Celtic Sun God, suggesting that at this locality there was worship to this god. As you drive into Clonbulloge, take the road to the left signposted for the Irish Parachute Club (there is a milestone at the top of the road). Drive down this road for 450m and in the field to the left you will see a large limestone rock. At first glance this appears to be just a stone lying in the field, however, on closer examination, it will be seen to have an unusual shape,

Plate D5:
Slumped and deformed glacial sediments near Portarlington.

Plate D6. This is known as a 'mushroom stone' or less commonly a 'wave stone'. Other similar stones can be found in Counties Offaly, Roscommon and Clare. (See Dunne and Feehan, 2002, for a full list of such stones). As mentioned in Section I of this book, at the end of the last glacial period, the midland lakes covered a larger area than today. Limestone rocks around the edge of the lakes would have been partially submerged and the parts of the rocks beneath the water would have been subjected to solution while the subaerial parts were not. Consequently, the lower part of such rocks are narrower and have similarities with the stalk of a mushroom, while the rock above the water appears like the head. The level that the water reached in the past is delineated by the flat surface, forming the base of the head. Studies of such stones allow us to understand better our palaeoenvironment by demarcating the edges of the lakes in the past. In addition, early humans inhabited the edges of these lakes and if we wish to find their habitation sites we need to know where the edges of the lakes were in the past, not where they are today. For the mushroom stone at Clonbulloge, the lake it was associated with has now totally vanished, but note the very flat nature of the surrounding terrain in which the mushroom stone lies.

Return to the main road and drive on through Clonbulloge on the R401 for 3.5 kilometres until you come to the 120MW power station and Bord na Móna works on your

Plate D6:
'Mushroom stone' near
Clonbulloge, County Offaly.

Plate D7:
One of the deep defensive ditches surrounding
Ballykilleen ringfort, County Offaly.

right. Milled peat is transported by small trains to the Bord na Móna factory, then carried by conveyor belt into the power station. Take the road to the left opposite the Bord na Móna factory and drive 1.5 kilometres to the brow of the hill. The wooded site to your left is the multivallate Ballykilleen ringfort. Access to the site is difficult. This large site is much more complex than is usual for ringforts comprising as it does three defensive concentric ramparts and intervening ditches, Plate D7. The location of the site has been chosen in order to provide commanding views of the surrounding terrain. Return to the main R401 road, turn left and continue towards Edenderry. After another 3 kilometres, if one turns right onto the road signposted for Drumcooly cemetery and drive to the top of the hill, another, much later, defensive structure can be observed which was sited at this location also because of its strategic position. An Anglo-Norman motte (*c.* 1200) is located at the crest of the hill (beside which a water tower has been constructed), Plate D8. Return to the main road, turn right and continue on to the T-junction, turn right and drive into Edenderry along the R402. Edenderry gets its name from the Gaelic 'Éadan Doire' meaning 'brow of the oakwood'. Almost immediately, you will pass over the Grand Canal, and on your left is the Catholic Church. You will shortly pass the Edenderry National School (built *c.* 1835) on your left, then take the next road on your left, signposted for Rhode.

Plate D8:
Anglo-Norman motte near
Edenderry, County Offaly.

Drive along this road for about 2 kilometres (R441), then on your right, you will come to Monasteroris Church (opposite a road to your left). Enter Monasteroris by the small metal gate that leads into the graveyard. Monasteroris was founded, as a Franciscan monastery in 1325, by the de Bermingham Anglo-Norman family. It is also referred to as Castro Petre (Peter's House) after Piers de Bermingham and Monasteroris is itself a Gaelised version of the 'Bermingham monastery'. The ruins of the parish church in the graveyard (St. John the Baptist) date mainly to the 16th century, although a portion is early 14th century (FitzPatrick and O'Brien, 1998). There is a large prominent Celtic Cross at the eastern side of the cemetery. This was erected in 1874 to commemorate Father Moses Kearns and Colonel Anthony Perry who were hanged in 1798 in Edenderry because of the prominent role that they played in the United Irishmen rebellion in that year. Other headstones in the vicinity mark the graves of Brigadier Thomas O'Connell who fought in the Irish Republican Army against the British in the early 1920s and Private J. Carroll, Royal Dublin Fusiliers, a British soldier who was killed in 1916 in the First World War. Some of the other graves date from the late 1600s to the mid-1700s.

Plate D9:
Remains of Monasteroris
Monastery, Edenderry.

The ruins of the Monasteroris monastery can be seen grouped on two small hillocks in the field adjacent to the cemetery, Plate D9. The building on the mound to the west (left as you look at it from the cemetery) is believed to be a dovecote, whereas those to the east include a gatehouse and farm buildings. Behind this mound and not visible from the cemetery are the footings of a regular grange precinct wall. A mid-17th century map of Monasteroris shows a water-wheel located on a mill-race. The line of this millrace is located to the west of the farm adjacent to the cemetery and it is seen to continue under the modern road.

Return to the T-junction with the main street in Edenderry, turn left and proceed into the centre of the town. On your right behind the long grassy bank and low limestone wall is the canal harbour opened *c.* 1802 which links the town with the main Grand Canal, which is approximately 1 kilometre to the south.

Farther along on the right a walkway leads to the Castropetre Church of Ireland Church, built in 1778 as a replacement for Monasteroris. The gateway (*c.* 1840) to the church is flanked by the heads of two stags which form part of the coat of arms of the Downshire family. Three family names dominated the Edenderry area from the 16th to the 19th century, the Colleys, the Blundells and the Downshires. In the mid-16th century Henry Colley was granted the lands around Edenderry (which was also known as Colleystown or Coolestown in his honour). One of his female descendants, Sarah, married into the Blundell family. Behind the present day Castropetre Church, located on a very prominent commanding high position (adjacent to a present day water tower), is Blundell's Castle, which was attacked and destroyed at the end of the 17th century. Moyses Hill came to northern Ireland in the 16th century and acquired lands, first around Carrickfergus and later in County Down (Hillsborough and Hilltown are named after the family). From the 18th century, the senior member of the Hill family carried the title of Marquis of Downshire and in 1786; Arthur Hill married a Mary Sandys who inherited a large part of the Blundell estate because her grandmother was the sister of Lord Blundell.

The most prominent building in Edenderry is the former Market House, built *c.* 1826 by the Downshires. It has had a chequered history, being used at different times as a courthouse and a ballroom. It was burned down in 1945 but has since been refurbished and is currently used by Offaly County Council. Drive past the Market House and on your left you will see Blundell House, built in 1813 by James Brownrigg, who helped to manage the Downshire estates.

Continue on the R402 west for 6 kilometres until you come to Carbury, Figure D1. Carbury (Carbrie), Carbury Hill or Castlecarbury features extensively in Irish literature. The name Carbury is derived from the O'Ciardha clan and in legend is Sidh-Nechtain, the fairy hill of Nechtan (Harbinson, 2003). The hill was clearly important in prehistoric times,

Plate D10:
Fortified house, mortuary chapel, and
graveyard on Carbury Hill, County Kildare.

because it was used for burials. Excavations of a number of ring-barrows near its summit in 1936 revealed 4 cremations and 15 burials with the former being possibly older. Grave goods included flint scrapers iron rings and pottery. The graves are believed to be later Bronze Age to early Iron Age in date (Willmot, 1938). The hill is formed of a ridge of more resistant limestone and consequently overlooks much of the surrounding territory. Good exposures of the limestone can be seen in a disused quarry. Croghan Hill, 22 kilometres to the west, is easily visible, as are the Wicklow Mountains 40 kilometres to the southeast. The source of the River Boyne, a river associated with significant archaeological sites and an important battle in 1690, lies just to the east of Carbury Hill.

The strategic importance of Carbury Hill was obvious to the Normans who established a motte near the summit and the area was initially ceded to Meiler FitzHenry, although later was in the hands of the de Bermingham family. The castles and houses that have been located here have been attacked at various times. For example, the castle was destroyed in 1475 by Red Hugh O'Neill, and a number of raids were carried out during the 1798 United Irishmen rebellion.

Walk up the hill past the present day Church of Ireland church. The hill, in front of you, is crowned with the ruins of a large house, containing a number of octagonal chimneys, Plate D10. Although part of this fortified house is 13th century in age, much of it dates to the late 1500s when Henry Colley was granted Carbury Manor. Carbury remained in the Colley family for successive generations and the mortuary chapel within the graveyard contains a wall-mounted stone tablet dedicated to a member of the Colley family and dated 1705. Mary Colley married Arthur Pomeroy in the mid-18th century and they lived in Newbury Hall which was built a short distance from Carbury Hill. (If you look back towards the road, the reddish building a short distance from the village is Newbury Hall). The roof is believed to have been removed from Carbury Castle in the late 1700s and the house has remained empty since then.

Return to Edenderry past the Market House and take the R401 road on your right for Kinnegad. This is opposite the present day Bank of Ireland which was the site of the original Hibernian Bank built in 1870. Note the entwined letters 'H' and 'B' at the top of the columns. Approximately 4 kilometres along this road, you come to Carrick Castle on your right. This was the site of a de Birmingham castle where in 1305 O'Conor Faly and about 20 of his clan were massacred after attending dinner. Continue for 3.5 kilometres until you come to Ballyboggan Bridge, which crosses the River Boyne and delineates the county boundary between Kildare and Meath. The river has been artificially straightened here, as a pronounced meander existed in the early 19th century. The Boyne is overlooked by the imposing ruins of Ballyboggan Priory (Plate D11). Aerial photographs show that the priory is surrounded by over 10 hectares of field markings, which show the positions of messuages (houses and plots), gardens and field boundaries. The Augustinian priory is believed to have been founded in the 13th century and was surrendered in 1537 to the English crown by the then Prior, Thomas (de) Bermingham. The priory contained a relic, supposedly part of the True Cross, and was an important site of pilgrimage for the veneration of the Cross. The relic was destroyed soon after the priory was surrendered. A 1m high sculpture, called a triptych, possibly of 15th century origin, was discovered hidden in Ballinabrackey Church, 6 kilometres to the west of Ballyboggan when that church was being demolished. It is possible that the triptych, which depicts the Virgin Mary and Jesus, was removed from Ballyboggan to prevent its destruction and lay hidden for nearly 400 years. An examination of the windows in the priory clearly shows different styles, representing various stages of rebuilding. Two aspects of the building are of some interest. One is the small carving of 2 heads on the southeastern corner of the priory, one looking south and one east (see inset Plate D11). As the wind comes mainly from the southwest, the south facing, more exposed head, is more eroded than the more sheltered east facing one. Secondly, the walls of the priory are characterised by a large number of small rectangular holes. These would have been used to secure the scaffolding employed during the construction phase of the building. Usually these are later 'made up', but here they have been left.

Plate D11:
Views of Ballyboggan Priory on banks
of the River Boyne, County Meath.
Inset shows detail.

Continue driving towards Kinnegad for another 500m and take the road on your right that leads to Clonard (5 kilometres). You will pass over the M4 motorway shortly before the junction with the R148 (formerly the N4 road). Turn right and park after 100m in front of the Monastery Inn, facing St. Finnian's (Finian) Catholic Church. Although today Clonard is a small village, it was one of the most important and influential ecclesiastical centres in Ireland for a period of about 700 years. Like many ecclesiastical centres, the Vikings plundered it at various times, mainly in the 9th century. Various structures and buildings have been associated with Clonard over many centuries: the Augustinian Abbey of St. Peter and St. Paul; ringfort, Round Tower, the high cemetery and the Abbey of St. Mary overseen by the Abbess Agnes, the first such location for canonesses in Ireland. Place-names such as the townland of Kilnagalliagh (Kill na gCailleach, the Church of the Nuns), Mulpheder – the Hill of Peter and Church Hill, are all associated with the early Church. Artefacts found in the locality include an 11th century crozier and a 9th century small house shaped shrine.

St. Finnian founded a monastic settlement at Clonard in the mid-6th century and he is often referred to as the 'Master of the Saints of Ireland' because of the large number of important saints who began their studies here. These are said to include St. Ciaran of Clonmacnoise, St. Brendan of Clonfert (see Itinerary B), St. Canice of Aghaboe (Itinerary F) and St. Colum of Terryglass (Itinerary H). The bishopric of Clonard maintained its ecclesiastical importance into the 12th century when it became the diocesan town of east Meath (Hickey, 1998). However, thereafter its importance waned and after the dissolution of the monasteries was given over to Sir William Bermingham by Henry VIII c. 1542. A "Clonard Heritage Trail" booklet can be obtained within the Monastery Inn and more information about the ecclesiastical history can be obtained there.

Cross the road and enter the Catholic Church. There is a superbly carved baptismal font located behind the main altar, dating to c. 1500, Plate D12. This was originally housed in the nearby Church of Ireland Church, but was presented to the Catholic congregation when the former church closed. The carved panels, on the font, include a number of figures such as angels, St. Peter, a bishop and scenes from the bible including the Flight from Egypt, Plate D13. Drive east through Clonard for 200m and take the road to your left. Immediately in front of you is an Anglo-Norman motte constructed c. 1180, Plate D14. The path across the road from the motte leads down to the disused Church of Ireland Church. This was built c. 1808 on the site of an earlier church and above the doorway is a carved head which possibly comes from this earlier church. The first edition 6 inch to 1 mile Ordnance Survey map of the Clonard area, published in 1836 records that the 'site of abbey' was at this location.

A geophysical investigation in 2004 uncovered many features in the surrounding fields, which may be related to the monastic settlement (Gibson and George, 2006). These

Plate D12:
Baptismal font, c. 1500 in date, in St. Finnian's Church, Clonard, County Meath.

include a 60m long sub-square enclosure adjacent to a 300m long palaeo-river channel. Three large areas, associated with anomalous magnetic readings were discovered, which indicated sites of enhanced anthropogenic activity. In addition, there are four distinct zones with large concentrations of high resistance values, suggesting that former buildings were located in these areas. Resistivity and ground penetrating radar show that one of these zones has characteristics which indicate the presence of an east-west aligned building approximately 7m wide in a north-south direction and about 15m long in an east-west direction. The alignment of this building suggests it may be a small chapel. Excavations carried out in the 1970s also found a number of shallow burials nearby (Sweetman, 1978). Return to the main R148 road, turn left and drive the 1 kilometre to the Leinster Bridge which crosses the River Boyne. (Approximately 500m along this road, set back in the fields, to your left, is a prehistoric tumulus). The building just past the bridge on the right is the former tollhouse and behind it are the remains of a fortified house, which was under the control of Thomas Tyrrell. It was attacked in 1798 and some of the graves of those attackers who were killed are buried in the nearby cemetery. Return back through Clonard to Kinnegad. Kinnegad, from the Gaelic 'Ceann Atha Gad' meaning 'Head of the Ford of Willow Twigs', has had a long reputation as a resting place for coaches traveling between Galway and Dublin. Take the bypass around Kinnegad, *initially* following the signposts for Galway. After passing over the N4 dual carriageway, go straight ahead at the roundabout, remaining on the *old* road to Galway and after 1.5 kilometres take the small road to your right. This is Clonfad, a former monastic site. Written on a relatively modern Celtic Cross at the side of the road is the inscription 'This cross marks the site of the Bishop's grave, a place of pilgrimage from early times. St. Etchen, buried in the cemetery founded the monastery of Clonfad. He ordained St. Columbkille to the priesthood. He died 11th Feb. 577. The monastery was destroyed by the Danes in the 10th century'. Nearby are the remains of a small church and graveyard within which is a 'rag tree'. Return to the main road and continue west through the Pass of Kilbride (a route through the bogs) to Rochfortbridge. Continuing on this road takes you to Tyrrellspass (Itinerary A). Alternatively turn left as you enter Rochfortbridge and drive to Rhode. This route takes you through the peatlands past the former peat-fired power station in Rhode on the R400. The high ground to your right is Croghan Hill, the extinct volcano discussed in Itinerary A. To return to Portarlington, go through Rhode and continue on the R400 south, Figure D1.

Plate D14:
Anglo-Norman motte at Clonard.

Itinerary E: North Central Irish Midlands

Approximate Distance: 120 kilometres
Ordnance Survey 1:50,000 Discovery Series Maps: 48, 47, 40 and 41.

This itinerary starts in Moate, County Westmeath, approximately 17 kilometres east of Athlone, Figure E1. Stop in the Main Street in Moate in front of, and on the same side of the road as, St. Mary's Church of Ireland Church. This was built *c.* 1782, about the same

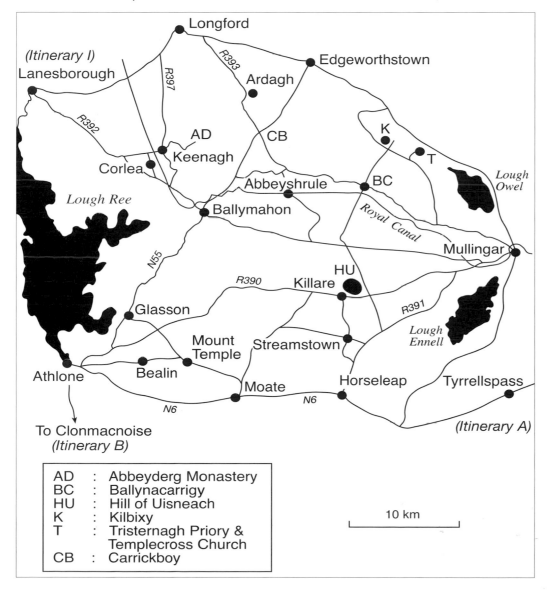

Figure E1:
Location map for Itinerary E.

time as some of the houses in the street were constructed. As you walk back towards the centre of town, you come to the Tuar Ard theatre and gallery. Go to the car-park at the back of the building and look out over the surrounding fields, the skyline is dominated by a glacial esker, part of which is currently being worked for sand and gravel deposits. Incidentally, the two wooden statues sculpted by Jackie McKenna show two people sealing a deal. Continue walking down the street until you come to St. Patrick's Catholic Church. It was built *c.* 1868 and there are two particularly interesting aspects to its construction. Firstly, it is relatively uncommon to find a Catholic Church is such a prominent central position in the main street of Irish towns. However, the location of St. Patrick's in Moate was formerly the Fair Green and consequently the site had not been built on. The site was donated by Lord Castlemaine (Westmeath Genealogy Project, no date). Secondly, the church is constructed of two different indigenous rock types. Grey limestone is employed for details around the doors and windows (and the large cross in the grounds) whereas blocks of Old Red Sandstone rock are used for the main construction.

Continue walking along the Main Street until you reach the courthouse built in 1831. This limestone building is now a local museum. The left-hand side of the archway contains some good examples of fossil crinoid fragments about 1m from the ground. Walk on until you are directly opposite the Grand Hotel entrance and go right down the lane. Immediately behind the houses that front onto Main Street on your right is an Anglo-Norman motte constructed around the end of the 12th century. This motte was built on top of an esker further enhancing its defensive capabilities. If you walk slightly farther down the lane, some of the glacial sediments can be seen. Return to the Main Street, turn right and continue walking for about 100m until you are near the old post office. Across the street, a large house (referred to as Moate Castle) can be seen behind an old wall. This was a 16th century tower house formerly occupied by the O'Melaghlin Gaelic family. The residence was granted to Peter Humphries in the 17th century and was extensively modified in the following centuries. The doorway into the courtyard on the northern edge of the house is surmounted by a medieval Sheela-na-Gig, a grotesque figure.

Cross the road to the same side as the former tower house, walk on in the same direction, past a former tannery (Dr Cuppaige's) and turn left at the first street on your left (signposted for Rosemount and Ballymore). Walk a few hundred metres to the Carmelite Church, built in 1870. Note, at the top of the small road on your right (Ave Maria Park) before you reach the church are the remains of the old jail, used in the 1700s. The Quakers, who made an important contribution to the wealth of the town from the mid-17th century, built some of the fine houses in the vicinity. If you walk just past the road junction on your left (Ballymore Road) and look out over the fields to your left, you can see the back of the former tower house. Behind this house is an old walled disused Quaker graveyard. The land was provided by John Clibborn who became a Quaker in the 1660s although he was originally very antagonistic toward them and once went to burn down their hall (Cox, 1981). Return to your car and drive to the Athlone (west) end of Main Street in Moate (to a place called 'The Gap', hence the name of the public house) and take the road to your right signposted for Mount Temple. In the past, the local indigenous Irish had to pay a toll in order to pass through the gap and sell their produce in Moate.

The land rises as you drive out of Moate and off to your left near the Dún Na Sí Heritage Park is Knockdomny, at an elevation 157m and where Old Red Sandstone rocks are at the surface. As you drive towards Mount Temple, the linear ridge of an esker, sometimes tree-lined, can be seen to your right, especially where the road takes a sharp left-hand bend. As you drive into Mount Temple, you will see Egan's public house at a corner on your right, which houses the Motte and Bailey Restaurant. (If you drive down this road for 200m the motte can be seen on your right, again, like Moate, situated on top of a mound of glacial sediments). Continue through Mount Temple (the golf course on your right was the former site of a castle and a police station *c*. 1800) and take the second road to your left past the Catholic Church, signposted for Athlone. Drive down this road for 4 kilometres to Bealin (Baylin). Note how the road descends as you come off the esker. In Bealin, drive past the school on your right and round the next corner take the small lane to your right. Drive up this lane for a few hundred metres and on your left, at the crest of a mound of glacial sediment is the Bealin Cross, Plate E1. The Bealin Cross has carved interlocking geometric patterns and hunting scenes, such as a man with a spea, and a dog biting the leg of deer. It was erected by Tuaghgal, abbot of Clonmacnoise who died in 811 AD and the cross is dated to around 800 AD. Return to the main road and drive west through Bealin into Athlone (see Figure E1). Cross over the dual carriageway bypass and park in Athlone near the castle on the west bank of the river (Plate E2).

Athlone is in the unique position in having evolved on both banks of the River Shannon and is thus in two provinces, Leinster in the east and Connacht in the west. For administrative purposes it is considered to be in County Westmeath in the Province of Leinster. The name Athlone is believed to derive from the Gaelic 'Ath Luain', the 'ford of Luan', although there are alternative stories as to who Luan was. The town was of strategic importance, controlling as it did a ford across the Shannon and as such it has an important military aspect to its evolution. Names such as Battery Heights, Bastion Street or Magazine Road preserve this military link.

A castle, built by the Ua Conchobair (O'Conor's) of Connacht, controlled the ford across the river in the mid-12th century. However, it was the arrival of the Anglo-Normans which led to a stone castle being constructed *c*. 1210 by John de Grey (Murtagh, 1994). Sweetman (2005) believes that the present curtain wall dates from this time. Over the

Plate E1:
9th century Bealin Cross at Bealin, County Westmeath.

following centuries, the castle, town and bridge were attacked often coming under the control of Gaelic chieftains. A new stone bridge was constructed over the Shannon *c.* 1567, and the castle's and town's fortifications were strengthened. However, during the 17th century, significant military action took place in Athlone. It was captured by Cromwellian forces in 1651 during the Confederate War and was besieged in 1690 and 1691 by Williamite troops. After the Battle of the Boyne in County Meath in 1690, Jacobite forces, loyal to King James II, retreated west and occupied Athlone. The attack in 1690, led by Lieutenant-General James Douglas, failed to take the town from the Jacobite forces under the command of Colonel Richard Grace. However, in 1691, Baron de Ginkel moved his army of 20,000 troops from Mullingar and besieged Athlone which fell after intense fighting (Murtagh, 1973). The castle fell into disrepair over the following 60 years but the fortifications were again improved *c.* 1800 in response to a possible attack during the Napoleonic War.

Plate E2:
Athlone Castle, County Westmeath.

Many of the buildings in the streets around the castle date from the 19th century, one (7 O'Connell Street) was built in 1836 for the National Bank and was later used as the residence of the Catholic Bishop (O'Brien, 1985), Plate E3. Located adjacent to the castle is the large Catholic Church of Saints Peter and Paul, built around 1937. Walk along the side of the river, down Grace Street towards the metal bridge spanning the Shannon. This railway bridge was built *c.* 1850 and is 180m wide. Around the corner is the impressive old railway station built at the same time, although the present railway station is now located on the far side of the river. The left-hand side of Grace Street is dominated by a military installation known as Custome Barracks, named after a Jacobite who fought in the 1691 siege. Old maps show that military barracks have been located in this part of Athlone for hundreds of years.

Return to the stone bridge and cross over the Shannon. This bridge was constructed in the mid-19th century and was opened in 1884. It originally had a section that could be opened to allow the movement of river traffic upstream but this has been removed. Turn left into Northgate Street and walk along it until you reach the Radisson SAS Hotel. This was the site of the North Gate, which allowed access through the defensive wall into the town. If you go up the small alley (Lucas Court) facing the hotel for a few hundred metres, you will come to the remains of part of the old wall built in the mid-17th century and which was breached in the 1691 siege (north bastion). Return to the end of the bridge passing on your way the Masonic Lodge built in 1810 and a Methodist Church built in 1864. Turn left into Church Street and walk as far as St. Mary's Church of Ireland Church. The present church dates from the early 19th century though it replaced earlier ones on the same site. The tower of one of these earlier churches, built *c.* 1622, is located beside the church. Continuing on past the church for 100m, the road diverges, then converges, with Dublingate Street going straight on and the Bawn, which is much narrower, going to the left. This was the site of another gate into the town. Return to your car and drive out of Athlone using the same route that you entered on but instead of turning right for Bealin continue on the N55 to Glasson (6 kilometres).

Glasson is the start of what is known as 'Goldsmith Country', which encompasses parts of Counties Westmeath and Longford. Oliver Goldsmith (1728-1774) born in Pallas wrote many poems and plays, including 'She stoops to conquer' and 'The deserted village'. Glasson was an estate village for the Waterston family. The 1844 schoolhouse, at the south of the town, is today used as a Heritage Centre. Drive northwards out of Glasson on the N55 to Ballymahon, a distance of 12 kilometres. On the way, you should note the remains of a limestone windmill tower on your left, behind a modern bungalow. Cross the River Inny and turn left (signposted the R392 for Lanesborough) and drive along the main street of Ballymahon. The main street is characterised by late Georgian houses and a limestone built courthouse/market house (now the public library) near which is a bronze statue of Oliver Goldsmith. The courthouse was on the first floor below which the market was conducted. It was built *c.* 1820 and the architect was Samuel Mullen who designed the Church of Ireland Church, also on the main street. The coat of arms on the courthouse belongs to the Shuldham family, who commissioned the building. Continue through Ballymahon, on the Lanesborough road for about 8 kilometres (passing over the Royal Canal twice), then take the road on your right signposted for Keenagh and Corlea Trackway. This road leads to the village of Keenagh and the surrounding area is peatland. After about 1 kilometre, take the road on your right, signposted for Corlea Trackway and

Plate E3:
7 O'Connell Street, Athlone,
former residence of bishop.

Detail of preserved oak planks from Iron Age trackway, Corlea, County Longford.

Plate E5:
19th century clock tower dedicated to Laurence King-Harman, Keenagh, County Longford.

drive to the Visitor Centre. A wooden trackway was discovered during the removal of peat and investigated by the Department of Archaeology of University College Dublin. The trackway was constructed during the Iron Age and is dated *c.* 148 BC (i.e. it is about 2150 years old). It was over 1 kilometre long, and about 80m of it have been conserved and preserved in situ in its original position within the Centre. It is about 4m wide, and the upper part is surfaced with split oak planks, Plate E4. Many of the planks were fastened using wooden pegs. The trackway, which must have been a prestigious feature of the landscape, appears to head towards Lanesborough, the nearest place to cross the River Shannon.

After visiting the Iron Age trackway, leave the Visitor's Centre and drive into Keenagh, again crossing the Royal Canal which reached Keenagh *c.* 1817. At the T-junction in Keenagh turn left, drive 100m and stop near the clock tower, Plate E5. The clock tower is 20m high and was built in 1878 to commemorate the local landlord Laurence King-Harman, who died in 1875. Take the road directly facing the clock tower and drive for a few kilometres to Abbeyderg cemetery. St. Peter's Augustinian monastery was founded here in the 13th century but was attacked and destroyed in 1567. A number of bishops from Ardagh are believed to have been buried here. Return to the Main Street, Keenagh, turn right and drive to Longford on the R397.

As you drive into Longford, proceed through the Main Street, over the bridge spanning the Camlin River and after a few hundred metres park on Battery Road near St. John's Church of Ireland Church. Various hypotheses have been put forward to explain how Longford got its name. The townland name, Aughafad, was possibly derived from 'Atha Fada' which is Longford in English. Longford was also known as Longphort Ui Fhearghail (stronghold of the O'Farrell's). This is the oldest part of the town; the church was built *c.* 1760 (with later modifications) and is on the site of a 15th century Dominican Abbey. Walk towards the front door of the church and look at the headstone to the right at the edge of the path near the door, Plate E6. It is dedicated to Private Joseph Ward V.C. who received the Victoria Cross, the highest gallantry medal awarded in the British Army, for action at Gwalior, India in 1858, when, as a member of the King's Royal Irish, he captured enemy cannon while under intense fire. Of the 168 Irish-born recipients of the Victoria Cross, only five are buried within the Irish Midlands; one each in Counties Offaly and Longford and three in County Westmeath. Thomas Flinn, from Athlone who died in the workhouse at Athlone in 1892 has the distinction of being the joint youngest person to ever have received the Victoria Cross. He was aged 15 years and 3 months when as a drummer boy, although wounded, he continued to fight on during an attack in 1857 in Cawnpore, India. Today the barracks (Connolly) opposite the church are occupied by the Irish army, although it has been a military site for may hundreds of years. Little now remains of the original installations except for part of the stables for the cavalry.

Walk back into town and after crossing the bridge note the fine pedimented building on your right before the road junction, presently occupied by Patrick J. Groarke & Sons. This was built *c.* 1840 and at one stage became a Gentleman's Club. Judges of the Assizes who visited, had on occasions, arrived at the club in full regalia, in open coaches escorted by a troop of cavalry.

Directly across the road from the Longford Arms Hotel is the four-bayed limestone Ulster Bank built *c.* 1865 by James Bell. Note the fossil shells above the doorway. Four carved sandstone 'riverine' heads contrast well with the grey limestone. Beside the Longford Arms Hotel is the three-storey courthouse built *c.* 1793 though added to in the 19th century. Return to your car and drive back through the Main Street and take the one-way system into Dublin Street. At the end of this street is the most impressive building in Longford Town, St. Mel's Catholic Cathedral. The cathedral was built in the mid-19th century renaissance style and is especially imposing because of its colonnaded façade and tall tower. The cathedral houses a little known diocesan museum, which contains, among their important ecclesiastical items, a book shrine dedicated to St. Caillin of Fenagh, Plate E7. An inscription on the shrine has been translated thus: 'A prayer for the man who

Plate E6:
Gravestone of Private Joseph Ward, V.C., note carving of Victoria Cross, St. John's Church, Longford Town.

Plate E7:
16th century Caillin book shrine housed in diocesan museum, St. Mel's cathedral, Longford.

enshrined this relic of Caillin, namely Brian, son of Eoghan O'Rourke and of Margaret the daughter of O'Brien. And the age of the Lord at that time was dated 1536. Ave Maria'. After visiting the cathedral, drive along the *old* Dublin Road (this is the road directly in line with Dublin Street, not the Ballinalee Road signposted for Dublin). After about one kilometre, take the R393 road, on your right, signposted for Ardagh. After 10 kilometres take the short road to Ardagh (it is bypassed by the R393), drive up into the centre and park near the clock tower. Ardagh has had a long ecclesiastical history and St. Patrick founded a monastery here in the mid-5th century. (You may have noticed in Longford Town that St. John's Church of Ireland was in the diocese of Ardagh). St. Mel was the first bishop of the diocese and he was a contemporary (some say relative) of St. Patrick. St. Patrick's Church of Ireland built *c.* 1810 is one of the dominant buildings in the centre of Ardagh. The entrance to the church exhibits a typical English feature, one that is relatively uncommon in Ireland. The entrance is through a small roofed gate called a lych (or lich) gate, Plate E8. In Old English 'lic' means corpse and it was here, before a burial that the clergy first prayed over the dead person. Just behind the church are the remains of St. Mel's Cathedral. This stone building dates from about the 8th century; note the projecting antae at the ends, typical of old Irish churches. The building, formed mainly of irregular blocks of sandstone, was repeatedly attacked over the centuries, in 1167, 1230 and finally in 1496 when a conflict arose between opposing families of the O'Farrell clan. One treasure escaped this destruction and was found buried adjacent to the cathedral in relatively recent times. This is a mid-10th century bishop's crozier (St. Mel's crozier) and

Plate E8:
Early 19th century St. Patrick's Church of Ireland Church with lych-gate, Ardagh, County Longford. Remains of 8th century cathedral behind church.

is presently housed in the diocesan museum in St. Mel's Cathedral Longford, Plate E9. It is formed of three pieces of yew wood connected by decorated knops. It is decorated in bronze and the designs include interlaced foliage and animal motifs (MacDermott, 1957). There is a later small metal figurine of a bishop holding a crozier set into the handle. Continue walking past the old cathedral and on the opposite side of the road you come to St. Brigid's Catholic Church built *c.* 1881 in a neo-Gothic style. St. Brigid, who is usually

Plate E9:
10th century crozier housed in diocesan museum, St. Mel's Cathedral, Longford. Found in Ardagh.

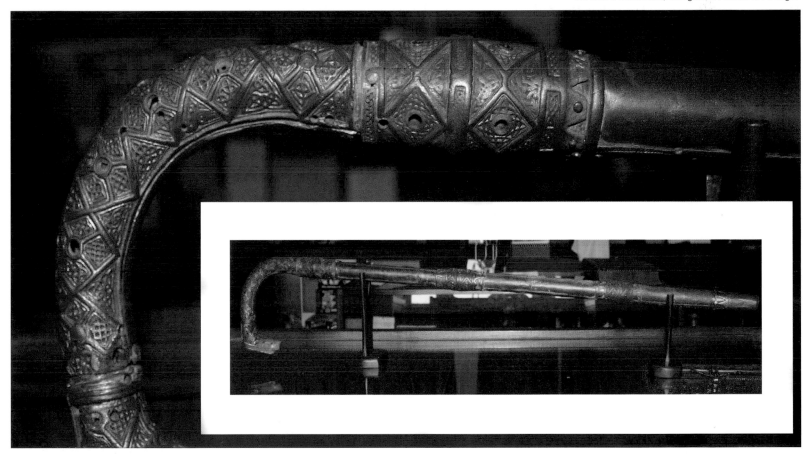

associated with County Kildare, is known to have spent some time in Ardagh. Further on, is an entrance to an estate and its gate lodge and a Heritage Centre. Return now to the centre of the village. A prominent architectural feature, adjacent to the village green, is the clock tower, Plate E10. The Fetherston family have been associated with Ardagh from 1703 until the mid-1920s. They built Ardagh House in the 1700s near the centre of the village, although it has been modified over the following centuries. It was to this house that Oliver Goldsmith was once directed under the mistaken impression that it was a lodging house rather than the home of an important family. Consequently he treated the family as servants, and this episode is said to have formed the basis of one of his most well known plays 'She stoops to conquer' in which an aristocratic lady who has been mistaken as a servant plays out this role in order to determine the character of a person in whom she is interested. The clock tower and the surrounding buildings were built *c.* 1863 in memory of Sir George Ralph Fetherston who died in 1853. Some of the adjacent buildings had an administrative function and were used as a courthouse, barracks and post office. Walk back down the road on which you drove into Ardagh. The remains of a medieval church and graveyard are located on your right and across the road and set back some distance is the old rectory (Glebe House).

Plate E10:
Clock tower in centre of Ardagh dedicated to Sir George Ralph Fetherston.

From Ardagh, take the road for Carrickboy (i.e. drive past the clock tower on your right down the hill) and at the junction with the main R393 road, turn left. As you entered Ardagh you drove uphill on one road and to leave it, you drive downhill on another. This elevated position is most likely why Ardagh is so named. In Gaelic, 'Ard Archadh' means 'high field'.

As you drive out of Ardagh, note the tree-covered high ground off to your right. This upland area is a region where the hard Old Red Sandstone is again exposed, thus the area erodes much slower than the surrounding limestone and consequently forms a hill. Drive on for about 3 kilometres and at Carrickboy Crossroad, go straight across the N55 road. The Gaelic for Carrickboy is 'Charraig Bhui', which translated means 'yellow rock' and refers to the nearby sandstone. Continue on this road (R393) towards Ballynacarrigy (also spelt Ballynacargy), but partway along it divert to Abbeyshrule, where it is signposted. You cross a hump-back bridge over the Royal Canal before you enter the town. Walk back along the towpath in order to see a good example of an aqueduct, where the canal is carried above the River Inny, flowing in a small valley below it. The village, as suggested by its name, contains an abbey (Cistercian), a substantial part of which remains. It was founded around 1150 by the O'Farrells and destroyed in 1476. Return to the R393 road and when you drive into Ballynacarrigy, take the road to the left at the first crossroads for 2.5 kilometres, until the road splits into three branches. The unroofed Kilbixy Church of Ireland Church can be seen near the junction, and nearby an older building and the impressive Sunderlin family mausoleum, built in 1798, Plate E11. The older building was a leper house and is also known as St. Bridget's (Brigid's) Hospital. Kilbixy was once a thriving settlement of streets and buildings. Follow the signs for Templecross Church (road to the right as you approach from Ballynacarrigy, see also Figure E1). Templecross Church is in a cul-de-sac and was turned into a Protestant Church in the 1600s. The plaque within the church above a tomb bearing a Latin inscription, dated 1620 is dedicated to Sir Henry Piers. It is possible to climb the stone spiral stairway and about 300m away the remains of the Augustinian Tristernagh Priory founded c. 1200 by Geoffrey (Galfridus) de Constantine can be seen, Plate E12. This remained in existence to the mid-16th century, when it was dissolved, and the lands were granted to the Piers family (McNamee, 1943). Much of the priory, including a 25m high octagonal steeple, survived until the late 18th century, when it was robbed out for the stone by Pigot Piers for his dwellings, adjacent to the priory. Most of his house is now also in ruins but a brick lined icehouse, which can be entered via a tunnel, is relatively intact (Plate E13).

Return to Ballynacarrigy, cross over the main R393 road and take the minor road (signposted to Castletown-Geoghegan). This road cuts through an old demesne and is flanked by extensive rhododendron bushes. When you reach the R390 road at Loughanavally, turn right, drive for 3 kilometres and stop at the lay-by on the right hand side of the road (note you will have passed a lay-by on the left side shortly before). The gate into the field leads to the Hill of Uisneach.

The Hill of Uisneach (also spelt Ushnagh) rises to a height of around 182m and provides excellent views in all directions. It is believed to have been occupied around 150 AD by Tuathal Teachtmhar and to have been the seat of the high king before it transferred to Tara (Zaczek, 2000). The Hill of Uisneach is associated with large pre-Christian assemblies especially the Celtic festival of Beltane (Bealtaine) in May when large fires were lit to welcome the summer and cattle herds were purified (Sheehan, 1996).

A large number of mainly prehistoric archaeological structures and natural features are concentrated in the vicinity of the hill. The most prominent natural one is the large glacial

Plate E11:
Sunderlin family mausoleum at Kilbixy, County Westmeath. Inset shows the family coat of arms.

Plate E12:
Remains of early 13th century Tristernagh Priory near Templecross Church, County Westmeath.

erratic, located on the southwest flank of the hill, Plate E14. This is known as 'Ail na Mireann', the 'stone of the divisions' and has traditionally been seen as where the five ancient provinces of Ireland met or the navel or centre of Ireland (though other places also claim to be the centre). It is also referred to locally as the Cat Stone as it is said to resemble a cat watching a mouse. Although a natural feature, there is evidence that it was seen as a significant object as it is surrounded by a man-made circular earthen bank about 20m in diameter.

Plate E13:
Brick-lined tunnel leading to ice house beside Tristernagh Priory.

Plate E14:
Ail na Mireann (stone of the divisions) on the Hill of Uisneach, County Westmeath.

MacAlister and Praeger (1928) describe 18 sites on the Hill of Uisneach including forts, tumuli, road/causeway, cairns and an enclosure. Part of this enclosure, which measures over 100m by 70m, contained a number of buildings, and was excavated in 1925-1926, and the results published by MacAlister and Praeger (1928). A number of periods of habitation were uncovered during the excavations, and some large pits were uncovered in an early period containing 'a thick bed of ashes, intermingled with stones of moderately large size, and with many animal bones'. Most of the bone found on the Hill of Uisneach was from cattle, which held great significance for the Celtic people. An iron knife found at the bottom of one of the pits came from the La Tène period of the Iron Age. Many iron artefacts were found and the authors report that 'the total absence of any object of Christian art is significant and the silver inlaid bronze pin, iron fibulae, sword-scabbard, and socket of a spear-head are all definitely late La Tène in character'. Here on the Hill of Uisneach we have clear archaeological evidence supporting the tradition that the hill was an important site for Celtic assemblies involving large fires and cattle. This, accompanied by its physical location – a high vantage point overlooking a large part of the country (and presumably other tribes),

Plate E15:
Pool (with glacial erratic boulder) high up on the flank of the Hill of Uisneach, County Westmeath.

all point to the Hill of Uisneach being of major significance. Interestingly, there was a total lack of pottery shards found during the excavation suggesting that the site may not have been inhabited in a domestic sense but that the site was used for ritual purposes.

The Hill of Uisneach does not contain one easily identifiable summit. If you proceed through the gate, keep to the left as you go up the hill (north) or alternatively use the old track near the house. (You can enter the field farther up through a stile). Some of the excavated areas are relatively flat platforms. As you continue walking upwards you come to a physical feature, one you would not expect near the top of a hill, a pool of water, Plate E15. The retreating glaciers have dumped some impermeable till in a hollow near the top of the hill, and that has allowed a small pool to form. Interestingly, other important Celtic sites in Ireland such as Emain Macha (Navan Fort) in County Armagh are associated with water bodies into which votive offering such as swords were placed. Proceed up to your left (as you approach the pool) towards the trigonometric point. Unfortunately this was built within another archaeological feature, a rectangular stone platform which has been partially destroyed during the construction of the concrete pillar, Plate E16. This is known as St. Patrick's Bed as he is said to have visited the Hill of Uisneach. The structure, having been placed in a very prominent position at the top of the hill, suggests that it was of some significance.

In order to visit the Ail na Mireann, return to your car and drive on towards Killare (see Figure E1). After 300-400m, pull in at the side of the road near the brown sign which states, 'Site of Celtic festival of Bealtane, ancient place of assemblies, St. Patrick's Church, sacred centre of Ireland in pagan times, site of Druid fire cult, seat of High Kings'. Cross over the road, enter via the gate and walk straight up the slope for about 250m, then look to your left and you should see the large stone. After you return to your car, drive the short distance to Killare. Note, the tree-covered Anglo-Norman motte to your right just behind the houses, which was attacked in 1187, and the defenders slain. Turn left at the crossroads, signposted for Streamstown. Almost immediately the topography starts to change, the road rises and extensive mounds of glacial sediments can be seen on your left, often separated by poorly-drained kettlehole depressions. The ridge on your left is known as Carns and the Ordnance Survey maps of the 1830s show a small settlement of about 14 buildings. However, the settlement could not be sustained throughout the mid-19th century famine and today is unpopulated, with only the shells of the houses remaining (O'Brien, 2000). When you reach Streamstown, turn left and drive the few kilometres until you intercept the R391. Turn right and drive the 4 kilometres to Horseleap. The topography around Horseleap is dominated by glacial landforms. In Horseleap, if you turn left, that will take you to Tyrrellspass (Itinerary A). Alternatively, turn right and drive back the 9 kilometres to Moate, on the N6, the start of Itinerary E. In Horseleap, there is a bronze figure of a rearing horse representing the reputed escape of Hugh de Lacy from a mob. As you leave Horseleap and drive towards Moate, the road is paralleled on the right by a long glacial esker ridge. (This is the esker shown in Plate 6, Section I of the book). On your left is a hill, formed of glacial sand, on which horizontal 'steps' or small terraces are well displayed. A natural process, known as creep, forms these, in which soil moves down steep slopes very slowly under the influence of gravity.

Plate E16:
Trigonometric pillar built into a prehistoric monument (known as St. Patrick's Bed) on the Hill of Uisneach, County Westmeath.

Itinerary F: South Central Irish Midlands

Approximate Distance: 130 kilometres
Ordnance Survey 1:50,000 Discovery Series Maps: 54 and 60.

This itinerary encompasses the most distinctive geomorphic region in the Irish Midlands: the Slieve Bloom Mountains, Figure F1. The average elevation for most of the midlands is around 100m, but heights of up to 527m (at Arderin) are reached in the mountains. The mountains trend approximately northeast-southwest with heights over 200m covering about 250 km^2. Analyses of the glacial sediments around the mountains indicate that the glaciers that moved over them came from a south-south westerly to westerly direction (Gallagher et al., 1996). Plate F1 shows a satellite image of the region and clearly illustrates the different vegetational patterns in the landscape. Pasture fields dominate east of the mountains and are shown in this false colour image as shades of red and orange.

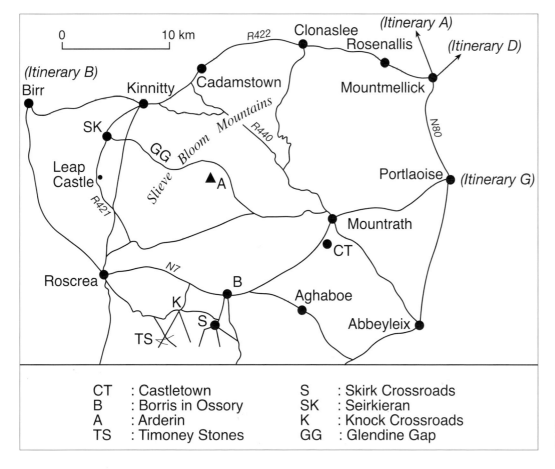

CT	: Castletown	S	: Skirk Crossroads
B	: Borris in Ossory	SK	: Seirkieran
A	: Arderin	K	: Knock Crossroads
TS	: Timoney Stones	GG	: Glendine Gap

Figure F1:
Location map for Itinerary F.

Plate F1:
Satellite image of the Slieve Bloom Mountains
(brown/blue/green area on left of image) and
surrounding area. P: Portlaoise; K: Kinnitty.

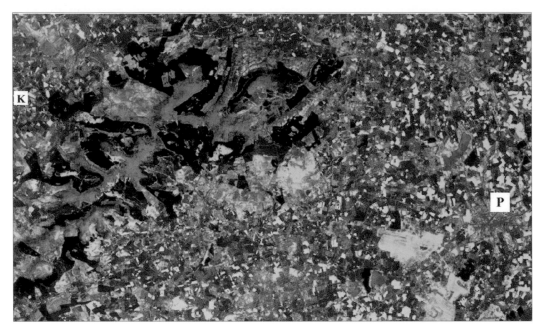

These patterns are absent in the Slieve Bloom Mountains which are characterised by coniferous plantations on the flanks of the mountains shown in black and mountain bog and heath displayed in dark green/blue.

There are a number of alternative routes that can be taken in this area. The route Portlaoise – Mountrath – Roscrea – Seirkieran – Kinnitty – Clonaslee – Mountmellick – Portlaoise encircles the Slieve Bloom Mountains and is described first. However at Seirkieran it is possible to drive east through the mountains via the Glendine Gap and then turn north to exit the mountains at Clonaslee. This alternative route through the mountains is described second.

The itinerary commences in Portlaoise, the administrative capital of County Laois. A fort was built in Portlaoise in 1548 in order to counter attacks being made by the O'More clan. This was known as Fort Protector or Fort of Leix (and later Fort of Maryborough) but was referred to as the 'Campa' by the indigenous Irish. In 1557, Counties Laois and Offaly were shired, the former being called Queen's County after Queen Mary and the latter King's County after King Philip. This was accompanied by attempts to plant English settlers. Portlaoise at this time was called Maryborough, a name it retained until the 20th century. The presence of such an important English garrison at Maryborough meant that the fort and the town, which grew up around it, were subjected to periodic attacks, especially during times of unrest (Loeber, 1999). The fort was attacked on a number of occasions in 1597-1600 by the O'Mores and again in the mid-17th century, being finally dismantled by Cromwellian forces *c.* 1652 (Deigan, 1999).

Park in the Market Square at the west end of the town near St. Peter's Church of Ireland consecrated in 1804. Proceed down Main Street as far as the large grey limestone courthouse on your left. Note the carvings on its façade, consisting of mace, swords, and sceptre, all symbols relating to the dispensation of justice. Turn left at the courthouse and proceed down the side street. The Dunamaise Arts Centre occupies the site of the old jail, in which many executions were carried out. Note the similarity of its carvings to those on the courthouse. The remains of the square tower of the old parish church of Maryborough, which is located within a graveyard can be seen behind the former jail.

Continue walking round to your right down Church Street. A section of the old fort wall and a round guard tower, which was located at its northeastern corner, still survive at this location, Plate F2.

Plate F2:
Guard tower of old fort at
Portlaoise, County Laois.

There is little of geomorphological interest within the town except part of a long esker (known as the Ridge of Maryborough), which runs from Portlaoise north to Mountmellick. It is located 200m along the N80 road signposted for Carlow or Stradbally past St. Joseph's Catholic Church at the east side of the town in an area known as The Downs. Return to your car and take the R445 road west to Mountrath, passing St. Peter's Church of Ireland Church on your right. After going through 2 roundabouts, the road joins the N7. After 5 kilometres, you come to Clonenagh Crossroads (just past a forested area) where there are lay-bys and ecclesiastical remains either side of the road. The ruins of a 16th century church in a graveyard can be seen on the left of the road whereas only a graveyard can be seen on the right. The latter area is believed to have been the site of a monastery founded in the mid-6th century by St. Fintan. A number of early Christian grave slabs and decorated stones have been discovered in this cemetery, Plate F3. Some of these are now located against the wall of the cemetery (on your left as you enter by the metal gate). A 'holy tree' is located in front of the cemetery adjacent to the road near which is a plaque installed by Laois County Council. The tree is practically dead due to metal poisoning, note the coins hammered into it as votive offerings. Return to your car and continue through Mountrath which was formed in the early17th century as a plantation town by Sir Charles Coote and which became a centre for linen and iron production (Feehan, 1983). After 3 kilometres, turn left, off the N7 into Castletown, which has been bypassed. On your left as you enter the village is a large corn mill, built *c*. 1800 on the north bank of the River Nore, which flows southwards from here to the sea. Note the sluice gates in the river, whose purpose was to control the water flow, needed to drive a waterwheel to produce power. The site of an Anglo-Norman castle is across the river. This was controlled by Gilbert de Clare, but was surrendered to Edward I in 1290. The MacGillapatrick (later

Plate F3:
Decorated early Christian stone from Clonenagh cemetery, site of monastery, County Laois.

Plate F4:
14th century Dominican priory, Aghaboe, County Laois.

Plate F5:
Late 12th century Anglo-Norman motte, Aghaboe.

Fitzpatrick) clan then took control of it and it was destroyed by Teige Fitzpatrick in 1600 (Sweetman et al., 1995).

Return to the main N7 road, turn left and continue towards Roscrea. After 8 kilometres take the R434 road to your left signposted for Durrow (and Aghaboe). Drive down this road for 6 kilometres to Aghaboe Priory. Presently, two churches are on the Aghaboe site, the present-day Church of Ireland rebuilt in the early 19th century and an older roofless nave and chancel Dominican priory dated *c.* 14th century, Plate F4. However, as in many other Irish midland ecclesiastical sites, there is a much older Christian tradition as St. Canice founded a monastery here in the 6th century. The Vikings attacked the site in the 9th and 10th centuries. Later, it later gained the attention of the Anglo-Normans, as is evidenced by the presence of a late 12th century motte in the adjacent field, Plate F5 and a nearby early 13th century an Augustinian priory for the canons regular. Most of this was destroyed in an attack by Dermot MacGillapatrick in the 14th century though parts of the belfry tower attached to the present-day church date back to this 13th century priory, Plate F6. The Dominican priory was founded on the site by Florence MacGillapatrick *c.* 1382 (Kennedy, 2003). Apart from the major ruins, there are a number of smaller features of interest. Badly eroded carved heads can be seen on the front of the present-day church and two elaborately decorated niches are located on the walls of the Dominican priory. There is also a modern plaque on the wall of the priory from the Austrian ambassador. This is to commemorate the link between Aghaboe and Austria. St. Virgil (Fergal) left Aghaboe in the 8th century as a missionary, and became the abbot of St. Peter's Monastery in Salzburg, Austria. Return to the main N7 road, turn left (note the remains of 'Derrin Castle' off to your right, an early 17th century structure) and drive the few kilometres to Borris in Ossory.

Plate F6:
Belfry tower at Aghaboe, part of which dates back to 13th century.

Plate F7:
Part of the bank surrounding the henge at Skirk, County Laois.

Plate F8: Standing stone in henge at Skirk.

Drive along the main street of Borris in Ossory and when you pass the church at the far end of the town, take the minor road to your left, signposted for Skirk and Errill. Drive 4 kilometres and park beside the roofless church at Skirk. This Church of Ireland Church was built *c*. 1831 to replace what is now a ruin in the adjacent cemetery, which may date back to the end of the 13th century. About 100m farther on from the church, on the same side of the road, is a shrubby elevated, circular area, about 90m in diameter. This is a henge, which dates back to around the early Bronze Age. It is surrounded by an external ditch (fosse) and a wide earthen bank. The interior of the henge is about 1m lower than its surrounding bank, Plate F7 and contains a 2m high standing stone, Plate F8. Access is difficult, although possible at a few locations around the perimeter. The prehistoric structure was modified c 1200 to produce a motte and bailey possibly by the de Rochefort Anglo-Norman family. Good views can be obtained from this elevated site (hence its use over the centuries for various structures) and from the road intersection in front of the henge, you may be able to see the remains of a tower house 1.5 kilometres to the southwest. This is located in the townland of Garranmaconly and was built in the 16th century, then controlled in turn by the Fitzpatricks, the Buckleys and the Vicars (Sweetman et al., 1995).

The next stop on this Itinerary is Roscrea in County Tipperary, which is in the Province of Munster. This can be reached most easily by retracing your route to Borris in Ossory, turning left and continuing along the N7 road for 10 kilometres. However, this would miss out one of the strangest collection of monuments in the Irish landscape, the Timoney Stones. Four kilometres west of Skirk, there are an estimated 300 standing stones in an area of less than 2km^2, Plates F9 and F10. The stones are scattered throughout many fields some singly, others in groups with no discernible pattern (though some have suggested 16 form a stone circle at Callaun). They tend to be formed of sandstone and vary in height from about 75 cm to over 2m. Their age, purpose and origin are unknown. To get to the stones from Skirk Church, return back towards Borris in Ossory for 200m and take the road to the left for 3 kilometres until you reach a church where five roads meet (Knock Crossroads). Take the second road on your left and drive along it for 2 kilometres until

Plate F9:
Examples of Timoney stones
in County Tipperary.

you come to another small crossroads. Some Timoney stones can be seen in the fields 300m up the road to your left and up a small track on your left 300m farther on. To reach Roscrea from here, return to Knock Crossroads and travel straight through them for 4 kilometres to the N7 road and turn left.

Roscrea has been an important ecclesiastical settlement since St. Cronan founded a monastery at nearby Monaincha in the late 6th century. It is located on the Slighe Dala, one of the major roads which radiated from Tara. The main monastic centre in Roscrea is in Church Street, where today's 19th century Church of Ireland Church is located. It consists

Plate F10:
Examples of Timoney stones
in County Tipperary.

Plate F11:
Round Tower at Roscrea,
County Tipperary.

of a Round Tower, Plate F11, a High Cross and the remains of the western façade of a Hiberno-Romanesque church, Plate F12. The Cross, adjacent to the façade, is a replica of the original St. Cronan's High Cross, which is housed in the Black Mills beside the Round Tower. The carving on one side is dominated by a figure representing the crucified Christ and the carving on the reverse side is believed to represent St. Cronan. The church dates from the 12th century. The top part of the *c.* 11th century Round Tower was removed in the late 18th century because it was being used as a firing position. It is formed to a large extent of large blocks of sandstone, many of which exhibit cross-bedding features (explained in Section D). The remains of a 15th century Franciscan friary can be found in Abbey Street. They are dominated by the bell tower constructed *c.* 1500 under the auspices of Maolrouny O'Carroll, Plate F13.

Plate F13:
Bell tower on 15th century Franciscan friary, Roscrea.

Plate F12:
Western façade of the late 12th century St. Cronan's Hiberno-Romanesque Church, Roscrea.

Plate F14:
Gatehouse at Roscrea Castle.

The strategic location of Roscrea has resulted in a military presence over the centuries, the most obvious manifestation of this is Roscrea Castle, built *c.* 1280. The castle consisted of a moated walled courtyard with southwestern and southeastern towers dominated by a large gatehouse, Plate F14. The castle was granted to the Earl of Carrick, Edmund Butler in 1315 and to a large extent remained under the control of the Butlers until the 17th century, although Cromwellian forces took it in 1650. Later, it was used as a Williamite base from which to launch attacks against the Jacobites *c.* 1690. The Duke of Ormond sold the castle (and Roscrea) to Robert Curtis in 1703. The Damer family built the 9-bayed house in the castle grounds *c.* 1720, but it, and the castle fortifications, housed the British army, for most of the time, until the early 20th century, Plate F15.

Take the R421 road out of Roscrea, signposted for Kinnitty (see Figure F1). After about 8 kilometres you pass Leap Castle on your right, Plate F16. This tower house, constructed in the early 16th century, has been attacked repeatedly and been considerably modified over the centuries by the addition of later Jacobean and Georgian structures. O'Brien and Sweetman (1997) report that it was initially the principal residence of the O'Carroll's of Ely, was captured in 1516 by the son of Gerald, Earl of Kildare, seized in 1558 by the Earl of Sussex, then retaken by William O'Carroll some months later. Five kilometres farther along this road, you will pass a 'rag tree' on your left, just before you come to Seirkieran monastic site on your right. St. Ciaran founded an early monastery here in the 5th century. The site is enclosed by an imposing double bank and ditch similar to the enclosures at other monastic sites such as Rahan (Itinerary B) or Killeigh (Itinerary A). There is the base of a High Cross within the cemetery and the bottom of a round tower can be seen from the path. The tower presently in front of the church is a much later gun turret, Plate F17. An Augustinian priory was established here in the early 13th century (little now remains), although the tall window on the east (back) wall of the present Church of Ireland Church, is believed to have come from it.

Plate F15:
Damer House within Roscrea Castle.

Continue driving for 4 kilometres until you reach the R440, turn right (east), drive into Kinnitty and park in the centre of the village near St. Finan's Church of Ireland. The church is believed to be on the site of a monastery founded in the mid-6th century. A 1.4m long slab of rock, whose surface has a range of carved spirals and lines over which

Plate F16:
Leap Castle, County Offaly.

are superimposed a number of crosses, was discovered here, Plate F18. This is known as the Kinnitty Stone and it may represent a pagan artefact, which has been 'Christianised'. It is now located within the entrance porch of the church (the key for which, may be obtained from Peavoy's corner shop). The Bernard family, who had a large estate around Kinnitty from the 18th century, have had a major impact on the village. The houses directly across the street from Peavoy's with the half doors and rounded windows were built for the workers on the estate. The 19th century Bernard mausoleum, to the rear of the church cemetery, was built in the shape of a large Egyptian pyramid, Plate F19. Drive east out of Kinnitty on the main R421 road for 1.5 kilometres until you come to Kinnitty

Plate F17:
Seirkieran monastic site, County Offaly.
Gun turret in the foreground.

Plate F18:
Kinnitty Stone, County Offaly,
courtesy of Caimin O'Brien.

Castle Hotel on your right, Plate F20. This was built by the Bernard family in the early 19th century on the site of an O'Carroll residence, part of which can still be seen behind the castle. Kinnitty High Cross stands to the side of the front entrance to the hotel, although portions of the upper part are missing, Plate F21. It is decorated with biblical scenes and contains a reference to Maelsechnaill, King of Tara in the mid-9th century (FitzPatrick and O'Brien, 1998).

Return to the main road, turn right and continue on through Cadamstown towards Clonaslee. Cadamstown was the location of another important O'Carroll stronghold, but the castle has since been destroyed. There are good exposures of Old Red Sandstone along the Silver River in Cadamstown, near the derelict mill adjacent to the bridge. Good views over the lowlands of County Offaly can be had to your left, as you drive along this road. You should also see (again to your left) ridges, quite near and parallel to the road, which are eskers formed at the end of the last glacial period. Shortly, you will come to Castlecuffe where the remains of a large early 17th century fortified house can be seen on the left. This was built by Sir Charles Coote and was named after his wife, Dorothea Cuffe. The house was destroyed in an attack in 1641, the same year that Mountrath, Portlaoise and Lea Castle were attacked (Loeber, 1999).

Continue on the R422 through Clonaslee, which is dominated by the 19th century former Church of Ireland Church (now a library) at the eastern end of the main street. A mill and millpond were located directly behind the church in the late 18th- early 19th-century. The most obvious derivation of the name is from the Gaelic 'Cluain na Sli' which translates as the 'meadow of the way (road)', although Feehan (1983) has suggested that, as it was formerly called 'Clonleslieu', a more correct derivation is 'mountain meadow' from 'Cluain na sleibhe'.

Six kilometres past Clonaslee, take the road to your right, signposted for Glenbarrow. Drive to the small car-park and walk down to the river. This valley,

Plate F19:
Bernard mausoleum, St. Finan's graveyard, Kinnitty.

Plate F20:
Kinnitty Castle Hotel,
County Offaly.

Plate F21:
Detail of Kinnitty High Cross.

within the Slieve Bloom Mountains, is the source of the River Barrow, one of Ireland's major rivers which flows east from here as far as Portarlington, then south to the sea. Excellent examples of the Old Red Sandstone and some of the features associated with it are exposed along the river as far upstream as the Clamphole Waterfall, a distance of about 1 kilometre. Plate F22 shows, in a bed of sandstone beside the river, very distinct curvilinear features. These are foreset beds seen in plan view (Plates 5 and 12 in Section I of the book show a side view of foreset beds). Walk to the Clamphole Waterfall, and, approximately 20m from where the steps lead down to the rocks, there are good examples of ripple marks formed in a similar manner to those formed on a beach, Plate F23. However, these are about 400 million years old. The rock layer at the side of the waterfall is not a thick homogeneous unit, but is formed of thin laminations because it is very shaley in character. This softer rock erodes easier and is partly the reason why the waterfall formed here. Rock was also removed from the river by quarrying and evidence of some boreholes can still be seen (Feehan, 1979, see also Plate F23). Some of the boulders here contain, within them, small lumps of white quartz, derived from older rocks. Glacial sediments are often exposed along the Glenbarrow valley, but may be hidden by dense vegetation. Return to the main R422, and drive on to Rosenallis. A well dedicated to St. Brigid, is situated in the main street. The first edition of 6 inch to 1 mile

Ordnance Survey map of Rosenallis in about 1841, records the site of a Round Tower beside the Church of Ireland Church. About 300 metres past the church on the road to Mountmellick, is the site of a Quaker graveyard, believed to be the oldest one in Ireland. The Quakers made a substantial contribution to the economy and business in the Rosenallis area from the mid-17th century onwards and it was the home of William Edmundson who died in 1712. A plaque on the wall to the left as one enters the graveyard carries the inscription 'Near this spot is buried William Edmundson the first member of the Society of Friends who settled in Ireland. Died 31st of 6th month 1712 (Old Style) aged nearly 85 years'. Continue on the R442 to Mountmellick, where you can turn south to return to Portlaoise, or travel northwest to Killeigh (Itinerary A) or northeast to Portarlington (Itinerary D). The Quakers also played a major part in the development of Mountmellick by bringing various enterprises such as linen, tanning and starching, to the town. Various Quaker families owned the Georgian houses in O'Connell Square. One of these, who originally settled in Mountmellick, the Bewleys, went on to found Bewley's Oriental Cafes based, on tea importation. The town contains a wide diversity of places of worship, including a Presbyterian Church, Catholic Church, a Quaker Meeting House, a Masonic Lodge and the Gideon Ouseley Memorial Methodist Church, mostly built in the 19th century.

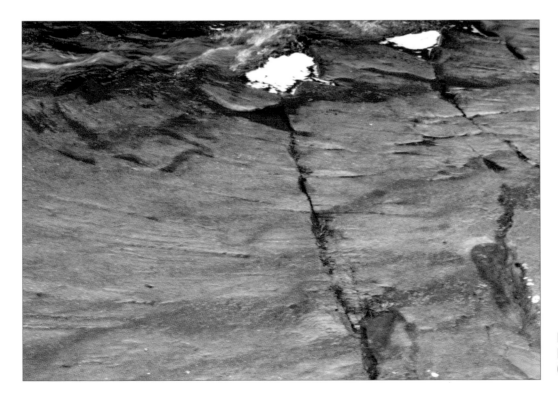

Plate F22:
Plan view of curvilinear foreset beds in sandstone, Glenbarrow, County Laois.

Plate F23:
Ripple marks in sandstone, Glenbarrow.

Alternative route from Seirkieran through Slieve Bloom Mountains

Turn right, onto a minor road, at the Clareen Crossroads just past Seirkieran following the signs for Glendine Drive. After 3.5 kilometres, at the next T-junction, turn right and after 500m, turn left up the narrow lane. There is little evidence of habitation along this lane, although in the past there were many small farmsteads and even a castle (Tulla) and a grouse lodge. After 2.5 kilometres, where the road splits; take the one to the right signposted for Glendine Drive towards Glendine Gap. The views out to the right show the rounded character of the Slieve Bloom Mountains caused by the erosion of the rocks during the last glacial period. The Silurian greywacke rocks in this part of the mountains are among the oldest in central Ireland and formed about 420 million years ago. They are exposed to the left of the road in a cutting (Plate F24), as are some of the unsorted till deposits dumped by the glaciers, Plate F25. Near the highest point of the Glendine Gap, the road cuts through a thick layer of blanket bog revealing a good section through the

Plate F24:
Silurian greywacke rock, Slieve Bloom Mountains, County Offaly.

peat. Shortly after passing the stone marking the boundary between Counties Laois and Offaly, you enter Glendine East and the road descends. The high ground off to your right is Arderin, the highest point in the Irish Midlands (527m). Glendine East has a broad U-shaped cross-section because the valley has been widened and deepened by the movement of ice down the valley in the last glacial period. Coniferous forests dominate the landscape and there are large bare areas where the trees have been felled for timber.

Continue through Glendine East until you reach a T-junction, turn left, signposted for Glenafelly Drive. Continue on this road for 2.5 kilometres and take the road to the left, again signposted for Glenafelly Drive. When this road intersects the R440, turning left takes you through the mountains to Kinnitty, see Figure F1. Alternatively, turn right (signposted 'The Cut') and drive the 1 kilometre to Burke's Crossroads and turn left for Clonaslee. This route takes you through 'The Cut', where the road runs along a narrow channel cut into the Old Red Sandstone rock. Drive on down the broad valley, which provides good views over the limestone Central Plain of Ireland, into Clonaslee, then turn right onto the R422 and continue on the itinerary.

Plate F25:
Glacial till deposits Slieve Bloom Mountains, County Offaly.

Itinerary G: Southeast Irish Midlands

Approximate Distance: 110 kilometres
Ordnance Survey 1:50,000 Discovery Series Maps: 54 and 55.

This itinerary commences in Portlaoise, the administrative capital of County Laois. See Itinerary F for a discussion on Portlaoise Town. Leave Portlaoise by going east past the prison and take the road on your left, signposted for Portarlington, which leads from the roundabout onto the R445 after about 1 kilometre. Turn left onto the R419 road, towards Portarlington (Figure G1). Drive past the thin-spired Coolbanagher Church on your right

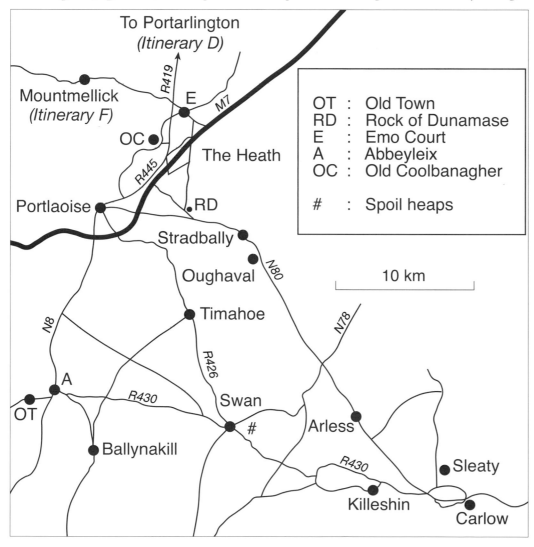

Figure G1:
Location map for Itinerary G.

(after 2.5 kilometres), then turn right for Emo Court, Plate G1. Emo Court is thought to be the second largest walled park in Europe. The original architect was James Gandon who also designed a number of important buildings in Dublin (Customs House, King's Inns and the Four Courts) and Daingean courthouse (see Itinerary A). Although construction began *c.* 1790 for the First Earl of Portarlington, John Dawson, many additions were made over the following decades, including the large green copper rotunda, designed by William Calbeck, and added in 1860.

Plate G1:
Emo Court, County Laois.

Return to the R419, turn left and stop at Coolbanagher Church (St. John the Evangelist) which is believed to be the only church constructed in Ireland that was designed by Gandon. The interior of the church was altered during the Victorian period, mainly by the conversion of the curved barrel-vaulted ceiling to its present open-beamed appearance. However, the high half moon windows, alcoved piers separating recessed neutral areas are all original, Plate G2. The font predates the church and is medieval in age. McParland (1985) in his book on Gandon's architecture states that 'when Coolbanagher was consecrated in 1785, there was no more nobly simple nor any more calmly grand church in the country'. The mausoleum at the rear (outside) of the church was built for the First Earl of Portarlington who died in 1798. Approximately 1.5 kilometres southwest of the present church are the remains of the old Coolbanagher Church located near a tower house (see Figure G1 for location). Part of this church may date back to the 13th century, as it has some Hiberno-Romanesque characteristics and an Anglo- Norman settlement under the auspices of Roger Mortimer developed here (Kennedy, 2003). A cross-inscribed stone slab mounted on the wall of the church suggests an even earlier Christian community in the area. Returning back towards the junction of the R419 and R445, the

Plate G2:
Interior of Coolbanagher Church, County Laois, showing view down central aisle towards altar, urn and alcove, and medieval font.
Church designed by James Gandon.

Plate G3:
Hums (line of low hills) in County Laois.

topography in front of you is dominated by a line of small isolated hills, typically 60-100m above the surrounding terrain, Plate G3. These are referred to as 'hums' and are believed to have formed due to karstic processes (see Section I of the book for a discussion of karst). It is thought that removal of limestone by the subsurface movement of water resulted in an eventual collapse of the overlying rock, leaving behind a few isolated hills of limestone. Interestingly, the word 'Coolbanagher' derives from the Gaelic 'Cuil Bheannachair' meaning 'corner of the pointed hills', an obvious reference to the hums. Upon reaching the intersection with the R445, take the small road opposite which takes you over the M7 motorway and follow the sign for 'The Heath' (see Figure G1). After driving over the cattle grid on the road and passing the graveyard on your right, take the road to your left at the next junction, signposted for the Golf Club. Drive a few hundred metres and stop near the school on your left. The area in front of you is known as 'The Great Heath' (of Maryborough) or more simply 'The Heath'. It is *c.* 200 hectares in size and in the past has been used for both military training and for horse racing. The area was also clearly of some significance in prehistoric times due to the large concentration of ring-barrows that are located within The Heath. Barrows are mounds of earth formed over burial sites and are believed to date from the Neolithic to the early Iron Age. Those barrows surrounded by a trench (fosse) and an outer circular bank are referred to as ring-barrows. Of the 14 known ring-barrows in County Laois, 9 are within the small area encompassed by the Great Heath (Sweetman et al., 1995). One is located at the intersection of the roads beside the school and a number are located within the golf course. They are typically about 15m in diameter with a slightly raised central domed mound, Plate G4.

Plate G4:
Prehistoric ring-barrow on the Great Heath, County Laois.

Return towards Portlaoise along the R445, and at the first set of roundabouts, take the road signposted for Carlow, and a few hundred metres farther on, take the road to your left for Carlow and Stradbally. This leads to another roundabout, where you should turn left onto the N80 road for Carlow. The land starts to rise and the hums are quite prominent on either side of the road. After about 4 kilometres, take the minor road to your left signposted for the Rock of Dunamase. The strategic location of this site is obvious as you drive towards the castle, Plate G5. It has commanding views over the surrounding area and controls the pass through to Carlow. The hum that it is situated on has near-vertical rock faces, which would have enhanced its defensive capabilities. Most of the castle seen today dates to the early Anglo-Norman period *c*. 1210 though archaeological excavation has revealed earlier fortifications possibly dating back to the 9th century (Sweetman, 2005). During the 9th century, the Vikings also attacked the site, and such is the strategic location of the Rock of Dunamase, it is probable that the site was occupied even earlier. The castle consists of a number of defensive 'rings' which had to be breached before the keep (the large building on the highest position of the Rock)

Plate G5:
Anglo-Norman castle on the
Rock of Dunamase, County Laois.

could be assaulted. Today, you enter the castle by an outer stone gateway which itself was protected by outer defences. This led into an inner defended courtyard and an inner gateway through which the keep could be reached, Plate G6. Bradley (1999) gives a brief account of its history. It is believed that Meiler FitzHenry built the keep before 1208 when William Marshall completed the remaining fortifications. The castle was later under the control of Roger de Mortimer, although it was subject to periodic attacks by the indigenous Irish. It was briefly under the control of the Confederate forces in the mid-17th century but was taken by Cromwellian forces, who destroyed it, so that it could not be retaken. Today, many of the large blocks of masonry still litter the site. Return to the main N80 road, turn left and proceed for 4 kilometres to Stradbally.

Stradbally was the site of a Franciscan monastery built *c.* 1447 by the Gaelic O'More family. This remained in existence for over 100 years, but was eventually destroyed by Francis Cosby who was granted the lands around Stradbally in 1563 during the 16th century plantation of County Laois (Cosby, 1999). The town itself consists for the most part of one long linear street with a number of old mill buildings along the river. Interestingly the Catholic Church, unlike those in many Irish towns, occupies a central position on the main street. Drive on through Stradbally and stop at the cemetery on your right about 1 kilometre from the village. This location is known variously as Oughaval or Nuachabhail ('New House'). It is the site of a 6th century monastery founded by St. Colman. Now, a medieval church stands on the site (Plate G7) though it has been modified over the centuries, most lately in the 19th century when it was altered in order to incorporate a burial vault in the nave for the Cosby family. Many of the headstones around the church date back to the mid-1700s.

Plate G6:
Inner gateway and fortifications on Rock of Dunamase.

Plate G7:
Medieval church at Oughaval, near Stradbally, County Laois. This was the site of a 6th century monastery founded by St. Colman.

Plate G8:
Sleaty Cross in southeast County Laois.

Continue on the N80 following the signs for Carlow. Four kilometres past the intersection with the N78, northwest of Arless, the road starts to rise. Note that, this little valley is most likely a former meltwater channel, formed at the end of the last glacial period. The rocks displayed in a small road cutting at this locality are not limestones, such as could be seen at the Rock of Dunamase, but friable shales. The rocks in the southeastern part of County Laois are mainly Upper Carboniferous in age rather than the Lower Carboniferous limestones that are present in the rest of the county, apart from in the Slieve Bloom Mountains. Drive on through Arless and Ballickmoyler to the bypass around Carlow Town and take the bypass road to your left at the Portlaoise Road roundabout. Continue on the bypass until you come to the Sleaty Road roundabout, and then turn left (signposted Knockbeg College). After about 1 kilometre, stop at the small ruined church on your right, just past the modern graveyard on your left. This site is associated with St. Fiacc and Kennedy (2003) records that it is one of the most important Christian centres in Leinster during the early Christian period, as it was the residence of the first bishop of Leinster. The church standing on the site is much later in date (medieval) and contains a large octagonal font. The site contains two granite crosses both of which are believed to be very early Christian in date. Granite does not occur locally at this site thus the crosses must have been transported to the site, or else glacial erratic material was used in their construction. One cross is quite small (*c.* 1.5m high) and is located near a tomb surrounded by railings whereas the other is much taller (2.8m) and is situated beside the church, Plate G8.

Return to the bypass, turn left and follow the signs for Rosslare until you come to the Hacketstown Road roundabout where you should turn left onto the R726, signposted dolmen, and drive about 3 kilometres to the Kernanstown (Brownshill) megalithic tomb. This Neolithic portal tomb has a capstone believed to weigh 150 tonnes, one of the largest in Europe, Plate G9.

Return to the Hacketstown Road roundabout and take the road into Carlow Town centre. Shortly you will pass 'Pollerton Castle' on your right, a possible modified tower house. The oldest extant building in Carlow is the early 13th century Anglo-Norman castle, little of which now remains, Plate G10. It originally had a rectangular keep with circular towers at the four corners and was constructed, for strategic reasons, on high ground overlooking the River Barrow. It was under the control of William Marshall and later

Plate G9:
Kernanstown portal tomb, Carlow.

his grandson, Roger Bigod, who died in 1270. It eventually passed into the hands of Richard Hartpole in the 16th century and to Donough O'Brien in the early 17th century (King, 1997). Like other castles in the Irish Midlands, it was captured by Confederate forces in the mid-17th century but was subsequently re-taken by Cromwellian forces. Near the castle, the spires of two churches dominate the skyline in the centre of Carlow. These are the Catholic Cathedral, built 1820-1833, and St. Mary's Church of Ireland Church, with different components built at different times; the nave in the early 18th century, the spire in the early 19th century and a late 19th century sanctuary (Garner, 1980). Across the river, in Ninety-Eight Street (off Maryborough Street) there is a memorial erected in 1898, to commemorate the deaths of 640 United Irishmen, killed in Tullow Street on 25th May 1798.

Plate G10:
13th century Anglo-Norman castle, Carlow.

Carlow has a range of administrative buildings, such as a courthouse, Town Hall and jail, mainly built in the 19th century. The jail was located in the Potato Market but has now been converted into Carlow Shopping Centre. A plaque states that it was constructed in 1750, extended in 1824 and closed in 1860. However, the former jail's archway has been retained as the entrance to the Centre, and the first building one sees upon entering is the house of the former governor of the jail, Plate G11. Many houses and buildings in Carlow have employed the Leinster granite for steps and window surrounds and the Governor's House is a good example of this practice.

Plate G11:
Governor's House in old jail at
Carlow Shopping Centre.

Plate G12: Hiberno-Romanesque doorway
at Killeshin, County Laois.

Return to the bypass and drive back to the first roundabout you encountered (Portlaoise Road roundabout). From here, take the R430 road signposted for Castlecomer and Abbeyleix. The road begins to rise as you drive onto the more elevated Upper Carboniferous rocks. Drive for 3 kilometres to Killeshin and take the road to the left signposted for Killeshin Church. St. Comgan founded a monastery here in the late 5th century and the site once possessed a Round Tower which was destroyed in the early 18th century. 12th century activity in the area is illustrated by a nearby Anglo-Norman motte and the Hiberno-Romanesque doorway of the church (Plate G12) with its triangular gable, which is similar to, though not as elaborate as, the one at Clonfert, County Galway (see Plate B6, Itinerary B). The four-ordered doorway contains elaborate carvings of human and animal heads, foliage motifs and chevron patterns, Plate G13. Either side of and within the doorway some carved lettering can be discerned, one of which has been interpreted as 'a prayer for Diarmait, King of Leinster' (Stalley, 1999).

Return to the R430, turn left, continue for 6 kilometres and take the road to the right signposted for Abbeyleix. Drive on for a few kilometres until you intersect the N78 at Newtown Crossroads. Take the road signposted for Swan. Swan is a relatively new settlement in County Laois, and is believed to have been named after the public house there. Throughout most of the Irish Midlands, the local rock is Lower Carboniferous limestone and industrial usage generally involved roasting it in lime kilns, Plate G14. However, around

Plate G13:
Details of Killeshin Church doorway.

Swan there are outcrops of Upper Carboniferous rocks and within them there are layers of fireclay and coal. The fireclays are used by Flemings Fire Clays Manufacturing Limited in Swan (located on the right in the red brick buildings as you entered the village) and the spoil heaps relating to the coal industry, which commenced in the 18th century, can be seen 3 kilometres east of Swan, near Slatt Crossroads, Plate G14. Drive through Swan and a few hundred metres farther on take the R 426road to your right for Timahoe (R426). Soon, you get good views of the hums that you saw earlier at Coolbanagher.

On reaching Timahoe, drive past the Catholic Church, take the road to your left, and park near the small church, now converted to a library. Timahoe is the location of one of the best preserved Round Towers in the country, Plate G15. The tower is 12th century and is built of grey limestone and red/brown sandstone blocks. It is over 29m in height, the walls are nearly 2m thick and the entrance is about 5m from the ground. The four-ordered doorway is formed of sandstone and is carved in the Hiberno-Romanesque style incorporating human heads. The tower is much later than the original monastery, founded here in the 7th century by St. Mochua. The name 'Timahoe' derives from 'Tigh Mochua' (Church of Mochua). The ruin adjacent to the tower was originally a church constructed in the 15th century. It was later altered and converted into a tower house. The Archaeological Inventory of County Laois records that large quantities of human remains were discovered around the tower house and that they may relate to a battle in 1598 when 1200 people were killed at this location. Situated near the Round Tower, on a limestone plinth, are a number of creatures whose purpose might seem at first puzzling, Plate G16. The work consists of a cockerel, a mouse and a fly sitting on a book. These animals are linked to St. Mochua, the founder of the monastery. St. Mochua was believed to have had three pets, a cockerel to wake him in the morning to say prayers, a mouse to lick his ear if he fell asleep and a fly, which walked along the line when he was reading from a book.

Leave Timahoe, driving towards Ballinakill (see Figure G1) and a few hundred metres outside Timahoe, take the minor road to your right. Large mounds of sediments, deposited in a fluvio-glacial environment, now forming mounds in the landscape, can be seen to the left of the road as you drive along. An Anglo-Norman motte was built on one of these mounds. Drive on to the Blandsfort Crossroads and go straight ahead (give way at this junction) – signposted for

Plate G14:
Lime kiln (top) and spoil heaps from coal extraction (bottom), near Swan, County Laois.

Ballinakill, 8 kilometres. Sediments, formed during the melting of the glaciers, predominate in this area. Rivers flowing into a lake have produced thick deposits (*c.* 8m) of fine-grained sand layers, which exhibit good examples of foreset and bottom set bedding, Plate G17. (Plates 5 and 12 in Section I also show examples of foreset beds). Continue straight through the next crossroads (signposted for Heywood Community School), and after 2 kilometres, turn left at the entrance to Heywood Community School beside the castellated former entrance to the demesne, Plate G18. Heywood House, built *c.* 1773 by Frederick Trench, was destroyed by fire in the mid-20th century. However, the grounds (which can be visited) retain some of the typical landscaping of this period. In the early 20th century, the then owner Colonel Hutchenson Poe, commissioned Sir Edwin Lutyens and Gertrude Jekyll, to create some small formal gardens. These at Heywood Demesne are considered to represent some of their best work in Ireland, Plate G19. A number of glacial landforms are located a short distance from the gardens near Mass Lough, a moraine, representing a standstill phase of the glaciers that once covered the region and an esker which has been exploited for its sand and gravel. (Note that, as you drove into the gardens from the main road, the tree-lined ridge to your left formed part of the moraine). Return to the main road and drive into the village of Ballinakill which developed around the castle that was built *c.* 1610 by Sir Thomas Ridgeway, though the lands had originally been granted to Alexander Crosby in 1570 (Bradley, 1999). The little that remains of the castle today can be seen from the grounds of the Catholic Church. In the 17th century, the village was noted for its ironworks, which produced cannon, and today, names such as the Ironmills River and Ironmills Bridge (southeast of Ballinakill), recall this tradition. The castle was attacked and captured by General Preston in 1643 and remained under Confederate control until recaptured by Cromwellian forces *c.* 1650 (Loeber, 1999). From Ballinakill, take the R432 road to Abbeyleix (5 kilometres).

As the name implies, Abbeyleix was the site of an abbey, in this instance a Cistercian one founded *c.* 1184 under the patronage of the O'More family (O'Brien, 1998). The site of this abbey was to the southeast of the town on the Ballycolla Road (R433) near Abbeyleix Demesne. The later area of settlement, that developed around the

Plate G15:
Round Tower at Timahoe, County Laois.

Plate G16:
Details of monument at Timahoe relating
to legend of St. Mochua.

Plate G17:
Glacial sediments, exhibiting foreset and bottomset bedding, near Ballinakill, County Laois.

Plate G18:
Former entrance of
Heywood Demesne,
Ballinakill,
County Laois.

Plate G19:
Early 20th century Heywood
Gardens designed by Edwin
Lutyens and Gertrude Jekyll.

abbey, is still known as Old Town (An Seanbhaile). There are no extant buildings relating to the abbey, although tombs of two of the O'More clan, dated 1486 and 1502, are presently located within the demesne (Kennedy, 2003). The family most associated with Abbeyleix were the Vesey (de Vesci) family. A crest commemorating them is displayed on the present Market House and the First Viscount de Vesci was responsible for the establishment of the new town of Abbeyleix in its present location in the mid-18th century. Many of the monuments in the area are to this family and architecturally Pembroke terrace represents the core of the 19th century town, Plate G20. This housed the police station, the bank and the post office and was given by Lord Pembroke to his daughter Emma when she married the 3rd Viscount de Vesci. A carpet factory, founded in 1904 across the road from Pembroke Terrace (near the Bank of Ireland) supplied some of the carpets onboard the Titanic, which sank in 1912. Return to Portlaoise by driving north out of Abbeyleix on the N8 road.

Plate G20:
Pembroke Terrace, Abbeyleix, County Laois.

Itinerary H: Southwest Irish Midlands

Approximate Distance: 115 kilometres
Ordnance Survey 1:50,000 Discovery Series Maps: 53, 59 and 58.

This itinerary circles Lough Derg, the largest lake on the River Shannon and encompasses three counties, County Tipperary east of the lough and Counties Clare and Galway, west of the lough. For the purposes of this itinerary, it is assumed that the route commences in Portumna at the northern end of the lough, Figure H1. County Tipperary is different from Counties Clare and Galway in that it was divided into Tipperary North and South Ridings in 1838, with Nenagh being the administrative centre for Tipperary North.

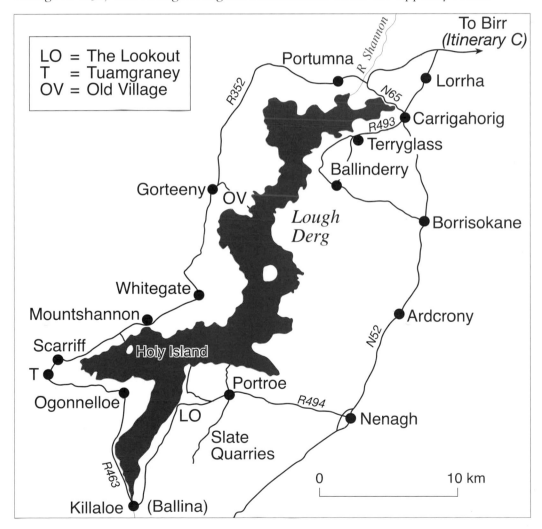

Figure H1:
Location map for Itinerary H.

Portumna, from the Gaelic 'Port Umna' meaning 'landing place of the tree', is dominated by two main building complexes, Portumna Castle and the Dominican priory. The castle was built *c.* 1618 by Richard Burke (the family name is also referred to as de Burgh, Bourke, or de Burgo) the 4th Earl of Clanricarde (Sweetman, 2005) and in essence consists of a rectangular building with four square towers at the corners, Plate H1. It was attacked during the Confederate War in the mid-17th century, and the lands seized by Cromwellian forces. It is surrounded by a walled garden and Delaney (2000) reports that it represents a transition from mainly older tall slender tower houses to later, squatter manor houses. The substantial remains of a Dominican priory are located close to the castle, Plates H2 and H3. This was formerly a Cistercian friary but was transferred to the Dominican order in the early 15th century under the patronage of Murcha O'Madden. Part of the cloister has been reconstructed, and today, the ruins consist of a nave and chancel church, cloisters and domestic buildings such as a kitchen and sleeping quarters. Most of these buildings date from the 15th century, although some of the windows may be 13th century. Some grave slabs for members of the Madden family, dating from *c.* 1670-1689, are mounted on the walls.

From Portumna, drive east across the bridge over the Shannon, and take the N65 for Nenagh. A small island in the River Shannon (Haye's island) is used to support one of the pillars of the bridge, part of which is periodically raised in order to facilitate the movement of boat traffic. Four kilometres farther on, take the minor road to the left signposted for Lorrha, drive for 3 kilometres and stop at the large Dominican priory on the left, Plate H4. Lothra is the Gaelic version of Lorrha, although there is no widely accepted explanation for the name. Lorrha was the site of a monastery founded in the mid-6th century by St. Ruadhan. It is recorded that St. Patrick travelled through Lorrha 100 years earlier. Monastic settlements, such as Clonmacnoise (Itinerary B), which were located near the River Shannon, were particularly susceptible to Viking raids as the river provided a means of easy access. Lorrha was destroyed in such an attack in 845 AD.

Plate H3:
View of Dominican priory looking through door, arches and window, Portumna.

Plate H4:
Dominican Priory. Lorrha,
County Tipperary.

Walter de Burgo founded the Dominican priory in 1269. It is dedicated to St. Peter who was martyred in 1252. The Dominicans remained at Lorrha for over 500 years until the late 18th century (Gleeson, 1915). The priory is about 48m long and 8m wide with walls that are over 1m thick. Its internal structure suggests that it had a tower at one time. Little now remains of the east window, however, what is left gives an impression of its massive size. There are two, large, elaborately carved, memorial plaques, dated *c.* 1690, in the priory, Plate H5. These are for members of the O'Kennedy clan who were an important Gaelic family in this part of Lower Ormond. A small wall plaque, dated 1689, is to Constantine Egan, one of the MacEgan clan.

Plate H5:
17th century O'Kennedy memorial plaque at
Dominican priory, Lorrha, County Tipperary.
Inset shows detail of coat of arms.

Drive into the centre of Lorrha, turn right and stop at the ruined church on your left across the road from St. Ruadhan's Well. The church was built in the mid-12th century by the Order of the Canons Regular of St. Augustine. It is most notable for its doorway with the carved head of a woman, Plate H6. This is later than the original building and is thought to be the wife of de Burgo, who founded the Dominican priory. Walk on up the road and enter the cemetery gate on your left. Two buildings can be seen at this site; the present-day Church of Ireland Church has been built onto a much older church dated *c.* 1000, Plate H7. This also has a newer doorway, in this case surmounted by a man's head, believed to be that of Walter de Burgo. The remains of two High Crosses, believed to date from the 8th century are also located in the graveyard. Gleeson (1915) suggested that the one which forms part of a pillar might mark the site of St. Ruadhan's grave whereas the other, which consists of a decorated cross base, may mark the grave of Congal I, High King of Ireland, who died at Lorrha in 710 AD. Walk on past the cemetery for 50m and you come to the remains of an Anglo-Norman motte dating from *c.* 1200. The motte is quite small and has probably been partially removed at some time.

Plate H6:
Augustinian priory, Lorrha. Inset shows carved head of woman over doorway.

Plate H7:
Present-day Church of Ireland Church and adjoining *c.* 1000 church on site of St. Ruadhan's monastery, Lorrha. Inset shows carved head of man over doorway.

Return to the N65, turn left and shortly after passing through Carrigahorig, take the R493 road to your right signposted for Terryglass from the Gaelic 'Tir dha Ghlas' meaning 'land of the two streams'. Carrigahorig was the site of a number of battles in 1548 when the Butlers were repelled, whilst attempting to extend their control over Lower Ormond. The topography here is very undulating due to glacial sediment deposition. Shortly on your right you come to the Catholic Church and cemetery. Note that all the headstones in the cemetery are identical. This was stipulated by Lucilia Larios y Tashara Hickie, who funded the building of the church. In the centre of the graveyard a Celtic Cross has been erected on a large boulder of granite (note the large pink feldspar crystals) beside which is a ballaun stone. The boulder is a glacial erratic moved by glaciers from the Galway area. However, it clearly had a religious significance as it originally stood outside the old church in Terryglass and was moved to its present position when the new church opened. It may have been used as a Mass Rock. All the graves in the cemetery face towards the granite boulder. Continue into Terryglass, where a monastic settlement was founded by St. Colum (son of Crimthain), in the mid-6th century. It, like Lorrha, was attacked by the Vikings but continued in existence until 1164 when it was burned. Terryglass differs from other places in the Irish Midlands (such as Killeigh, Clonard, Kells or Clonmacnoise) in that later monastic orders such as the Augustinians, Dominicans or Franciscans did not have a community at this early Christian site. Near the Church of Ireland Church (now a private residence), there are the remains of a medieval church, part of a tower house and bawn (Murphy, 1997). Within walking distance of the centre of the village is the quay, beside which are located St. Augh's Well and Oldcourt Castle, Plate H8. The castle, which overlooks Lough Derg, has four squat corner towers, was built in the early 1200,s and is referred to a 'towered keep' by Sweetman (2005).

Drive through Terryglass towards Ballinderry and then turn left at the crossroads signposted for Borrisokane. As you drive along this road you will see on your left a small roadside quarry displaying Carboniferous limestone rocks and further along the road a

tower house, Plate H9. This is known as Tombricane Castle, an O'Kennedy fortification, where Owen O'Kennedy was killed during a rebellion in 1600. In Borrisokane, turn right onto the N52 road and drive south towards Nenagh. The 'Borris' in Borrisokane (and Borris in Ossory on Itinerary G), refers to an Anglo-Norman garrison or settlement.

When you reach the Nenagh bypass, turn left at the Borrisokane roundabout, drive along the R497 into Neneagh and park near the centre of town. The name 'Nenagh' is believed to derive from 'Aonach Urmumhan' meaning 'assembly of Ormond' (Grace 1993). An early Christian monastery was located south of Nenagh but it was the Anglo-Normans who have had the most visible impact on the town. Theobald FitzWalter was granted land in Tipperary in the late 12th century. He built a castle in the early 13th century at Nenagh, which is near the boundary of Upper and Lower Ormond, in order to consolidate his control over the territory. He was appointed Chief Butler of Ireland, and, over time, the family became known as the Butlers. The most distinctive landmark in Nenagh is the castle keep, which is about 30m in height though the upper part is a much later addition, Plate H10. The walls of the lower part are about 5m thick. Parts of the rest of the castle that still

Plate H10:
Keep of Nenagh Castle, County Tipperary.
Upper crenellated part is recent addition.

remain are the eastern tower of the gateway and parts of the gatehouse. Most of the wall that once surrounded the castle and some watchtowers have been destroyed. As with other important castles in the Irish Midlands, Nenagh Castle was attacked and occupied by opposing factions over the following centuries. It was attacked in 1550 by Teige O'Carroll, taken by Owen Roe O'Neill's forces in 1648 and was under Cromwellian control in 1650. In the late 17th century, another O'Carroll (Long Anthony), seized it in 1688, although by 1691, it was in the hands of Williamite forces.

A building, comparable in scale to the castle, is Nenagh prison. This was constructed *c.* 1842 and consisted of a central octagonal governor's house from which seven cell blocks, each holding male prisoners, radiated, Plate H11. The jail also housed a female wing and a laundry. The jail is located beside the courthouse and is connected to it via an underground passageway. Such an arrangement also existed for Tullamore courthouse and prison, which were built around the same time. The jail was in existence for less than 50 years and the building complex

Plate H11:
Governor's house at Nenagh prison.

was taken over, around 1887, by the Sisters of Mercy, who turned the cell blocks into classrooms. The entrance to the jail was the location of the cells of those who were condemned to death, Plate H12. In all, 17 men were executed here. The condemned man was led from an execution room, through a door behind the present-day religious statue above the entrance, and publicly hanged on a scaffold. The Governor's House is now the location of Nenagh Heritage Centre.

A Franciscan friary was built near the castle in the mid-13th century under the patronage of the Butler family, Plate H13. It was considered to be one of the most important Franciscan houses in Ireland and is about 45m long and 8m wide. The friary was suppressed during the 16th century, being granted to Robert Collum, *c.* 1588, although the Franciscans had returned by *c.* 1687, when the Catholic James II was king, but it fell into disrepair during Penal times.

Plate H12:
Entrance to Nenagh prison, once the location of public hangings.
Inset shows one of the condemned cells located behind the statue.

Plate H13:
Mid-13th century Franciscan friary, Nenagh.

Plate H14:
Example of slate produced at Portroe quarries, County Tipperary. 5m high.

Return to your car and leave Nenagh on the same road as you entered. When you reach the Borrisokane roundabout on the bypass, turn left, and, at the Portroe Road roundabout, take the road for Portroe on your right (R494 road). As you drive towards Portroe, the elevation increases quite sharply. Heights, in the vicinity of Nenagh, average 70m, whereas the Arra Mountains on your left are up to 450m above sea level. The highest parts of the mountains are formed of hard resistant Silurian rocks, mainly the Slieve Bernagh Formation greywackes (Archer et al., 1996). However, in the Portroe area, the silts and mudstones developed a slaty cleavage, which led to the development of an extensive slate industry (Royal Irish Mining Company). The old workings of the slate quarries are 3 kilometres along the road to the left at the crossroads in Portroe, Plate H14. Return to Portroe, continue driving on the R494 towards Ballina and stop at the viewing place, known as 'The Lookout', 4 kilometres beyond Portroe. This vantage point allows an excellent view of the lower part of Lough Derg, Plate H15. The mountains on the far side of the lough are the Slieve Bernagh Mountains, which reach heights in excess of 500m above sea level. As reported in Section I of the book, the presence of mountains, either

side of the lough, is the reason why the southern part of the lough decreases dramatically in width. The mountains are formed of hard resistant *non-soluble* rocks, so the lough is narrow, as it takes a long time to wear these rocks away mechanically whereas to the north, the soluble limestone can be dissolved away more quickly. The small island near the far shore is Holy Island, on which you may be able to make out a Round Tower. The

Plate H16:
13th century St. Flannan's Cathedral at Killaloe, County Clare.

small roofless church that can be seen down near the shore below 'The Lookout' is located at Castletown. This forms part of the 18th century Castlelough Demesne owned by the Parker family who have a large vault in the graveyard. Some of the smaller grave slabs relate to Welshmen, who had come from Wales (Bangor) to work the slate quarries near Lough Derg, mostly in the 19th century. A much older gravestone, located beside the church, refers to Morine Carrol, a parent of the late 16th century bishop of Killaloe (Murphy, 1997). Near the church are the remains of a tower house, which was occupied by the MacBrien clan.

Continue to Ballina, cross the bridge into Killaloe (County Clare) and park near the cathedral, Plate H16. Killaloe became the 'cathedral town' for the Diocese of Killaloe, which was formed in 1111 at the Synod of

Plate H17:
Late 12th century Hiberno-Romanesque doorway in St. Flannan's Cathedral. Insets show details.

Rathbreasil (Cashel, County Tipperary). The course of the River Shannon at Killaloe has been extensively altered over the centuries. The river used to tumble down a small waterfall, making navigation impossible. In winter, the water would back-up, causing flooding, and various deepening and widening schemes were undertaken in the mid-19th century (Kierse, 2001).

Killaloe gets it name from the Gaelic 'Kill Dalua', the 'Church of Lua' (also Dalua or Malua). Lua founded a monastery near Roscrea in the 6th century, and is often identified with Killaloe. The present cathedral is dedicated to St. Flannan an 8th century saint and is mostly 13th century in date, though the tower has had its height increased in the 19th century. St. Flannan's Well is located in the bank premises, across the road from the cathedral, suggesting that the original ecclesiastical site was probably much larger than today. It is believed that earlier cathedrals were located on the same site; there was initially the 'Great Church' of Brian Boru, and a later late 12th century one was built by Donal Mor O'Brien, King of Munster (Owen, 1992). There is evidence on the site for a significant ecclesiastical structure of this age. Enter the cathedral, and the 'window' to your right is in reality a late 12th century Hiberno-Romanesque doorway of four orders, consisting of chevron patterns, honeysuckle designs and beasts, Plate H17. The large Celtic Cross in the cathedral was found in pieces near Kilfenora, County Clare, and is thought to date from the 11th-12th century. The irregular block near the doorway is an ogham stone that is believed to be unique in that it contains both ogham writing and runes relating to a person called 'Toroqr', Plate H18. Two other points of interest in the cathedral are the 13th century rectangular basin font (Plate H19), and the 12m high East Window, containing stained glass depicting Christ the Good Shepherd and the 12 Apostles.

The oldest building on the site is not the cathedral but the earlier, *c.* 12th century St. Flannan's Oratory beside it, Plate H20. Note the similarity of this oratory to the one at Kells in County Meath (see Plate C16, Itinerary C). Drive to the Catholic Church in Killaloe, which is on an elevated, commanding position, and is thought to be the site of Brian Boru's palace. He was High King of Ireland in the early 11th century. Located within the

Plate H18:
Ogham stone in St. Flannan's Cathedral.

Plate H19:
13th century basin font in St. Flannan's Cathedral.

Plate H20:
St. Flannan's Oratory (*c.* 12th century) in grounds of St. Flannan's Cathedral.

Plate H21:
St. Lua's Oratory, Killaloe.

Plate H22:
Castlebawn tower house near
Ogonnelloe, County Clare.

grounds of the church is St. Lua's Oratory consisting of a 9th -10th century nave and a later chancel, Plate H21. This building originally stood on a small island downstream from Killaloe. However, in the late 1920s, the Shannon Hydroelectric Scheme (Ardnacrusha) resulted in the raising of the level of the river below Killaloe, submerging the island and the surrounding land.

From Killaloe take the R463 road north towards Scarriff. Shortly after going through Ogonnelloe, stop at the viewing place overlooking Lough Derg. A good example of one of the many tower houses which ring the lough can be seen, Plate H22. This is Castlebawn tower house (or Simon's Castle), and is built on a small island about 150m offshore. It was constructed in the mid to late 16th century by Owen McNamara (Cody, 1998). Continue on to Tuamgraney and park near St. Cronan's Church occupied by the East Clare Heritage Centre. The name is believed to derive from Tuaim Greine, which has been variously translated as the hill of the Sun or the tomb of Grian, a pagan Sun goddess (Madden, 2000). St Cronan and St. Colman established a monastic settlement here in early Christian times. The church is considered to be one of the oldest in Ireland, though various building styles and ornamentation are evident. The small bell tower at one end is relatively recent but the doorway (Plate H23), constructed of 'Cyclopean' blocks, dates back over 1,000 years to when the church was initially constructed in the 10th century under the auspices of Cormac Ua Cillin (Madden, 2000). Parts of the church date to the

Plate H23:
10th century doorway in St. Cronan's
Church, Tuamgraney, County Clare.

12th century and various Hiberno-Romanesque characteristics are evident on some of the window surrounds. The tower house beside the church was an O'Grady stronghold built in the mid-16th century. Drive a few hundred metres past the church to the intersection with the R352. A large natural outcrop of limestone containing a memorial to those from East Clare, who fought in the Irish War of Independence, is located at the junction. The limestone here exhibits excellent examples of a karst landform known as rinnenkarren, Plate H24. These are parallel trough-shaped grooves (runnels) over 1m in length formed by the solution of limestone by rainwater as it is funnelled down the sloping surface.

Plate H24:
Karst runnels formed on limestone
surface, Tuamgraney.

Madden (2000) records that Scarriff developed around a strategically placed O'Grady castle, which controlled a ford over the River Graney. The name Scarriff derives from the Gaelic for shallow and presumably relates to the shallow ford. It thrived as a market town and was also an important centre for iron manufacture in the 17th century. Proceed towards Mountshannon along the R352 and 5 kilometres past Scarriff take the road to the right signposted Holy Island. The principal structure that can be seen on Holy Island (Inis

Cealtra: Island of the Burial Place) from the shore is the *c.* 10th-11th century Round Tower, Plate H25. However, this small island (which can be visited by boat from Mountshannon) contains a large number of ecclesiastical structures. A monastery was founded here by St. Colum (son of Crimthain) who also founded the monastic settlement at Terryglass in County Tipperary. The island contains the *c.* 10th century St. Caimin's Church with later 12th century additions, St. Mary's Church (13th-14th century), St. Bridget's Church (*c.* 12th century) and the much later Church of the Wounded Men believed to be associated with the O'Grady clan. In addition, there are parts of High Crosses, ballaun stones and a graveyard containing many 11th-12th century grave slabs (Madden, 2004). The island, like other ecclesiastical centres near the Shannon, was raided and plundered by the Vikings. Return to the main road and turn right and continue to Mountshannon. Today, Mountshannon Town is located within County Clare but the First Edition (mid-19th century) of the 6 inch to 1 mile Ordnance Survey map shows that then, it was in County Galway. The town is a relatively new settlement and came into existence in the mid-18th century when Alexander Woods built a number of houses for workers in the flax growing and linen industries which he established there (Madden, 1993). The most substantial historic building that remains is the Market House in the main street, Plate H26

From Mountshannon, continue through Whitegate and return to Portumna. Note, that at Gorteeny, 7 kilometres past Whitegate, the road to the right leads down to Lough Derg to a place called the 'Old Village'. This is the site of a pre-famine village (near Dooras graveyard) though today only one small house retains much of its original form, Plate H27.

Plate H26:
Market House in Mountshannon,
County Clare.

Plate H27:
Small thatched house, retaining many
original features, at the 'Old Village',
Gorteeny, County Galway.

Itinerary I: Northwest Irish Midlands

Approximate Distance: 100 kilometres
Ordnance Survey 1:50,000 Discovery Series Maps: 40, 41 and 43.

This itinerary in the northwest Irish Midlands takes in parts of two counties; Roscommon and Longford, and commences in Roscommon Town, Figure I1. Roscommon comes from the Gaelic 'Ros Comáin' meaning 'Woods of Coman'. St. Coman founded a monastery at

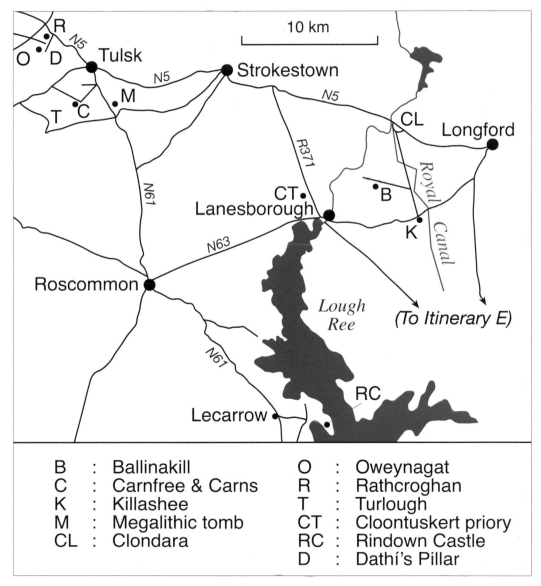

B	:	Ballinakill	O	:	Oweynagat
C	:	Carnfree & Carns	R	:	Rathcroghan
K	:	Killashee	T	:	Turlough
M	:	Megalithic tomb	CT	:	Cloontuskert priory
CL	:	Clondara	RC	:	Rindown Castle
			D	:	Dathí's Pillar

Figure I1:
Location map for Itinerary I.

Roscommon in the mid-8th century, although, unlike some other locations in the Irish Midlands, its exact location is not known. Traditionally it is believed to have been on the site presently occupied by St. Coman's Church of Ireland Church. Such a continuity of worship is known from other locations in the Irish Midlands. For example a church occupies the site of an early Christian monastery in Roscrea (Itinerary F), Killeigh (Itinerary A), Rahan (Itinerary B) and Seirkieran (Itinerary F).

Four buildings dominate Roscommon Town; the castle, the friary, the jail and the one presently occupied by the Bank of Ireland. Roscommon Castle is an Anglo-Norman fortification, built towards the end of the 13th century under the auspices of Robert de Ufford, Plate I1. It is essentially rectangular in plan view (40m x 50m) with the addition of four D-shaped towers at its four corners and a twin-towered gateway. Sweetman (2005) believes that the gatehouse is 'almost certainly the largest in Ireland'. The area around the castle was once very boggy and was occupied by a lake, which was the site of an earlier crannog. The townland, Loughnaneane, is named after the lake that once existed here (Lough Nea or Nen). Water from the lake was used to fill a defensive fosse around the castle. Such an imposing structure was of considerable strategic importance and as such even before it was completed, it was attacked by Aodh O'Conor son of Felim O'Conor, King of Connacht.

Plate I1:
Roscommon Castle,
Roscommon Town.

The castle came under the control of the O'Conors by the mid-14th century and remained in their hands for 200 years. It was returned to Anglo-Irish forces in the late 16th century and the castle and lands were granted in the 1570s to Sir Nicholas Malbie who was appointed Governor of Connacht. Large-scale modifications of the castle took place at this time, which essentially turned the castle into a large fortified house. Red Hugh O'Donnell attacked it at the end of the 16th century, then it was held by the Confederates during the mid-17th century conflict, but it was taken in 1652 by Cromwellian forces and burned down in 1690.

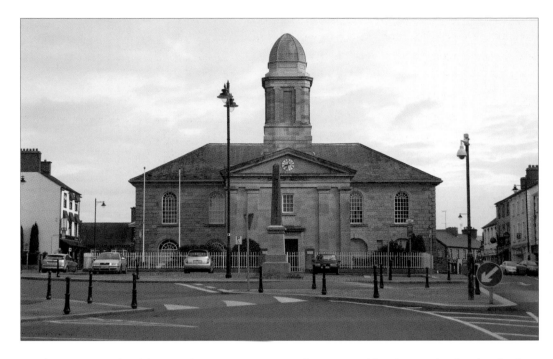

Plate 12:
Mid -8th century former Courthouse
in Roscommon Town.

The imposing building in the Square is currently occupied by the Bank of Ireland, Plate 12. This was constructed in the 1760s and was originally used as a courthouse/Market House, but for much of the 19th century was a Catholic Church. It ceased being a place of worship in the early 20th century when the Catholic Sacred Heart Church was opened in 1903. Two other structures are evident in the Square, the façade of the old gaol, which was renowned for its female hangwoman, 'Lady Betty', and the former 19th century Presbyterian Church with its 'Star of David' window, which currently houses the County Museum (John Harrison Memorial Hall).

Plate 13:
Dominican Priory,
Roscommon Town.

In the 13th century, the castle would have dominated the northern part of Roscommon Town, while an equally imposing Dominican priory would have dominated the southern part, Plate 13. This was founded by Felim O'Conor (King of Connacht) *c*. 1253 and consecrated to the Blessed Virgin. It was destroyed in the early 14th century and much of today's building is from the 15th century. Felim died in 1265 and the building houses a 13th century effigy, which currently rests on, a 15th century tomb, decorated with 8 mail-clad knights, Plate 14. These are known as gallowglasses and were essentially mercenaries.

Plate I4:
15th century tomb within Dominican Priory, Roscommon town decorated with eight mail-clad knights.

From the bypass around the town, take the N63 road east towards Lanesborough and Longford. Lanesborough is named after George Lane who was granted land in this area in the 1600s. Its Gaelic name 'Beal Atha Liag' means 'Mouth of the Ford of the Stone' It is located where the River Shannon enters Lough Ree, and thus, it was of strategic importance for crossing the river. Like Roscommon, Lanesborough also had a priory (situated at Cloontuskert, 2.5 kilometres along the R371 road, see Figure I1). Today, little remains, although a large number of decorated stones and architectural feature, such as columns and window and door surrounds, are preserved in the cemetery. Some early

Christian cross-inscribed slabs have been found at the site, one of which may be 8th-9th century in date (Fanning and Ó hÉailidhe, 1980). Cross the Shannon and continue on the N63 road to your left towards Longford. Lanesborough is dominated by the peat-fired power station, a local landmark visible from great distances. The peat is obtained from the surrounding bogs, and transported to the power station by small railways. After 7 kilometres, take the road to your left in Killashee, then after 2 kilometres, take the narrow road to your left and drive down it for 3 kilometres to the graveyard on your left. This is Ballinakill cemetery and is the site of what is known locally as the Grey Friars monastery, where it is though that St. Ernan founded a 6th century monastic settlement. Some early Christian grave slabs discovered here have been mounted on a wall, near which is a stone basin similar to one at the early Christian Gallen Priory, Ferbane, County Offaly, Plate 15. Return to Killashee (Cill a Sidhe: Church of the Fairy Mound or Woods of the Fairies), turn left and drive on to Longford. Longford has been discussed earlier in the book (see Itinerary E). From the Main Street in Longford take the N5 west signposted for Westport. As you approach the Shannon (after 9 kilometres), take the road to your left, signposted for Clondara (Cloondara) where the Royal Canal from Dublin terminates (see Figure 15 in Section II of the book). There is an unusual dry dock and the public house is named the Richmond Inn after Lord Lieutenant Richmond who opened the harbour (Delany, 2000). As you drive through Clondara, over the canal bridge, note the roofless church, located adjacent to the newer one. A number of interesting grave slabs are displayed near the entrance to the cemetery.

Continue through Clondara, rejoin the N5, cross the River Shannon and drive through Termonbarry (Tarmonbarry) to Strokestown. Termonbarry, from the Gaelic means 'Churchlands of Barry' and refers to an early monastic settlement founded nearby by St. Barry. When you reach the roundabout in Strokestown, you will see that the town is characterised by a wide avenue linking the (former) Church of Ireland Church at the western (left) side of town with Strokestown House at its eastern end, which can be accessed through the Gothic arch. The

Plate I5:
Part of grave slab (top) and stone basin (bottom) discovered near graveyard at Ballinakill, County Longford.

land around Strokestown was granted to the Mahon family in the 17th century but the town and the Palladian style house were not laid out until the mid-18th century, Plate 16. Today, it houses a museum, dedicated to the mid-19th century famine, which resulted in a massive decrease in Ireland's population due to emigration and death. Ironically, the landlord during the famine, Major Denis Mahon, was assassinated because of his forced evictions.

Plate 16:
Strokestown House, Strokestown,
County Roscommon.

Drive past the Church of Ireland Church, west on the N5 for 10 kilometres to Tulsk and stop at the cemetery. The high ground that can be seen to your left as you drive to Tulsk is the Slieve Bawn Mountains formed mainly of sandstone. Although there is little documentary evidence about Tulsk before the 1400s, it is located on one of the ancient roads of Ireland (Slighe Assail) and a number of other roads converge on it (Doran, 2004). It was the site of an O'Conor Roe castle built *c.* 1406. The Discovery Programme has carried out extensive fieldwork and excavations in Tulsk over the last number of years, and interested readers should consult Brady and Gibson (2005) and Brady et al. (2005) for further details. The cemetery is the site of a Dominican priory, built in the mid-15th century, consisting of a chancel and nave and a later transept. Sir Richard Bingham, Governor of Connacht, during the reign of Elizabeth I, built a later tower house onto the chancel in *c.* 1582. The oldest known graves in the cemetery date to around the 1670s. A number of later mausoleums are also within the cemetery walls. One, belonging to the Grace family, and in the form of a small church is Victorian in date, although the Dowell mausoleum, with its very thick slated roof, may be older, *c.* 1710. A raised earthwork can be seen in the field directly across from the graveyard. It is slightly oval in shape (36m by 27m) and parts of it are up to 5m above the surrounding terrain. Excavations here, based on geophysical work, showed an external battered stone façade of a rectangular tower (Plate 17) and the presence of an external fosse (defensive ditch). Finds suggest a 16th century date consistent with the date of the tower house in the cemetery. A seasonal spring beside the earthwork may have provided a water supply.

Plate 17:
Excavation of raised earthwork at Tulsk, County Roscommon showing buried stone façade.

The area surrounding Tulsk has one of the largest concentrations of archaeological structures to be found in the Irish Midlands. Over 200 features are known, many prehistoric in age. They include megalithic tombs, ring-barrows, standing stones, Bronze Age tumuli, banked avenues and ringforts. Many of the larger structures are circular or oval in shape, have diameters of *c*. 100m, and can only really be appreciated from the air. The Heritage Centre in Tulsk contains a range of such aerial photographs. It is not possible here to detail all these features, but two areas will be discussed which provide examples of most of them: Rathcroghan and Carnfree. Extensive descriptions and further information can be obtained by consulting Herity (1983, 1984 and 1987) and Waddell (1983). In addition, Herity (1991) has provided a guide to many of the structures.

Drive through Tulsk westward on the N5 for 5.5 kilometres and stop beside the school on your left. This is the farthest northwestern extent of this itinerary. The surrounding area and associated archaeological structures are generally accepted as the site of Cruachain (today termed Rathcroghan or Ráth Cruachan). Waddell (1983) provides an excellent discussion on the various texts that refer to Cruachain. It is considered to be a sacred royal site on a par with Tara in County Meath, a burial place for kings and a gathering place for great assemblies. It also features in the great epic tale known in Gaelic lore as the Táin Bó Cúailnge, the Cattle Raid of Cooley. Directly across the road from the school is Rathmore, a raised circular mound *c*. 28m in diameter and 6m high, surrounded by a wide

Plate I8:
Oweynagat Cave entrance near Tulsk.
(Entrance is about 1m high).

ditch across which are two causeways, allowing access to the structure. Return towards Tulsk for 200m, and take the first road on your right. On your left (facing the water tower) is Rathbeg ring-barrow, which is surrounded by two banks and ditche. Continue along this road for a further 350m and on your right is the large circular enclosure known as Rathnadarve (Fort of the Bulls) where, in the epic Táin, the bulls fought. The structure is almost circular has an internal diameter of *c*. 85m, is surrounded by a bank and enclosed by a broad fosse (ditch). Continue past Rathnadarve and take the next narrow lane on your left. Drive down it to the end, past the house on your right. On your right, near a

Plate I9:
Aerial photograph showing Rathcroghan mound (top) and other nearby circular monuments. Photograph courtesy of Gerry Bracken.

metal gate, at the base of a large bush at the edge of the field, is the entrance to a small cave, Plate 18. This is Oweynagat also called the Cave of the Cats. It is possible to enter this cave, at your own risk, but you will need a lamp. It is often very muddy and quite low in places. The entrance to the cave is artificial (souterrain) and within an earthwork (now largely destroyed). The entrance lintel is formed of an ogham stone and the sides are flanked with slabs of rock (orthostats). The ogham stone has been interpreted as '(the stone) of Fraech, son of Medb'. Once inside, the cave turns to the left after a short distance, and proceeds for about 70m. The latter part of the cave is a natural geomorphological feature formed by solution of the limestone. It may have exploited a vertical fracture as it is quite narrow (about 1m) but in places, it is up to 7m high. In Celtic legend, the cave is associated with the afterlife and the animals that exited from the cave were associated with destruction. Condit and Moore (2003) suggest that the cats may refer to Bricriu's feast in which three cats challenge three of Ulster's mythical heroes. Note that in the field directly across the lane, near the gorse bushes, there is another small cave. Return to the main N5, turn right towards Tulsk and drive 600m and stop at the car-park on your right at Rathcroghan mound, Plate 19. This mound is believed to be the focus of the cluster of monuments that occur in this locality. It is about 6m high and 88m in diameter, Plate I10. Detailed geophysical work carried out by the National University of Ireland, Galway, has shown that it is surrounded by an enclosure 370m in

Plate I10:
Rathcroghan mound, focal point of the Cruachain complex of monuments.

Plate I11:
Dathí's Pillar, Rathcroghan.

diameter and that circular structures exist on its summit. Return to your car, continue towards Tulsk and take the first road on your right. Drive down this road for 200m and off to your right you will see a tapered pillar of sandstone approximately 1.8m in height, Plate I11. It is located within a ring-barrow and charcoal from it has been radiocarbon dated to *c.* 150 BC (Waddell, 1983). The site is traditionally thought to be the location where King Dathí (allegedly the last pagan king of Ireland) was buried. The monument is within a limestone region but the stone itself is formed of sandstone. The nearest such sandstone is at least 7 kilometres away, though it may have originated as a glacial erratic.

Return towards Tulsk on the N5 and at the crossroads there, take the N61 road to your right for Roscommon. After about 1.8 kilometres take the narrow road to your right and then turn left after 250m (note, that cultivation ridges can be seen in the field to the left when the sun is low). Drive along this road for 1 kilometre and stop where the road turns sharply to the right, after reaching the top of a steep incline. There are a number of monuments and standing stones in various fields on the left side of the road. The largest known feature is the ecclesiastical site at Carns, which is recognised as a site visited by St. Patrick (Herity, 1991). Today the site is dominated by a 150m diameter circular enclosure and old maps record the existence of a church and graveyard, Plate I12. A geophysical investigation of this site by the Environmental Geophysics Unit of the National University of Ireland, Maynooth revealed a much more complex hidden landscape for Carns consisting of a number of concentric enclosure boundaries suggesting it was an important site for an extended period of time, Plate I13. Excavations in 2006, by

Plate I12:
Carns ecclesiastical site, near Tulsk, Image courtesy of the Discovery Programme.

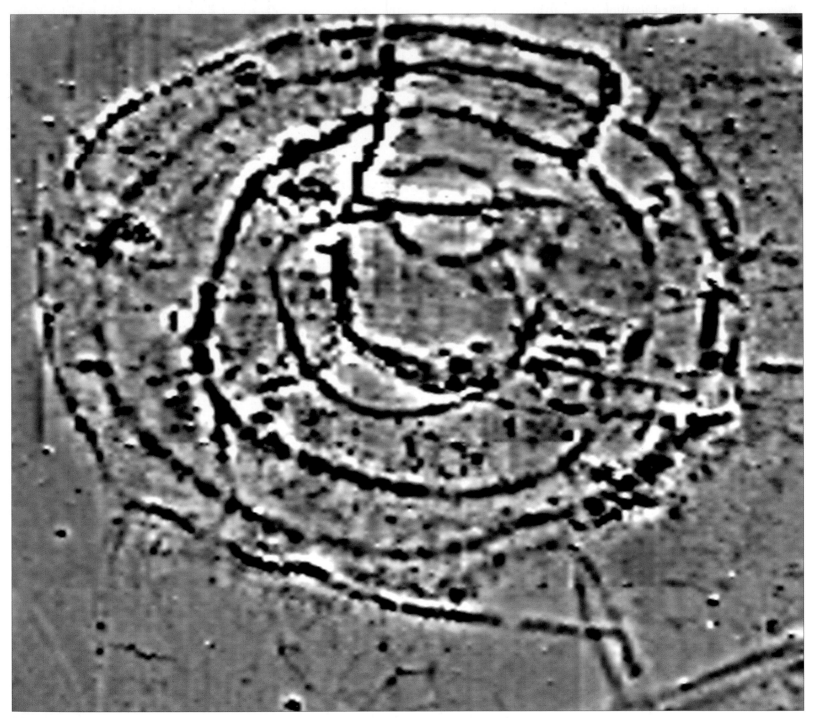

Plate I13:
Magnetic image from geophysical investigation of Carns revealing a much more complex hidden landscape than previously thought.

the Discovery Programme, revealed a number of burials within this site and discovered an unknown ogham stone. The conical mound of the Bronze Age tumulus of Dumha Sealga can be seen from Carns and is located about 400m to the west, Plate I14. Nearby, in a prominent elevated location, is Carnfree, a small mound (apparently also dating back to the Bronze Age) that, in historic times, was the site where members of the O'Conor clan were inaugurated as Kings of Connacht, Plate I15 (Herity, 1991). This mound occupies the highest position in this region and affords a spectacular 360 degree vista.

Return to the N61 road, turn right and drive towards Roscommon. After about 2 kilometres (in the townland of Sheegeeragh) on your left, about 100m into the field, you may notice a small group of limestone slabs. These have been identified as a megalithic tomb but today little structural details can be discerned. (Turning right at the next crossroads and driving for 3 kilometres, brings you to a turlough on your right). Continue towards Roscommon. As you approach the town, you come to the Anglo-Norman castle discussed at the beginning of the itinerary. You may extend the itinerary by visiting another Anglo-Norman castle and its associated borough, at Lecarrow, south of the town – see Figure I1. Take the N61 for Athlone and turn left into Lecarrow. Drive past the school (note the good views of Lough Ree) and after 2 kilometres park where the road takes a sharp right near the sign for Rindown (Rindoon) Castle. The castle and its associated settlement were built on a peninsula jutting out into Lough Ree, which surrounded it on all sides, except the landward one. The castle was built at one of the narrowest part of Lough Ree which both facilitated crossings of the lough and movement of boat traffic along the lough. A defensive wall, with associated guard turrets and gate, over 500m long and 3m high, was built across the landward side to complete the defences, Plate I16. The settlement and Rindown Castle were protected by the wall, which Graham (1988) has suggested may date

Plate I14:
Bronze Age Dumha Sealga tumulus, Carnfree, near Tulsk.

Plate I15:
Carnfree, inauguration mound of the O'Conor clan.

Plate I16:
Defensive wall cutting off peninsula on which Rindown Castle and town were established, Lecarrow, County Roscommon.

from *c.* 1251. The castle is believed to have been built by Geoffrey de Marisco *c.* 1227. A large defensive ditch was cut across the peninsula and around the castle to form a moat. Various building phases can be determined for the castle, which still today retains large pasts of its gatehouse, hall-keep and curtain wall, Plate I17 (Sweetman, 2005). The settlement and castle were attacked by the O'Conor clan in 1251, 1270 and 1315 (Graham, 1988). Apart from the castle, the ruin of a priory church of the Fratres Crucifieri order remains standing (Delany, 2000). At the end of the peninsula are the 6m high remains of a circular tower. Its form suggests that it was a windmill and is believed to have been in existence in 1636, so making it the oldest surviving example in Ireland (Claffey, 1980).

Plate I17:
Rindown Castle, Lecarrow.
Inset shows details of entrance.

References

Aalen, F. H. A., Whelan, K. and Stout, M. (1997). Atlas of the Irish Rural Landscape. Cork University Press. ISBN 1 85918 095 7.

Andrews, J. H. and Davies, K. M. (1992). Irish Historic Towns Atlas. No. 5: Mullingar, (editors) J. H. Andrews and A. Simms, Royal Irish Academy.

Archdall, M. (1786). *Monasticon Hibernicum*. Published by L. White: Dublin.

Archer, J. B., Sleeman, A. G. and Smith, D. C. (1996). Geology of Tipperary. Published by Geological Survey of Ireland. ISBN 1 899702 06 7.

Bellamy, D. (1986). The Wild Boglands: Bellamy's Ireland. Country House Publishers Dublin.

Bradley, J. (1999). Early urban development in County Laois. Pages 257-282. In: Laois, History & Society, (editors) P. G. Lane and W. Nolan, Geography Publications ISBN 0 906602 46 7.

Brady, N., Connon, A., Corns, A., McNeary, R., Shanahan, B., and Shaw, R. (2005). A survey of the priory and graveyard at Tulsk, Co. Roscommon. In: Discovery Programme Report 7. Pages 40-58. ISSN 1649 7295.

Brady, N. and Gibson, P. J. (2005). The earthwork at Tulsk, Co. Roscommon: topographical and geophysical survey and preliminary excavation. In: Discovery Programme Report 7. ISSN 1649-7295. Pages 65-75.

Brindley, A. L. and Lanting, J. N. (1998). Radiocarbon dates for Irish Trackways. The Journal of Irish Archaeology. V. IX. Pages 45-68.

Brindley, A. L., Lanting, J. N. and Mook, W. G. (1989). Radiocarbon dates from Irish fulachta fiadh and other burnt mounds. The Journal of Irish Archaeology. V. V. Pages 25-33.

Byrne, F. J. (2005). The Viking Age. Pages 609-634. In: A new history of Ireland volume I Prehistoric and early Ireland, (editor) D. O'Croinin, Oxford University Press. ISBN 0-19-821737-4.

Byrne, M. (1998). Tullamore: the growth process, 1785-1841. Pages 569-626. In: Offaly, History & Society (editors) W. Nolan and T. P. O'Neill, Geography Publications ISBN 0 906602 90 4.

Claffey, J. A. (1980). Rindoon windmill tower. Pages 84-88. In: Irish Midland Studies, (editor) H. Murtagh, The Old Athlone Society, ISBN 0 9503428 1 5.

Clarke, P. (1992). The Royal Canal – the complete story. Elo Publications Dublin. ISBN 0 9519593 2 8.

Cody, P. (1998). Castlebawn in Sliabh Aughty East Clare Heritage Journal no. 8. Pages 20-22.

Cogan A. (1874). The ecclesiastical history of the diocese of Meath ancient and modern. Volume I. W. B. Kelly: Dublin.

Condit, T. and Moore, F. (2003). Ireland in the Iron Age. Archaeology Ireland Heritage Guide No 21.

Cosby, I. (1999). The English settlers in Queen's County, 1570-1603. Pages 283-326. In: Laois, History & Society, (editors) P. G. Lane and W. Nolan, Geography Publications ISBN 0 906602 46 7.

Cox, L. (1981) Moate, Co. Westmeath. A history of the town and district. Printed by Alfa Print Ltd., Athlone.

Coxon, P. (2001). Cenozoic: Tertiary and Quaternary, until 10,000 years before present. Pages 388-427 In: The geology of Ireland, (editor) C. H. Holland, Dunedin Academic Press. Edinburgh.

Cronin, T. (1980). The Elizabethan colony in Co. Roscommon. Pages 107-120. In: Irish Midland Studies, (editor) H. Murtagh, The Old Athlone Society, ISBN 0 9503428 1 5.

Daly, L. (no date). Austin Friars (52 pages).

D'Arcy, G. (1969). Portrait of the Grand Canal. Transport Research Associates. Dublin.

D'Arcy M.R. (1974). The saints of Ireland. Irish American Cultural Institute: St. Paul Minnesota.

Davies, G. H. and Stephens, N. (1978). The geomorphology of the British Isles: Ireland. Methuen & Co. Ltd. ISBN 0 416 84650 5.

Deigan, M. (1999). Portlaoise: Genesis and Development. Pages 689-708. In: Laois, History & Society, (editors) P. G. Lane and W. Nolan, Geography Publications ISBN 0 906602 46 7.

Delany, R. (1986). A celebration of 250 years of Ireland's Inland Waterways. The Appletree Press Ltd., Belfast. ISBN 0 86281 129 5.

Delany, R. (2000). The Shell Guide to the River Shannon. Published by Era-Maptec Ltd., Dublin. ISBN 1 873489 90 0.

Doran, L. (2004). Medieval communication routes through Longford and Roscommon and their associated settlements. Proceedings of the Royal Irish Academy. V.104C. Pages 57-80.

Duffy, S. (2000). The concise history of Ireland. Gill and MacMillan. Ltd. ISBN 0 7171381 0 0.

Dunne, L. A. and Feehan, J. (2002). The origin and significance of mushroom stones in lowland karst regions. Irish Journal of Earth Sciences. V. 20. Pages 33-40.

Earl of Rosse (1982) Birr castle. Irish Heritage Series: 37. Published by Eason and Sons, Ltd, Dublin, ISBN 900345 48 5.

Edwards, N. (2005). The archaeology of early medieval Ireland, c. 400-1169: Settlement and economy. Pages 235-300. In: A new history of Ireland volume I Prehistoric and early Ireland, (editor) D. O'Croinin, Oxford University Press. ISBN 0 19-821737 4.

Egan, O. (1986). Tyrrellspass past and present. Published by Tyrrellspass Town Development Committee.

Fanning, T. and Ó hÉailidhe, P. (1980). Some cross-inscribed slabs from the Irish Midlands. Pages 5-23. In: Irish Midland Studies, (editor) H. Murtagh, The Old Athlone Society, ISBN 0 9503428 1 5.

Feehan, J. (1979). The landscape of Slieve Bloom: a study of its natural and human heritage. ISBN 0 9054711 1 3.

Feehan, J. (1983). Laois: an environmental history. Ballykilcavan Press, Stradbally. ISBN 0 9509188 0 6.

Feehan, J. and O'Donovan (1996). The Bogs of Ireland. UCD. The Environmental Institute.

FitzPatrick, E. and O'Brien, C. (1998). The medieval churches of County Offaly. Government of Ireland ISBN 0 7076 5081 X.

Flanagan, L. (1990). A chronicle of Irish saints. Blackstaff Press: Ireland.

Friel, M. (1997). Here lies: A guide to Irish graves. Poolbeg Press Ltd, Dublin. ISBN: 1 8537 713 4.

Gallagher, C., Thorp, M. and Steenson, P. (1996). Glacial dynamics around Slieve Bloom, Central Ireland. Irish Geography. V. 9, no. 2. Pages 67-82.

Garner, W. (1980). Carlow Architectural Heritage. An Foras Forbartha. ISBN 0 9061 20 38 1.

Geissel, H. (2006). A road on the long ridge. CRS Publications, Newbridge, Ireland. ISBN 0 9547295 1 X.

Gibson, P. J. and George, D. M. (2006). Geophysical investigation of the site of the former monastic settlement, Clonard, County Meath, Ireland. Archaeological Prospection V. 13. Pages 45-56.

Gleeson, J. (1915). History of the Ely O'Carroll Territory. M. H. Gill and Son Ltd, Dublin.

Grace, D. (1993) Nenagh. Pages 114-119 In: Tipperary County: People and Places, (editor) M. Hallinan. Kincora Press, Dublin ISBN 0 9521003 0 4.

Graham, B. J. (1988). Medieval settlement in Co. Roscommon. Proceedings of the Royal Irish Academy. V. 88C. Pages 19-38.

Harbinson, P. (2003). Treasures of the Boyne Valley Gill and MacMillan. ISBN 0 7171 3498 9.

Herity, M. (1983). A Survey of the Royal Site of Cruachain in Connacht. I. Introduction, the monuments and topography. Journal of the Royal Society of Antiquaries of Ireland. V. 113. Pages. 121-142.

Herity, M. (1984). A Survey of the Royal Site of Cruachain in Connacht. II Prehistoric monuments. Journal of the Royal Society of Antiquaries of Ireland. V. 114. Pages 125-138.

Herity, M. (1987). A Survey of the Royal Site of Cruachain in Connacht. III. Ringforts and Ecclesiastical Sites. Journal of the Royal Society of Antiquaries of Ireland. V. 117. Pages 125-141.

Herity, M. (1991). Rathcroghan and Carnfree. Celtic Royal Sites in Roscommon. Printed by Colour Books Ltd. 38 pages.

Hickey E. (1998). Clonard: the story of an early Irish monastery. Published by Hickey: Leixlip Ireland.

Hogan, M. and Short J. (1994) Birr Heritage Town: A Guide. Published by Birr Historical Society.

Holland, C. H. (2003). The Irish Landscape. Dunedin Academic Press. Edinburgh.

Hylton, R. (1999). Portarlington and the Huguenots in Laois. Pages 415-434. In: Laois, History & Society, (editors) P. G. Lane and W. Nolan, Geography Publications ISBN 0 906602 46 7.

Jackson, J. S. (1967). The Clonfinlough Stone: a geological assessment. Pages 11-19. In: North Munster Studies, (editor) E. Rynne. Published by the Thomond Archaeological Society, Limerick.

Johnson, S. (1997). Johnson's Atlas & Gazetteer of the railways of Ireland. Midland Publishing Ltd. ISBN 1 85780 044 3.

Karst Working Group of Ireland (2000). The Karst of Ireland. Published by Geological Survey of Ireland. ISBN 1 899702 41 5.

Kearney, J. (1992). The long ridge. Towards a history of Killeigh. Esker Press Tullamore.

Kearney, J. (2003). Notes on the history of Daingean.

Kelly, M. J. (1991). The last days of the Colleys on Carbury Hill. Journal of the County Kildare Archaeological Society. V. 17. Pages 96-98.

Kennedy, J. (2003). The monastic heritage & folklore of County Laois. Lisheen Publications, Roscrea. ISBN 0 9542331 5 8.

Kenny, M. (2005). Coins and coinage in pre-Norman Ireland. Pages 842-851. In: A new history of Ireland volume I Prehistoric and early Ireland, (editor) O'Croinin D. Oxford University Press. ISBN 0 19 821737 4.

Kerrigan, P. M. (1998). Castles and fortifications of County Offaly c. 1500-1815. Pages 393-438. In: Offaly, History & Society, (editors) W. Nolan and T. P. O'Neill, Geography Publications ISBN 0 906602 90 4.

Kierse, S. (2001). The Killaloe Anthology. Boru Books ISBN 0 9512279 5 5.

King, T. (1997). Carlow, the manor & town 1674-1721. Irish Academic Press. ISBN 0-7165-2634-4.

Lafferty, S., Commins, P. and Walsh, J. A. (1999). Irish Agriculture in Transition. Published by Teagasc, Dublin. ISBN 1 84170 063 0.

Larsen, A. (editor) (2001). The Vikings in Ireland. Roskilde Ship Museum, Denmark. ISBN: 87 85180 42 4.

Loeber, R. (1999). Warfare and architecture in County Laois through seventeenth century eyes. Pages 377-413. In: Laois, History & Society, (editors) P. G. Lane and W. Nolan, Geography Publications ISBN 0 906602 46 7.

Lucas, A. T. (1967). The plundering and burning of churches in Ireland, 7th to 16th century. Pages 172-229. In: North Munster Studies, (editor) E. Rynne. Published by the Thomond Archaeological Society, Limerick.

Lydon, J. (1998). The Making of Ireland. Routledge Publishers. ISBN 0 41501348 8.

MacAlister, R. A. S. and Praeger, R. L. (1928). Report on the excavation of Uisneach. Proceedings of the Royal Irish Academy v. XXXVIII, section C. Pages 69-127.

MacDermott, M. (1957). The crosiers of St. Dympna and St. Mel and Tenth century Irish metal-work. Proceedings of the Royal Irish Academy. V. 58. Pages 167-195.

Madden, G. (1993). For God or King. The history of Mountshannon, Co. Clare 1742-1992. Published by East Clare Heritage. ISSN 0791-4571.

Madden, G. (2000). A history of Tuamgraney & Scariff since earliest times. Published by East Clare Heritage. ISBN 0 9529511 50.

Madden, G. (2004). Holy Island: A history. Published by East Clare heritage. ISBN 0 9529511 0 X.

Malcomson, A. P. W. (1998). A variety of perspectives on Laurence Parsons, 2nd Earl of Rosse. Pages 439-484. In: Offaly, History & Society (editors) W. Nolan and T. P. O'Neill, Geography Publications ISBN 0 906602 90 4.

Manning, C. (1994). Clonmacnoise. Published by the Office of Public Works. Dublin/ ISBN 0 70760388 9.

McDermott, C. (1998). The prehistory of the Offaly Peatlands. Pages 1-28. In: Offaly, History & Society, (editors) W. Nolan and T. P. O'Neill, Geography Publications ISBN 0 906602 90 4.

McNamee, J. J. (1943). Ardagh and Tristernagh. Ardagh and Clonmacnois Antiquarian Society Journal. V. II, no. 9. Pages 3-17.

McParland, J. (1985). James Gandon. Studies in Architecture volume XXIV, (editors) John Harris and Alastair Laing. Published by A, Zwemmer Ltd. ISBN 0 302 02576 6.

Middlemass, T. (1981). Irish Standard Gauge Railways. David & Charles (Publishers) Ltd.

Mitchell, F. and Delaney, C. (editors) (1997). The Quaternary of the Irish Midlands. Irish Association for Quaternary Studies Field Guide No. 21. ISBN 0 947920 24 2.

Mitchell, F. and Ryan, M. (1998). Reading the Irish Landscape. Town House Dublin.

Morris, J. H., Somerville, I. D. and MacDermot, C. V. (2003). Geology of Longford-Roscommon. Geological Survey of Ireland. ISBN 1 899702 45 8.

Murphy, N. (1997). A trip through Tipperary lakeside. Relay Books, Nenagh. ISBN 0 946327 21 1.

Murtagh, H. (1973). The sieges of Athlone 1690 and 1691. Published by Old Athlone Society.

Murtagh, H. (1994) Irish Historic Towns Atlas. No. 6: Athlone, (editors) J. H. Andrews and A. Simms, Royal Irish Academy.

O'Brien, C. (2006). Stories from a sacred landscape. Offaly County Council. ISBN 1 85635 489 X.

O'Brien, C. and Sweetman, P. D. (1997). Archaeological Inventory of County Offaly. Dublin Stationery Office. ISBN 07076 3819 4.

O'Brien, G. (1985). Athlone Tourist Trail. Published by Old Athlone Society.

O'Brien, J. and Guinness, D. (1992). Great Irish Houses and Castles. Published by George Weidenfeld & Nicolson Ltd., London. ISBN 0 297 83141 0.

O'Brien, K. (1998). Abbeyleix: life lore & legend. Franamanagh Books. ISBN 0 9532604 0 2.

O'Brien, S. (2000). Carns, Killare, A forgotten Westmeath Famine Village. Rathlainne Publications, Mullingar. ISBN 0 9537941 0 5.

O'Conor, K. (1999). Anglo-Norman castles in County Laois. Pages 183-212. In: Laois, History & Society, (editors) P. G. Lane and W. Nolan, Geography Publications ISBN 0 906602 46 7.

Ó'Corráin, D. (2000). Prehistoric and Early Christian Ireland. Pages 1-52. In: The Oxford Illustrated History of Ireland, (editor) Foster R. F. Oxford University Press ISBN 0 19 289323 8.

O'Keeffe, T. (2000). Medieval Ireland: An Archaeology. Tempus Publishing Ltd. ISBN 0 7524 1464 X.

O'Keeffe, T. (2003). Romanesque Ireland. Four Courts Press Ltd. ISBN 1-85182-617-3.

Orme, A. R. (1970). The World's Landscapes: Ireland. Longman Group Ltd. ISBN 0 582 31155 1.

O'Kelly, M. J. (2005). Bronze-Age Ireland. Pages 98-133. In: A new history of Ireland volume I Prehistoric and early Ireland, (editor) D. O'Croinin. Oxford University Press. ISBN 0 19 821737 4.

O'Riordain, S. P. (1935). Bronze Age burials at Crookedwood, County Westmeath. Journal of the Royal Society of Antiquaries of Ireland. V. 65. Pages 102-112.

Orme, A. R. (1970). The World's Landscapes: Ireland. Longman Group Ltd. ISBN 0 582 31155 1.

Owen, E. (1992). St. Flannan's Cathedral Killaloe. Ballinakella Press, 31 pages.

Phillips, W. E. A. (2001). Caledonian deformation. Pages 179-199. In: The Geology of Ireland, (editor) C. H. Holland, Dunedin Academic Press, Edinburgh.

Potterton, M. (2005). Medieval Trim. Four Courts Press. ISBN 1 85182 926 1.

Powell, J. S. (1996). 1696-1996 St. Paul's Church, Portarlington. The French Church. Portarlington and Monasterevin, Parish of the Church of Ireland. ISBN 0 9528218 0 X.

Quinn, D. B. (1998). Clara: a midland industrial town 1900-1923. Pages 799-830. In: Offaly, History & Society (editors) W. Nolan and T. P. O'Neill, Geography Publications ISBN 0 906602 90 4.

Raftery, B. (2005). Iron-Age Ireland. Pages 134-181. In: A new history of Ireland volume I Prehistoric and early Ireland, (editor) D. O'Croinin, Oxford University Press. ISBN 0 19 821737 4.

Richardson, H. (2005). Visual Arts and Society. Pages 680-713. In: A new history of Ireland volume I Prehistoric and early Ireland, (editor) D. O'Croinin, Oxford University Press. ISBN 0 19 821737 4.

Roche, R. (1995). The Norman Invasion of Ireland. Anvil Books. ISBN 0-947962-81-6.

Ryan, B. (2003). Dear old town: a history of Ferbane in the 18th and 19th centuries. White Grass Publications ISBN 0 9514459 5 2.

Sevastopulo, G. D. (2001). Carboniferous (Dinantian). Pages 241-288. In: The Geology of Ireland, (editor) C. H. Holland, Dunedin Academic Press, Edinburgh.

Sevastopulo, G. D. and Jackson Wyse, P. N. (2001). Carboniferous (Silesian). Pages 289-312. In: The Geology of Ireland, (editor) C. H. Holland, Dunedin Academic Press, Edinburgh.

Sheehan, J. (editor) (1996). Beneath the shadow of Uisneach. Published by Ballymore-Bohr History Project. ISBN 0 9521923 3 0.

Simms, A. and Simms, K. (1990). Irish Historic Towns Atlas. No. 4: Kells, (editors) J. H. Andrews and A. Simms, Royal Irish Academy.

Simms, K. (2000). The Norman Invasion and the Gaelic Recovery. Pages 53-103. In: The Oxford Illustrated History of Ireland, (editor) R. F. Foster, Oxford University Press ISBN 0 19 289323 8.

Smith, C. (1992). Late Stone Age Hunters of the British Isles. Routledge. ISBN 0 415 07202 6.

Stalley, R. (1999). Hiberno-Romanesque and the sculpture of Killeshin. Pages 89-123. In: Laois, History & Society, (editors) P. G. Lane and W. Nolan, Geography Publications ISBN 0 906602 46 7.

Stout, G. and Stout, M. (1997). Early landscapes from prehistory to plantation. Pages 31-63. In: Atlas of the Irish Rural Landscape, (editors) F. H. A. Aalen, K. Whelan and M. Stout. Cork University Press. ISBN 1 85918 095 7.

Stout, M. (2000). The Irish Ringfort. Four Courts Press. ISBN 1 85182 582 7.

Sweetman, P. D. (1978). Excavation of medieval 'field boundaries' at Clonard, County Meath. Journal of Royal Society of Antiquaries of Ireland. V. 105. Pages 10-21.

Sweetman, P. D. (2005). The medieval castles of Ireland. The Collins Press ISBN 1 903464 0 3.

Sweetman, P. D., Alcock, O. and Moran, B. (1995). Archaeological Inventory of County Laois. Dublin Stationery Office.

Taylor, G. and Skinner, A. (1778). Maps of the Roads of Ireland. Reprinted 1969 Irish University Press, Shannon. ISBN 7165 0063 9.

Waddell, J. (1983). Rathcroghan – a royal site in Connacht. The Journal of Irish Archaeology. V. 1. Pages 21-44.

Westmeath Genealogy Project (no date). Moate Heritage Trail. 15 pages. Printed by the Westmeath Examiner.

Whittow, J. B. (1995). Geology and Scenery in Ireland. Penguin Books.

Willmot, G. F. (1938). Three burial sites at Carbury, Co. Kildare. Journal of the Royal Society of Antiquaries of Ireland. V. 68. Pages 130-142.

Winckworth, T. (no date). All Saints Church, Mullingar. Westmeath Examiner Ltd, Mullingar.

Zaczek, I. (2000). Ireland Land of the Celts. Collins and Brown Ltd. ISBN 1 85585 765 0.

Index

A

Abbeyleix 22, 73, 173, 191, 200, 203, 205, 206, 244

Aghaboe 59, 69, 156, 173, 176, 177

Anglo-Norman 5, 6, 50, 51, 68, 69, 70, 85, 93, 100, 116, 118, 127, 135, 143, 144, 148, 150, 151, 156, 158, 160, 161, 172, 176, 177, 178, 192, 195, 196, 198, 199, 200, 202, 211, 213, 226, 237, 244

Ardagh 59, 65, 76, 159, 164, 166, 167, 168, 243

Athlone 2, 6, 8, 16, 24, 35, 39, 59, 72, 79, 80, 81, 84, 87, 103, 159, 161, 162, 163, 164, 237, 239, 240, 241, 243, 244

Augustinian 67, 71, 91, 92, 102, 120, 128, 154, 156, 164, 169, 177, 183, 211, 212, 247

Augustinian priory 91, 92, 102, 120, 154, 177, 183, 211, 247

B

Ballaun stone 60, 62, 85, 122, 212, 223

Ballinakill 202, 203, 204, 225, 229

Ballyboggan Priory 71, 154, 155

Ballynacarrigy (Ballynacargy) 159, 168, 169

Ballycumber 27, 122, 125

Banagher 56, 59, 80, 84, 103, 107, 108, 111, 112

Barrow 13, 39, 40, 43, 51, 54, 64, 75, 146, 148, 153, 185, 186, 194, 195, 198, 232, 233, 234

Baylin (see Bealin)

Bealin 159, 161, 163

Birr 8, 46, 59, 73, 80, 84, 88, 103, 104, 105, 106, 118, 173, 207, 240, 242

Blanket bog 28, 36, 44, 188

Boher 103, 123, 124, 125

Bog – see blanket bog and raised bog

Bord na Móna 34, 35, 36, 95, 149, 150

Boyne 39, 40, 57, 62, 74, 75, 134, 136, 146, 153, 154, 155, 157, 162, 241

Bronze Age 24, 50, 51, 55, 56, 63, 102, 120, 128, 153, 178, 232, 237, 244

C

Calcium Carbonate 19, 29

Carboniferous 13, 14, 16, 17, 19, 20, 29, 31, 43, 95, 96, 198, 200, 202, 212, 245

Carbury Hill 152, 153, 154, 242

Carlow 2, 6, 7, 8, 53, 54, 59, 64, 80, 84, 86, 176, 191, 195, 198, 199, 200, 241, 242

Carnfree 225, 232, 237, 241

Carns 172, 225, 234, 235, 236, 237, 244

Carrick 31, 154, 182

Cave of the Cats – see Oweynagat Cave

Celtic/Celts 6, 51, 52, 57, 60, 100, 146, 148, 151, 158, 169, 171, 172, 212, 218, 233, 241, 246

Clara 36, 79, 80, 103, 122, 125, 244

Clare 6, 7, 8, 17, 37, 38, 43, 54, 59, 61, 65, 68, 84, 86, 149, 176, 207, 217, 218, 220, 221, 223, 224, 239, 243

Clonard 6, 55, 58, 59, 61, 63, 64, 65, 69, 75, 91, 107, 126, 146, 156, 157, 158, 212, 241, 242, 245

Clonaslee 173, 174, 185, 189

Clondara 76, 225, 229

Clonenagh 176

Clonfert 58, 59, 64, 65, 67, 84, 103, 108, 109, 110, 111, 156, 200